_____ *Fourth Edition*

Materials and Components of Interior Architecture

J. Rosemary Riggs, Allied member ASID
Brigham Young University, Emeritus

Prentice Hall, Englewood Cliffs, New Jersey 07632

Library of Congress Cataloging-in-Publication Data

Riggs, J. Rosemary.
 Materials and components of interior architecture / J. Rosemary
Riggs.—4th ed.
  p. cm.
 Previous eds. published under title: Materials and components of
interior design.
 Includes bibliographical references and index.
 ISBN 0-13-186842-X
 1. Building materials. 2. Household appliances. 3. Plumbing—
Equipment and supplies. 4. Interior decoration. I. Riggs, J.
Rosemary. Materials and components of interior design. II. Title.
TA403.R523 1996
698—dc20   95–7025
                                                           CIP

Acquisitions editor: Elizabeth Sugg
Editorial assistant: Kerri Ribik
Editorial/production supervision and
  interior design: Linda B. Pawelchak
Copy editor: Melanie Stafford
Cover design: Marianne Frasco
Production coordinator: Ed O'Dougherty

Front Cover. Denver International Airport, Denver, CO. The Roybal
Corp. Architect. Hensel Phelps Construction, General Contractor.
Barb McKee and Darrell Anderson, Designers. Bauer Floor Cover-
ing, Wichita, KS., Tile Contractor. Concourse Floor: Dal-Keystone
Porcelain Ceramic Mosaic Custom-Designed Murals and Borders in
Assorted Colors. Photograph Courtesy Jim Blecha, Jim Blecha Pho-
tography, Denver, CO.

Previously published as *Materials and Components of Interior Design*

Printed in the United States of America
10 9 8 7 6 5 4 3 2 1

ISBN 0-13-186842-X

Prentice-Hall International (UK) Limited, *London*
Prentice-Hall of Australia Pty. Limited, *Sydney*
Prentice-Hall Canada Inc., *Toronto*
Prentice-Hall Hispanoamericana, S.A., *Mexico*
Prentice-Hall of India Private Limited, *New Delhi*
Prentice-Hall of Japan, Inc., *Tokyo*
Simon & Schuster Asia Pte. Ltd., *Singapore*
Editora Prentice-Hall do Brasil, Ltda., *Rio de Janeiro*

Contents

Foreword

In the past, interior design was an afterthought. Interior decorators applied finishes to the building shell, with little more than a visual effect upon the basic architecture of the building.

Today, we architects and interior designers operate from a different understanding. Our interrelationship with each other and with end users, contractors and subcontractors, landscape architects, facility managers, and others begins early in the process. It starts as a commonly understood need and ends as materials that are recycled, reused, or refurbished to satisfy that need.

We are becoming increasingly aware that our design choices will affect the health of the users and the sustainability of the planet. But making good choices in the process of creating good design requires education, initially to train us to understand the thought process, and ongoing to keep us abreast of the social and physical changes swirling about us. This book serves both levels of education: It introduces students to many alternatives available in interior design and allows experienced designers to update their knowledge base.

In this fourth edition, Rosemary Riggs carries on her tradition of innovation. The first edition introduced students to new and more varied ideas about finishes. Her intent was to make the workplace more comfortable, pleasant, and efficient—to create a better quality of life for end users. Now the concepts of sustainability and sustainable materials extend that quality of life further. And why must designers do it? Because design is our lives, our livelihoods. If we don't do it, who will? The implementation of sustainable strategies is a natural part of the decision-making process called Design. To think of it as any less is irresponsible.

If we accept the definition of sustainability as "meeting our needs today without compromising our children's needs tomorrow," then the questions we need to ask as we read this book and consider finishes are very evident: Where does the material come from? How is it manufactured and shipped? How long does it last? Can it be recycled at the end of its useful life? How much energy does it consume?

Many goals to sustainability like those listed below could be incorporated into a typical interior design project. Use those that are feasible and applicable on your next design project:

Use flooring made from natural materials instead of synthetic materials.

Use nonendangered species of wood.

Retain as much existing construction and furniture as feasible. Consider using salvaged items.

Use new products such as lawn seating and toilet partitions made from recycled plastics.

Use carpet made from recyclable nylon fibers.

Use carpet pad made from recycled tire rubber.

Use steel studs and other products with recycled steel content.

Use gypsum board with recycled content.

Use insulation with recycled glass content or made from recycled paper.

Use plumbing fixtures that conserve water and turn off automatically.

Use vegetation and plant materials that minimize water consumption.

Use daylighting to carry light into interior spaces and minimize the need for electrical lighting.

Use light-colored finishes to maximize the effect of available lighting.

Use lighting fixtures that conserve energy and turn off automatically.

Use operable windows and skylights for natural ventilation.

Optimize glazing in windows and skylights for energy savings.

Use solar collectors for heating water.

Use raised floor and demountable wall systems that are reusable.

Use products made locally or regionally that require minimal resources to ship.

Use low-VOC adhesives, paints, stains, sealers, and sealants.

Ventilate materials off-site to reduce offgassing on-site.

Recycle all demolition and construction waste materials (wood, steel, glass, cables, conduit).

Design new tenant spaces to include collection areas for recyclable materials.

Although this list is not comprehensive, it will help you to start thinking in the right direction. Any one of the items will contribute to the sustainability of the earth, and the more of them you use, the greater the contribution. As you read this book, you will discover other materials and products that will meet the goals in the list. "Process" is a key word because interior design is an evolving art. It may be your own practice that one day is the proving ground for the next innovation to be added to this list and advance the profession in efficiency, aesthetics, and social responsibility.

John B. Carter, Associate
Gensler and Associates/Architects

Preface

While teaching an introductory class in interior design, I noticed that the students usually chose paint or wallpaper for the walls and always used carpeting on the floor, as though these were the only suitable treatments for walls and floors. I felt a need to break the cycle by exposing students to the fascinating world of materials—and so this book started to take shape.

I was unable to find a book that fully covered the exciting nonstructural materials available to the interior designer. Some authors concentrated on historical aspects of the home, both in architecture and furniture. Some emphasized upholstered furniture, draperies, and carpets, while still others stressed the principles and elements of design and color and the aesthetic values that make up a home. However, no one concentrated on the "nuts and bolts" of interior design. Some books purporting to cover all types of flooring did not even mention wood floors, while others had only one or two paragraphs on the subject. This and the previous editions address these issues. New in this fourth edition is a chapter on environmental concerns, which should be of prime interest to those designers (most of us) who believe that the environment is something precious and worth saving.

In the past, the interior design profession has dealt mainly with the more decorative aspects of design. Today it has become increasingly necessary for interior designers to be knowledgeable not only about the finishing materials used in the design field, but some of the structural materials as well. Many interior designers are working for, or with, architects, so it is important that they understand the properties and uses of all materials. Thus the *raison d'être* of this textbook.

Most sales representatives realize that the interior design student of today is the customer of tomorrow, but there are still some who do not understand the scope of the interior design field. Many interior designers are women and I have found that the ability to talk knowledgeably about materials earns the respect of others in the profession.

Installation methods have been included because, unfortunately, there are some contractors (luckily only a few) who will use the cheapest method of installation, one that may not be the best for that particular job. The installation methods discussed in the text come from manufacturers, associations, and institutions involved in producing each product. Knowledge of the correct installation procedures will ensure a properly installed project. The instructor's manual has many true examples of problems with products that have been improperly installed.

The fourth edition of this textbook emphasizes environmental responsibility and recycling as a way to help cope with the growing landfill problem.

Throughout this new edition, for those particularly interested in environmental concerns, products and manufacturers will be mentioned that are participating in some way in recycling processes. (See Chapter 1 on Environmental Concerns.)

With most of the rest of the world on the metric system, and with the attempt of the U.S. government to stress the transition to the metric system, designers will find increasing use of millimeters, meters, grams, and kilograms as measurements for length and weight. The wallcovering industry has already converted to metric or European measurements. Some of the other manufacturers, particularly those who sell to Canada and other foreign countries, now list their products in two systems, inches and metric. There is a chart at the beginning of Appendix A with handy conversion tables.

In doing my research and talking to many manufacturers, I have found a growing awareness of customers' needs and wishes. Dependability is one of the things consumers require. This is reflected in the many warranties provided by manufacturers, in one case, a lifetime structural guarantee on a wood floor.

All disciplines have their own jargon; and in order to communicate properly with contractors and architects, it is necessary to be able to understand their language. When designers or prospective builders read and study *Materials and Components of Interior Architecture,* they will be able to talk knowledgeably with architects and contractors about the uses of materials and their methods of installation. This understanding will also enable them to decide for themselves which materials and methods are best, without being unduly influenced by personal bias or ease of installation.

This book can also serve as a reference for designers who are already practicing, because it brings to their attention new materials on the market and improvements in current ones, many of which have won 1994 awards. The appendices are a useful reminder of manufacturers and their products. When a product is unique to one manufacturer, that manufacturer's name and product have been mentioned. Wherever possible, generic information has been used. A contractor who read this book believes that contractors would also benefit from using it as a reference tool.

In arranging the subject matter, I placed the chapter on environmental concerns first, as all chapters on materials stress environmental concerns. The chapter on paint comes second, since all types of surfaces—floors, walls, and ceilings—may be painted. Then, starting from the bottom up, the logical progression is a chapter on carpet (the most used covering for floors). Here special thanks are due the Carpet and Rug Institute, without whose help the carpet chapter could not have been written. Chapter 4 deals with all the other types of materials for floors.

Many of the same materials used for flooring also appear in Chapter 5, but this time they are used on walls; the installation, finish, and, of course, maintenance do vary. Chapter 6 covers ceilings, areas that are either painted or ignored. Chapter 7 includes all the other components that make up a well-designed room, including mouldings, doors, hardware, and hinges.

Chapter 8 could not have been written without the assistance of the Architectural Woodwork Institute. It is an explanation of what goes into the structure and design of fine cabinetry. This chapter will enable designers to provide rough drawings of cabinetry that is as economical as possible to construct. Chapter 9 covers kitchens. With the background of the previous chapter, it enables a designer to make an intelligent selection of the appropriate cabinetry. This chapter also covers the various appliances and the newest innovations in kitchen design. Chapter 10 describes bathrooms, both residential and institutional. The last two chapters were included because designers will be called on more and more to assist in the renovation of homes—including the very expensive kitchen and bathroom areas. These remodeling jobs will probably cost about 10 percent to 15 percent of the house value. A full bath added to the older, three-bedroom, one-bath house will not only guarantee recouping the cost of improvements, but even increase resale value.

A glossary of words that are boldfaced in the text is placed at the end of each chapter to make it easier to relate to other words from the same subject matter. It is also added as an aid for students studying for exams. Appendix A is a listing of manufacturers and associations that sell or represent the products mentioned in the chapters. Appendix B lists the names and addresses of the manufacturers named in the text. Every effort has been made to make this list as up to date as possible, but businesses do change names and locations.

While compiling the index, I realized that it can be aid in preparation for comprehensive exams, such as a final or the NCIDQ exam. I have listed in parentheses all the words in the glossaries for two reasons. First the page number enables users to find the word (the usual purpose of an index). Second, the students can test themselves to determine if they are familiar with the word and its meaning.

If one manufacturer seems to be given more emphasis than another at times, it is not necessarily because its product is better than others on the market, but that the manufacturer has been extremely helpful in providing information and brochures, checking sections for accuracy and, most importantly, providing photographs with which to illustrate the various sections.

I am indebted to the many, many manufacturers and trade organizations that have so willingly provided me with technical information and brochures from which I have been able to compile an up-to-date summary. As previously mentioned, I am deeply indebted to the Carpet and Rug Institute for granting permission to quote material found in its extremely informative *Specifier's Handbook*. This handbook has been the basis for much of the information contained in the carpet chapter.

I have found the trade organizations to be very helpful and particularly wish to thank the Architectural Woodwork Institute for many drawings as well as technical information. Other trade organizations that assisted me with preparation of the text were the Door and Hardware Institute and the Hardwood Plywood Veneer Association.

In order to be as accurate and current as possible with the information contained in the text, I was assisted by many professionals, one of whom was Robert Hanks of Bridgepoint Corporation, who realized that proper maintenance is vital to the durability of carpeting. I particularly want to thank Prentice Hall's former Editor-in-Chief for Education, Career Technology, Priscilla G. McGeehon, who gave me wonderful encouragement and allowed me to use, for the first time, color photographs.

I would also like to thank the reviewers for this edition: Kathleen Johnson, Hesser College; Sandra Slade, Bassist College; Jan Slaubaugh, Weber State University; Hank Stembridge, Savannah College of Art and Design; and Betty Treanor, Southwest Texas State University.

Most of all I wish to thank my husband, sculptor Frank Riggs, for his support and encouragement and for many of the line drawings in the text. I am also grateful to him for not complaining about meals served at odd times during the writing of this new edition.

Introduction

For too many years, the fields of architecture and interior design have been treated as two separate disciplines involved in creating a pleasant living environment. The architect planned the exterior and interior of the home, often with little attention to where the furniture was to be placed. The interior designer had to contend with such things as walls that were not long enough to allow placement of furniture, or heating vents placed directly under the bed or some other piece of furniture. On the other hand, designers would ruin the architect's plans by using the incorrect style of furniture, thereby spoiling the whole concept of the building.

Today, these problems are being resolved with many architects having interior designers on their staff. The result is that both disciplines cooperate from the very beginning of the project.

From the interior designer's point of view, this cooperation involves learning and appreciating the language and problems associated with architecture. The American Institute of Architects (AIA) is the professional organization for architects; The American Society of Interior Designers (ASID) and the International Interior Design Association (IIDA) are the professional organizations for interior designers. It is because of the professionalism of these organizations that the fields of architecture and interior design have gradually become aware of the necessity for closer cooperation. This book is dedicated to fostering that cooperation.

Trademarks

Envirosense is a registered trademark of the Envirosense Consortium

Gridset is a registered trademark of Rockland React Rite

Intersept is a registered trademark of Porter Paints

Syndecrete is a registered trademark of Syndesis

BASF Nylon 6ix™ and Again™ are trademarks of BASF

Zeftron is a registered trademark of BASF

Clean Air Choice™ and Lifemaster™ 2000 are trademarks of the Glidden Corp.

Spred® 2000 is a registered trademark of the Glidden Corp.

Ecolon and Duratron are registered trademarks of Image Carpets Inc.

Jacuzzi is a registered trademark of Jacuzzi Whirlpool Bath Inc.

Delfino is a trademark of Jacuzzi Whirlpool Bath Inc.

Hartex is a registered trademark of Leggett & Platt

Marblesque is a registered trademark of Summitville Tile

Protect-All is a registered trademark of Oscoda Plastics

CottonBac is a registered trademark of Ruckstuhl (USA) Ltd., d/b/a Larsen Carpet

Vicrtex is a registered trademark of Forbo Industries

Ever Clean is a trademark of Sherwin Williams

Perma-White is a registered trademark of Wm Zinsser & Co. Inc.

Portersept is a registered trademark of Porter Paints

Aquafleck is a registered trademark of California Products Corp.

Duroplex is a registered trademark of Triarch Industries

Omniplex is a registered trademark of Seagrave Coatings Corp.

Playfield is a registered trademark and Country Club Collection is a trademark of Playfield International, Inc.

Scotchgard is a registered trademark of the 3M Company

Teflon is a registered trademark of E.I. DuPont de Nemours Co. Inc.

Spillblock is a registered trademark of E.I. DuPont de Nemours Co. Inc.

Weardated is a registered trademark of Monsanto Co.

Traffic Control is a trademark of Monsanto Co.

UltraBrite is a trademark of Harris-Tarkett

Timeless, PermaGrain, and Paragon are registered trademarks of PermaGrain Corp.

Bruce and WearMaster are registered trademarks of Bruce Hardwood Flooring

Hydroment is a registered trademark of Bostik

HARDIBACKER is a registered trademark of James Hardie Building Products Inc.

Plaza is a registered trademark of Johnson Wax

DELPHI, VISTABRIK, and PC are registered trademarks of Pittsburgh Corning

FIRM-STEP is a registered trademark of Kentile

Johnsonite and Permalight are registered trademarks of Johnsonite Corp.

ComfortTech is a trademark of Johnsonite Corp.

Clorox is a registered trademark of The Clorox Company

Masonite is a registered trademark of Masonite Corp.

Ipocork is a registered trademark of Ipocork Inc.

EndBlock and Encurve are trademarks of Pittsburgh Corning

VUE, PC, PC GlassBlock, HEDRON, TRIDRON 45° BLOCK, and KWiK'N EZ are registered trademarks of Pittsburgh Corning

SHEETROCK is a registered trademark of U.S. Gypsum Company

Softforms is a registered trademark of Pittcon Industries

FRESCO is a trademark of Pittcon Industries

Anaglypta and Lincrusta are registered trademarks of Mile Hi Crown

Quantex is a trademark of MDC Wallcoverings

NEOCON is a registered trademark of National Exposition of Contract Interior Furnishings

Koroseal is a registered trademark of The B.F. Goodrich Co.

Flexwood is a registered trademark of Flexible Materials

Velcro is a registered trademark of Velcro USA Inc.

Tedlar and Corian are registered trademarks of E.I. DuPont de Nemours & Co. Inc.

Vicrtex is a registered trademark of Forbo Industries

Prefixx is a trademark of Divers Tech General, Wallcovering Division

Peg-Board is a registered trademark of The Masonite Corp.

Wilsonart and SOLICOR are registered trademarks of Ralph Wilson Plastics Co.

COLORCORE is a registered trademark of Formica Corporation

Formula 409 is a registered trademark of The Clorox Co.

Glass Plus is a registered trademark of Dow Brands

Mr. Clean is a registered trademark of Procter & Gamble

Fill 'n Glaze is a trademark of the 3M Company

Restoration Glass is a trademark of Bendheim Corp.

VITRICOR is a registered trademark of Nevamar

Cirrus Borders and Compässo are trademarks of USG Interiors

Classique is a trademark of Chicago Metallic Corp.

Barrisol is a registered trademark of Barrisol North America Inc.

AutoCAD is a registered trademark of Autodesk

Corian is a registered trademark of E.I. DuPont de Nemours & Co. Inc.

Gibraltar is a registered trademark of Ralph Wilson Plastics

Focal Point is a registered trademark of NMC Focal Point Inc.

Specicast is a trademark of NMC Focal Point

QuarryCast is a registered trademark of Formglas Interiors Inc.

Intelock is a registered trademark of InteLock Technologies

Light Touch and Quick Space are registered trademarks of General Electric

Frigi-Foam is a registered trademark of Frigidaire

UtraStyle is a trademark of Frigidaire

Ceran is a registered trademark of Schott Glaswerke

Kohler Coordinates is a trademark of Kohler

Soft Scrub is a registered trademark of The Clorox Company

Martex is a registered trademark of Martex Towels

GE Monogram is a registered trademark of GE Company

Duostrainer, Black Black, and Assure are registered trademarks of Kohler

Spacemaker Plus is a trademark of GE Company

Nuvel is a trademark of Formica Corp.

Perma-Edge is a registered trademark of Ralph Wilson Plastics

ScotchBrite is a registered trademark of the 3M Company

Swanstone is a registered trademark of Swan

Re-Bath is a registered trademark of Re-Bath

PowerPro, Water Rainbow, and Fiore are registered trademarks of Jacuzzi Corp.

J-Dream and J-Shower tower are trademarks of Jacuzzi Corp.

Environment, Habitat, Delfino, Precedence, Freewill, Revival, and Pillows are trademarks of Kohler

Riser is a registered trademark of Moen

____ *Chapter 1*

Environmental Concerns

The Center for Environmental Study states,

> We stand at a crossroads. For the first time in history, we face the prospect of irreversible changes in our planet's life support systems. The growing human population and the by-products of our industrial and technological society threaten our planet's air, water, climate and biodiversity. These threats present a challenge to our society—to learn to live in harmony with our planet.

Members of the design community and the manufacturers they work with can, if they wish to, lead the way in helping to save this country from overburdened landfills. This can be achieved in both the manufacturing process itself and in the disposal of the product after it is no longer needed. An example would be using linoleum instead of vinyl flooring. Linoleum is a product manufactured from natural materials and will, at the end of its use, gradually biodegrade.

On July 28, 1992, the Federal Trade Commission (FTC) announced guidelines for environmental marketing claims. The guidelines are recommendations, not enforceable regulations. They are intended to reduce consumer confusion and prevent false or misleading use of common environmental terms. The FTC defines "recycled content" as materials that have been recovered or diverted from the solid waste stream, either during the manufacturing process (preconsumer) or after use (postconsumer). Scrap produced from manufacturing processes in which the end product is not for consumer use is commonly referred to as "postindustrial."

The increasing awareness of indoor air quality issues and the growing incidence of Sick Building Syndrome (**SBS**) affecting worker comfort, well-being, and productivity highlight the vital need for improved workplace air quality worldwide.

Probably the most well-known example of environmental concern are the precautions taken when dealing with any form of asbestos. Before the mid-1980s, one of the ingredients used in the resilient flooring industry was asbestos. This mineral has been proven injurious to health; therefore, the Resilient Floor Covering Institute (RFCI), a trade association of resilient flooring manufacturers, has developed a set of recommended work practices for the removal of resilient flooring, regardless of whether or not it contains asbestos. Following RFCI's recommendations will ensure that the removal of an older resilient floor complies with Environmental Protection Agency (**EPA**) and Occupational Safety and Health Administration (**OSHA**) regulations regarding the handling of asbestos-containing materials, should it be determined that removal is necessary.

Asbestos is hazardous to health when it becomes "friable" or free-floating and airborne, as in a dust form. However, asbestos used in resilient flooring manufactured prior to the mid-1980s is firmly encapsulated in the product as a result of the manufacturing process. The EPA has determined that encapsulated, or nonfriable, asbestos-containing products are not subject to extensive regulatory requirements as long as they remain in that state. Resilient flooring, either vinyl composition tile or sheet vinyl, is nonfriable provided it is not sanded, sawed, or reduced to a powder by hand pressure.

To ensure that any asbestos present in resilient flooring does not become dislodged and friable, the RFCI has recommended work practices that specifically prohibit sanding, dry scraping, mechanically pulverizing, or beadblasting the resilient flooring or felt backing. In other words, workers should refrain from any procedure that produces a dust.

Common substrates used today in kitchen cabinet and furniture applications are particleboard and Medium Density Fiberboard (MDF). Because products manufactured with these materials are known to emit minute quantities of formaldehyde, the following information is supplied by the National Particleboard Association (NPA), based on the NPA Technical Bulletin—Formaldehyde Emission Barriers:

Urea Formaldehyde (UF) adhesives are used in most particleboard and MDF products worldwide. UF resins are easy to work with, and provide a strong, durable, and cost-effective bonding system. Acting as the cross-link or "polymerizer" in UF resins, formaldehyde enables the adhesive to bond the wood particles and fibers together.

Over the last 10 years, new resin technology and improved manufacturing controls have dramatically reduced formaldehyde emissions. Using less formaldehyde in combination with chemical scavengers, manufacturers can still produce high quality board products. . . .

Particleboard and MDF are ideal substrates for laminate and coating products. Because the boards are dimensionally stable and flat, have tight thickness tolerances and a smooth surface, particleboard and MDF are the preferred choice of designers for new laminating, fabricating, and finishing ideas.

Most laminates, overlays and finishes provide protection against water damage stains, and the general hazards of every day use. High pressure laminates and veneers can increase board stiffness. Most of these surface treatments also act as barriers and reduce formaldehyde emissions from the particleboard/MDF core.

When deciding whether or not to use barriers for emission reduction, consider whether these environmental factors exist:

High temperatures
High humidity
Low ventilation rates.

High temperatures or high humidity increase formaldehyde emissions, while low ventilation can trap emissions in a room. If these conditions may be encountered, barriers can provide an effective means of protecting the substrate as well as reducing potential formaldehyde emission levels.

After manufacturing, emission levels from UF bonded boards can be reduced two ways: Aging, and applying barriers such as laminates, veneers, overlays or coatings.

In UF board products, emission levels are always the highest immediately after manufacturing—then quickly dropping or "decaying" as the boards age.

Research shows that average emission levels from unfinished or unlaminated boards drop by about 25 percent after the first month and by 50 percent after 7 months. Over time, these levels approach and maintain background or household formaldehyde levels.

Effective barriers can reduce emission levels by 95 percent or more. Barriers are particularly effective when applied to products that already have low emission levels.

Barriers are most effective when all surfaces are treated. For maximum emission reduction, edges, notches, and holes also need to be edge banded, laminated, finished or covered with hardware. This is because edge emissions are higher than surface emissions. Filling and sanding edges well before finishing and between coats prevents the **wicking-in** of wet coatings.

Good barrier properties include:

A continuous laminate or coating—For laminates this generally translates to good adhesion to the board. For finishes, multiple coats may be necessary to obtain a continuous, low defect finish.

Research shows that two coats that are each 1.0 mils (0.001") thick are up to ten times as effective as one coat 2.0 mils thick. The second coat will fill many of the pinholes and other minor imperfections of the first coat.

Enough flexibility to move with the wood—otherwise, delaminating and cracking can occur during cyclic humidity changes. This will not only impact the barrier effect, but will detract from the product appearance.

An inherently low permeability to vapors—for example, oil based paints are often less permeable than latexes and high pressure laminates are almost impermeable.[1]

More information concerning barriers can be found in the NPA Technical Bulletin—*Formaldehyde Emission Barriers.*

Envirosense is a consortium of international companies who are uniformly concerned with bringing common sense into the design, construction, furnishings, operation and maintenance of buildings. Their goal is to allow environmental engineering and indoor air quality disciplines to be represented in proactively implementing a total systems approach to a more comfortable and productive environment. Consisting of architects, designers, engineers, consultants, manufacturers, owners, developers and maintenance firms, the consortium is raising the awareness of Indoor Air Quality **(IAQ)** issues. More importantly, it is providing viable solutions and products that not only remedy existing problems, but also can help prevent indoor air quality from deteriorating in the future.

Systems Approach

The Envirosense consortium represents the first complementary "systems approach" to solving IAQ problems using coordinated solutions that satisfy, and in some cases pioneer, environmental standards while maintaining energy efficiency. Based on a "design-to-disposal" perspective, the concept encompasses three major sectors which, while seemingly distinct, are in fact, inextricably interwoven:

Building Systems—design, construction, operation, monitoring. [This section is in the architects and construction province and as such is not something with which interior designers are involved directly.]

Product Systems—manufacture/installation/performance.

Maintenance Systems—cleaning/approved products/training . . .

Comprehensive pre-building IAQ consulting concepts and proactive IAQ inspection and monitoring programs have been developed. These ser-vices, when integrated with innovative electronic monitoring systems, provide property owners with unparalleled safeguards concerning the well-being of their buildings.

Product Systems—Manufacture/ Installation/Performance

Independent researchers have implicated bacterial or fungal contamination in over 40 percent of SBS cases and virtually all Building Related Illness **(BRI)** problems. Also, of primary concern to the consortium are unwanted emissions from a variety of sources. Therefore, two major contributors to poor indoor air quality—microbial contamination and volatile organic compounds **(VOCs)** emissions—were selected as solution priorities.

The challenge was the apparent paradox that most products used for treating microbial contaminants were themselves toxic. Some contained heavy metals, most used carriers or aerosols, to dispense the active ingredients. High concentrations of such products can expose the product applicators and/or building occupants to risks, and possibly create long term problems with respect to the ultimate disposal of the treated products.

Since bacteria and fungi routinely settle and multiply on exposed interior surfaces, consortium members aimed research at creating an effective, environmentally friendly antimicrobial shield which could be incorporated into fabrics, carpets, plastics, paints, adhesives, wall coverings, lacquers, floor and ceiling surfaces, and air filters. The agent had to be very low in toxicity to animals, plants and humans during manufacture, biologically active throughout the life of the products, and yet be easily neutralized for safe disposal.

Results of this research produced an ideal, versatile antimicrobial complex providing a protective, durable "inhibitory zone," or germ barrier, that can be added in the manufacturing process to a wide variety of interior finishing and furnishing materials.

Maintenance Systems—Cleaning/ Approved Products/Training

Even a building utilizing proper design and superior interior products must be maintained by well trained and adequately equipped staff.

A "green list" of environmentally friendly cleaning materials has been identified. Products have been certified as environmentally safe, biodegradable, water soluble and not only meet, but exceed, current standards. Cleaning service operatives receive training in the proper use of these specially formulated materials to ensure that optimum cleaning is accomplished while minimizing the risks of exposure from residues of these compounds. Alternatively, the approved cleaning products and training in their use is offered to building owners with in-house cleaning staffs.

Conclusion

Envirosense embraces a total systems approach which includes the building design, operation, environmental control and monitoring, product specifications and performance and a well thought-out maintenance program. This coordinated solution is the key to helping building owners and users to positively impact the quality of their indoor environment.

It is anticipated that buildings adopting the Envirosense concepts will be recognized as environmentally friendly structures. Occupiers and tenants will progressively be more selective about their choice of buildings, and investors have already started to appreciate the value of incorporating environmental concerns in their property portfolios.[2]

The following information from Interface, a member of Envirosense, shows what a responsible company can do in setting standards for other manufacturers to follow:

Interface is dedicated to offering alternatives which ensure that we do not contribute to the environmental problem, but that we contribute to the solution. Interface's environmental efforts are focused on three critical areas:

Materials, Processes, and Programs

Interface Flooring Systems (IFS) is committed to conforming to the spirit and to the letter of sound environmental practices. Prior to any process or material change, we undertake an evaluation of the environmental impact the change may have on any area of our business, including product quality, commercial use, or Mother Earth.

Our commitment to this environmental effort is evidenced by the investment in a state of the art testing laboratory at our Interface Research Corporation facility. We are able to test for VOCs and **off-gassing** as well as other critical factors related to the environment. An example of our commitment is the development of Gridset® adhesive which is manufactured by our subsidiary Rockland React Rite. Gridset establishes new industry standards for VOC and off-gassing emissions of adhesives which have historically been a major source of VOCs. Gridset produces less than half the VOCs in proposed EPA standard for VOC emissions. . . .

In addition to Gridset, all of the recommended chemicals used in the Interface Service Management (ISM) maintenance program have been thoroughly tested and certified as environmentally responsible. Interface invites and welcomes comparison of its environmental efforts (and investment therein) with those of any other companies in the field.

Proactive Solutions to Indoor Air Quality Problems Through the Envirosense Consortium

Indoor Air Quality, Sick Building Syndrome, and Building Related Illness are all real issues of growing concern and importance in today's work place. Interface offers real solutions today through its Envirosense Consortium.

The Interface led Envirosense Consortium delivers a family of products, ranging from interior fabrics, plastic components, wall coverings, upholstery fabric, paints, coatings, and laminates, to flooring, ceiling tile and **HVAC** components, which, collectively, demonstrably inhibit the growth of microorganisms, and thereby offer an enhanced interior environment for today's commercial building.

Intersept®, an EPA-registered antimicrobial, the active agent incorporated into all Envirosense products, is a durable, environmentally friendly, broad spectrum antimicrobial which inhibits the growth of microorganisms and controls bacteria and fungi—major sources of indoor air quality contamination.

Recycle/Reuse—A Continuing Process

Interface has created a worldwide multi-disciplinary task force which is dedicated to identifying and implementing programs and processes to reduce waste generation, increase the percentage of materials recycled, and increase the proportion reused in the manufacture of products and other applications. Our thrust goes beyond this internal effort, to include our customers in recycling and selective replacement programs, reducing the impact on land fills.

At present, Interface recycles up to 50 percent of the waste from manufacturing. Throughout the world, we are aggressively seeking additional opportunities to reduce the waste generated, as well as to find methods of increasing the percentage of materials recycled.

During 1992, Interface introduced a new packaging system which employs a two piece box containing a high percentage of recycled materials. This new box configuration allows our customers to pack used carpet tiles in the boxes in which they receive new tiles, so the tiles can be returned to Interface for recycling.

Once the carpet life has been exhausted, Interface recycles the material in an environmentally sound manner. At present, two methods exist:

1. Closed loop reuse of the material, by separating components and using these in the manufacturing of new carpet or other industrial products. Projects are currently under way to recycle nylon polymers by depolymerizing type 6 nylon fiber to **caprolactam,** and extruding first quality fiber from it. This initiative differs from more commonly known recycling efforts as it is a "closed loop" process which ensures the new polymer is the same as the original.
2. Environmentally friendly disposal; several initiatives are underway, in conjunction with the major fiber suppliers, to turn old carpet materials (broadloom or tile) into recyclable materials, used outside the carpet industry.[3]

Following is a list of those manufacturers of products covered in this textbook who are members of Envirosense Consortium, Inc.: Bentley Mills, carpet; General Polymers Corp., epoxy and terrazzo flooring systems; Interface Flooring Systems Inc./Huega USA, carpet systems for commercial, institutional, health care, retail, hospitality, and residential markets; Interface Research Corp., Intersept antimicrobial compound, licensing of Envirosense program; Interface Service Management, carpet maintenance and appearance-retention programs; Porter Paints (Division of Courtaulds Coatings, Inc.), paints, coatings, and adhesives for wall coverings; and USG Interiors, Inc., ceiling tile systems.

Another example of environmental concern would be the world conference of the PVC (polyvinyl chloride) industry where participants pledged to expend efforts in 1994 to encourage three types of recycling:

> Mechanical recycling, where used products such as bottles are made into new products such as furniture and irrigation pipe.
>
> Chemical or feedstock recycling, which converts vinyl into basic chemicals for reuse in new production.
>
> Thermal recycling, where vinyl's heat content is recovered in waste-to-energy process and used to generate steam for electricity, thus reducing society's reliance on fossil fuels.

Syndecrete® is a restorative product, reconstituting materials extracted from society's waste stream to create a new, high-valued product. Syndecrete was developed by Syndesis as an alternative to limited or nonrenewable natural materials such as wood or stone and synthetic petroleum-based solid and laminating materials. Like standard concrete, Syndecrete is chemically inert and is not subject to out-gassing. Syndecrete can incorporate 41 percent recycled or recovered materials from industry and postconsumer goods. Fly ash, a powder residue that results from the combustion of pulverized coal in electric power-generating plants, is added by 15 percent to displace the cement base. Polypropylene fiber, a recovered off-fall scrap with a three-dimensional reinforced matrix, increases the tensile strength of the product and gives it a physical property akin to wood.

Aggregates, added to vary the texture and appearance of the product, have included recycled materials such as metal shavings, postconsumer plastic re-grinds, recycled glass chips, and scrap wood chips, creating a contemporary reinterpretation of the Italian tradition of terrazzo. Scrap materials are actively sourced from local businesses and curbside recycling centers.

Syndecrete is certified as a recycled product by the Californians Against Waste Foundation and has been referred by environmental consultants for use by chemically sensitive persons. Products discussed in this textbook and manufactured by Syndesis include counter tops, tiles, sinks, bathtubs, and showers.

Gensler and Associates Architects, one of the world's largest architectural and interior design firms, is taking a stand for environmentally sound design. An example of this is the design of the Los Angeles offices of HBO (Home Box Office). They recycled all demolished materials, including wood, paper, glass, plastics, copper, and aluminum. Recycling bins were placed on each floor of the construction area. This is in accordance with the goals mentioned in the Foreword.

The carpeting was laid with low-toxicity carpet adhesive and special, solution-dyed, nontoxic carpeting was installed with carpet manufacturers accelerating the off-gassing process before installation. The carpeting was shipped off-site and was ventilated for 48 hours with massive amounts of fresh air. Linoleum, while more expensive, was used instead of vinyl composition flooring and low-biocide, low-fungicide paints were also used. Where possible, existing furniture and ceiling tiles were reused and repainted with **non-bridging** paint.

The following companies manufacture products that are covered in this textbook and are all involved in recycling or preserving our planet in some way. The list is alphabetical.

1. In 1994, Azrock Industries introduced their Exotic Luxury Vinyl Tile, which resembles exotic woods that grow in and around the world's rain forests. Their original contribution to The National Arbor Day Foundation's Rain Forest Rescue program preserved 1 million square feet of forest. They also contributed enough funds to preserve an additional 2,500 square feet of rain forest every time Exotic Luxury Vinyl Tile was specified and registered.

2. BASF Nylon 6ix™ Again™ is BASF's nationwide recycling program for commercial carpets. Through the inherent strengths of Nylon 6ix, they have succeeded in patenting a process for recycling old BASF carpet fiber into new carpet nylon. All Zeftron® carpets manufactured after February 1, 1994 that meet BASF's qualifications are eligible for the program. Once a qualified carpet has reached the end of its useful life, the end user may return it to BASF for recycling. As a "closed loop" process, carpet that would be landfilled may be continually reused as new carpet fiber. BASF guarantees that all Nylon 6ix fiber returned to them will be converted into new nylon carpet fiber or other useful products. BASF will not landfill or incinerate any of the Nylon 6ix fiber they recover from the carpets submitted to the 6ix Again program.

The end user must supply a copy of the purchase receipt for verification of the carpet style and purchase date and must pay for shipping to the collection centers. These shipping costs will probably be approximately the same as landfill dumping fees.

Once the nylon polymer is converted back to raw caprolactam and then repolymerized, the resulting polymer is indistinguishable from virgin material. BASF has tested identically constructed carpets made from chemically recycled fiber and virgin fiber and found no discernible differences.

3. Pollution is the enemy of the environment. To fight this enemy, Bentley Carpet has empowered its Environmental Coordinator to monitor and evaluate all emissions, effluents, chemical handling, and disposal at all its manufacturing facilities. Air emissions are monitored to prevent the discharging of harmful quantities of chemicals; water effluents are checked regularly for any traces of chemicals and/or solids to make sure that all dyes are exhausted from discharged water that is monitored to keep it in the neutral zone of 7 ph $\pm$ 1; solvents used for cleaning carpets, even in small amounts, are collected and recycled; yarn **tailouts** are sold, rather than discarded, to small tufters for making carpet; latex waste has been reduced by the installation of latex recycling equipment.

4. Congoleum received the Pennsylvania State 1993 Governor's Waste Emission Award for its achievement in reducing and preventing the generation of waste through its use of water-based inks at its Marcus Hook, Pennsylvania, sheet vinyl flooring manufacturing plant. The water-based system eliminates the emission of potentially harmful solvent fumes, eradicates the need for hazardous waste disposal and landfill space, and saves the company upward of a million dollars a year.

5. Domtar Gypsum, manufacturers of gypsum board, recycle manufacturing-generated waste. They are also accepting gypsum waste from construction sites at two plants in the United States and two Canadian plants, with two other plants in the process of developing waste-acceptance programs.

6. Dura carpet cushion manufactured by Dura Undercushions Ltd. is produced with a cellular structure made from ground tire scrap rubber granules bonded with latex. A typical truck tire will produce 5 or 6 yards of Duracushion with just the addition of a little latex and backing made from cellulose and fiberglass, both made from natural products. Ninety percent of every yard is recycled tire rubber, and Dura Undercushions are recyclable into more Dura Undercushions.

7. The Glidden Company's technological and environmental breakthrough in paints is the first latex paint without petroleum-based solvents. The Clean Air Choice™ paints—Spred® 2000 and its companion brand for professional painters, Glidden Lifemaster™ 2000—use a unique resin that allows the petroleum-based solvent to be eliminated in the formula.

Solvents in traditional latex paints have two primary functions: They assist film forming and increase workability. In film forming, the resin particles flow together and act as a binder, holding pigment particles together in a continuous, durable film. Workability is the ability paint has to be applied smoothly and evenly before it dries.

In all latex paints, the resin and pigment adhere to the surface after the paint has dried. In traditional latex paint technology, the resin particles are softened by a petroleum-based solvent so that they fuse together to form a continuous film on drying. The resin used in Spred® 2000 and Lifemaster™ 2000 employs a unique latex technology known as heterogeneous technology. In effect, the softening process required to fuse the resin particles is built right into the resin, eliminating the need for petroleum solvent. This new formula keeps the paint from drying too fast, allowing the painter time to load paint on the applicator and "work" the product on the surface without visible brush strokes or roller marks.

8. IMAGE Carpets Inc. uses PET (polyethylene terephthalate) polyester for 100 percent of the face fibers in their Ecolon® products and for a majority of the face fibers used in Duratron® products. PET is made from recycled soft drink and ketchup bottles; PET fibers are naturally stain resistant as demonstrated by the use of PET to make ketchup bottles. Tire manufacturers also use polyester, which shows the durability of this material. IMAGE extrudes its own PET fibers for its own products.

9. Jacuzzi Whirlpool Bath provides several options that reduce the amount of water needed to operate its whirlpool baths. First, the jets are placed low in the bath for beneficial hydrotherapy. This also means that the water level only needs to be just past the top of the jets; the bathtub does not have to be completely full for operation. Jacuzzi® now manufactures the new Delfino™ whirlpool bath/spa combination. Although this unit is large, it comes with an inline heater and filter system so it does not have to be drained with each use.

10. Leggett & Platt manufactures Hartex® carpet cushion from 100 percent recycled fibers. It is made from recycled carpet fiber such as **strike offs,** thread waste, and other soft-backed waste that are by-products of the broadloom carpet manufacturing process. The company operates a 90,000 square foot facility in Dalton, Georgia, where, each year, over 15 million pounds of carpet waste are accumulated, baled, and then distributed to shredding and processing plants.

After processing, the fiber is shipped in bales to the Hartex manufacturing plant in Villa Rica, Georgia. The fiber is then blended and run through a needling loom where it is punched through a woven polypropylene innerliner.

11. Marblesque®, from Summitville, is an eco-friendly porcelain paver offering the natural beauty of marble without the high price tag. Marblesque is produced from a waste product that previously overloaded landfills and is now manufactured in a new Summitville plant designed to recycle virtually all waste products that were previously discharged into rivers and mountainous landfills. The company has also created a system for reuse of its own unprocessed manufacturing wastes. Accordingly, this is a paver for consumers in search of products from environmentally responsible companies.

12. Oscoda Plastics, Inc., manufactures Protect-All® from 100 percent recycled materials. It is an all-purpose protective covering for floors and walkways. Protect-All provides superior shock absorbency, excellent traction even when wet, yet it is highly resistant to the abuse of golf spikes and cleats, and is ideal for locker rooms, weight rooms, pro shops, laboratories, etc. Sheets are 5 feet by 30 inches, 5 foot square, and 5 feet by 8 feet. Also available are 18-inch interlocking tiles that easily snap together, for temporary floor protection.

13. Porter Paints now formulates Intersept into a line of paint products. Intersept is a unique antimicrobial agent that prevents the growth of fungi and bacteria on the applied paint film. Portersept HVAC 3830 is specifically designed for use in HVAC systems and can be applied to metal and insulated surfaces. This water-based product is typically sprayed on and is very fast drying. The Intersept remains effective against the growth of microbes on the paint film for as long as the paint film is intact and the surface is clean.

14. Ruckstuhl (USA) Ltd., d/b/a/ Larsen Carpet, has developed the CottonBac® with natural properties

specifically designed for superior installation of coir and sisal as a better backing for area rugs and a product that is wholly biodegradable. The adhesive used between the cotton and carpet pile is an SBR latex, free of heavy metals and other toxic agents. When replacement is necessary, the carpet can be taken up easily and disposed of without environmental concern since coir, sisal, and the CottonBac are biodegradable.

15. Vicrtex® from Forbo Industries, Inc., uses an extrusion process, rather than calendered or plastisol coating, in the manufacture of its wallcoverings, a process that does not use solvents. Vicrtex wallcoverings won an ASID award in 1993.

16. Ralph Wilson Plastics is currently converting its press operations to reusable steel plates for imparting finish to high-pressure decorative laminate. This conversion will eliminate the use of release paper and aluminum foil, which will result in a savings of approximately 14 million pounds of these materials each year. Currently these materials are sold for reclamation and recycling. The company also thermally destroys in excess of 95 percent of its VOC stack emissions.

ENDNOTES

[1]NPA Technical Bulletin, *Formaldehyde Emission Barriers,* National Particleboard Association, 1991.

[2]Envirosense™, *A "Total Systems" Approach,* Envirosense Consortium, press release, pages 1–3.

[3]Interface, *Environmental Responsibilities,* press release, pages 14–17.

GLOSSARY

BRI. Building Related Illness. A variety of illnesses that have been attributed to toxic fumes inside a building.

Caprolactam. The white crystalline cyclic amide that is one of the components from which nylon is made.

EPA. Environmental Protection Agency.

HVAC. Heating, Ventilating, and Air Conditioning, almost always written using initials.

IAQ. Indoor Air Quality. The result of measuring the air inside a building for toxic emissions.

Non-bridging. A paint that will not cover the small holes in an acoustical tiled ceiling. (See Chapter 6, page 120.)

Off-gassing. The process by which toxic fumes are emitted from carpet, when it is newly laid.

OSHA. Occupational Safety and Health Administration.

SBS. Sick Building Syndrome. The symptoms of an illness caused by toxic emissions inside a building.

Strike-off. A small sample run off for color or pattern.

Tailouts. Short cones left on tufting machines.

VOC. Volatile Organic Compound. Toxic emissions from solvents in paints and other ingredients used in manufacturing.

Wicking-in. Absorption of liquids into a material, in this case the absorption of paint into the substrate.

_____ *Chapter 2*

Paints and Finishes

It is only since 1867 that prepared paints have been available on the American market. Originally, paint was used merely to decorate a home, as in the frescoes at Pompeii, and it is still used for that purpose today. However, modern technology has now made paint both a decorative and a protective finish.

The colors used are also of great psychological importance. A study made by Johns Hopkins University showed that planned color environments greatly improved scholastic achievement. Many major paint companies now have color consultants who can work with customers on selection of colors for schools, hospitals, and other commercial and industrial buildings. Today, paint is the most inexpensive method of changing the environment.

Paint is commonly defined as a substance that can be put on a surface to make a film, whether white, black, or colored. This definition has now been expanded to include clear films.

CLASSIFICATION OF PAINTS AND THEIR COMPONENTS

Most paints are classified according to their **vehicles** or **binders**—in other words, whether the contents of the vehicle or liquid portion is water, oil, varnish, or dissolved synthetic **resins**.

Oil Paints

This type of paint is no longer manufactured. It was the original coating used for both exterior and interior use. Today, as a result of modern technology, alkyds have replaced oil paints.

Alkyds

Alkyds are oil-modified resins that dry faster and are much harder than ordinary oils. Drying results from both evaporation of the **solvent** and **oxidation** of the oil. The more oil there is in the formula, the longer it takes to dry, the better the wetting properties, and the better the elasticity. Alkyds dry quickly and evenly, are durable for both interior and exterior applications, are easy to apply, and are moderately priced. However, alkyd-based exterior paints, when compared to latex exterior paints, do show poorer gloss and color retention and tend to yellow over time.

Freshly made alkaline surfaces such as concrete, masonry, or plaster must be treated with an alkali-resistant primer before an alkyd is applied. Fumes of some alkyd paints are odorless but are toxic and flammable until the surface has dried. Therefore, the area should be very thoroughly ventilated. Alkyd paint is the most durable of the common finishing products.

Solvent-containing coatings can be used safely if overexposure is avoided and proper protective equipment is used. The disposal of all types of coating materials is controlled by government regulations.

To comply with the volatile organic compounds (VOC) emissions laws, more solids are being added, which makes the paint heavier bodied; and therefore it takes longer to dry.

In many areas of the country, the amount of VOC, expressed in pounds of VOC per gallon, is restricted. Sherwin-Williams has four pages at the beginning of its "Painting and Coatings Systems," that illustrate by means of primary red, green, and blue, which of its products are VOC compliant in those states with very strict regulations.

OSHA and the EPA both have strict rules governing not only the manufacture of paint but also its application. Check the appropriate regulatory agency for the VOC limits in your area, since some local agencies, particularly in California, have even more stringent regulations in place.

Latex

Latex binders are synthetic materials that may vary in hardness, **flexibility,** and **gloss** retention. There are several types of latex binders including styrene butadiene, poly-vinyl acetate, acrylics, and vinyl acetate-acrylics; the pure acrylics are the preferable choice. Drying results from **coalescence** of latex particles as the water evaporates from the film. Advantages of latex paint over alkyds include the ease of application, freedom from solvent odor, fast drying and recoating, minimal fire hazard, blister and peel resistance, and ease of cleanup (requires soap and water only).

Because of ease of application, the temptation may be to make the paint go further; thus, coverage may not be as heavy as needed for a good job.

Several paint companies have developed very durable latex paints because of the VOC restrictions. Sherwin-Williams has produced Ever Clean™, a new stain-resistant interior latex wall paint, available in flat and satin, that gives the washability and durability performance usually found in glossy enamel finishes. The paint dries to a virtually nonporous film, preventing absorption of stains into the paint finish.

Perma®-White mildew-proof bathroom wall and ceiling paint from Wm Zinsser & Co., Inc., features a 5-year mildew-proof guarantee. It is also scrubbable and blister- and peel-proof.

On page 7 Clean Air Choice™ paints from The Glidden Company are described.

There are several finishes or **lusters** available in both alkyds and latex:

Flat. Velvety, with a rich, soft-looking surface for walls requiring little washing.

Eggshell or Satin. Slightly higher light reflectance for walls in residential areas where finger marks need removing.

Flat or Eggshell Enamel. Dull luster for washable surfaces.

Semigloss. Just enough sheen for contrast with flat-finished surfaces. Used in kitchens, bathrooms, nurseries, and school rooms in order to give greater resistance to wear and washing.

Gloss or High Gloss Enamel. Very shiny surface giving easy washability. However, the higher the gloss, the more likely it is to show surface discrepancies. This is true with both walls and woodwork and demonstrates the importance of proper surface preparation.

The classification of paints according to gloss ratings depends on the ability of the surface to bounce back varying amounts of light beamed on it, and these readings show the relative reflectance of the coated surface as compared with a smooth flat mirror (Table 2–1). The ratings in Table 2–1 measure the light reflectance of the surface only. Table 2–2 shows the percentage of light reflected by different hues and their different values.

TABLE 2–1
**Standard Gloss Range for Architectural
and Special Coatings**

NAME	GLOSS RANGE	TEST METHOD (ASTM D-523)
Flat	Below 15	85° meter*
Eggshell	5–20	60° meter
Satin	15–35	60° meter
Semigloss	30–65	60° meter
Gloss	Over 65	60° meter

*Angle at which light is reflected.

Source: Consumerism Subcommittee of the N.P.C.A. Scientific Committee acting with the Subcommittee D01.13 of the American Society for Testing and Materials (ASTM).

Pigments

Pigments confer the following properties: color, **hiding power** or opacity, and protection and corrosion repression on iron and steel. Pigments are the minute solid coloring parts of paints, and different pigments have different purposes. **Titanium dioxide** is the best white pigment for hiding power. Other pigments, whether organic or inorganic, merely add color to the

TABLE 2–2
Percentage of Light Reflected by Colors

COLOR	PERCENTAGE OF LIGHT REFLECTED
White	89
Ivory	77
Canary yellow	77
Cream	77
Orchid	67
Cream gray	66
Sky blue	65
Buff	63
Pale green	59
Shell pink	55
Olive tan	43
Forest green	22
Coconut brown	16
Black	2

paint. The third type, such as **calcium carbonate,** is inert, acting mainly as a filler. Masonry paints have a larger percentage of calcium carbonate than other paints.

Solvents

Solvents, when used in paints, are liquids that dissolve the resins or **gums** or other binder constituents. These liquids are mineral spirits in the case of alkyds, water for latex emulsions, alcohol for shellac, and lacquer thinner for lacquers. These solvents are used as thinners and are also used to clean the paint equipment and clean up any spills. Turpentine was used as a solvent before mineral spirits came on the market, but it is not used today due to VOC compliance, toxicity, high cost, and strong odor.

TYPES OF COATING PRODUCTS

Enamels

Enamels are pigmented paints that produce a hard, glossy, durable surface, with the pigments ground finer in order to provide a smooth texture. In the standard architectural coatings, the highest sheen is produced by an alkyd enamel, but many lacquers and urethanes can also achieve high sheens. Enamels come in semigloss and gloss, but a flat appearance can be produced by adding a **flatting** agent, though this addition can affect some performance properties.

Enamels and other paints should be applied to a properly prepared surface. A glossy surface will not have **tooth** and should be sanded with sandpaper or a liquid sanding material before application of another coat of paint.

As a result of the VOC laws, latex enamels have been greatly improved and one advantage is that latex enamels do not yellow.

Primers

A primer is the first coat applied to the **substrate** to prepare for subsequent finishing coats and may have an alkyd or latex base. Some primers also serve as sealers and function on porous substrates such as some woods, and particularly on the paper used on **gypsum board.** These nonpenetrating sealers prevent the waste of paint caused by absorption of the porous materials and provide a good base for the final coats. Other primers are specially formulated for use on wood surfaces where the natural dyes in the wood might cause unsightly stains. Some finish coats are self-priming, while others require a separate primer. The manufacturers' specifications will give this information.

Portersept with Intersept surface sealer can be used as a sealer under wallcoverings, reducing damage to drywall during removal, and as a premium quality primer under paints for plaster, wood, drywall, and metal. The Intersept controls the growth of microorganisms on the paint film.

Flame-Retardant Paints

Flame-retardant paints differ from conventional paints in that they are able to slow down the rate of combustion. Some of these fire-retardant paints are intumescent, which means that they form blisters and bubbles—thus forming an insulating layer—while others give off a gas that excludes air from the surface, thereby extinguishing the flames.

Flame-retardant paints are specified for public buildings, especially offices and hotels. After the tragic hotel fires of the early 1980s, it may become necessary to seriously consider these paints, which, while not fireproof, do reduce the flammability of the substrate.

For many commercial painting contracts, a Class A fire rating, defined as a **0–25 flame spread,** is required by law. Included in some technical data are the amounts of smoke developed and fuel contributed. As more people die in fires from smoke inhalation, perhaps the smoke development figure is more important than the flame spread figure. All major paint companies have flame-retardant paints and these manufacturers should be contacted for more specific information.

There is a great deal of misunderstanding about flame ratings and flame-retardant paints. The flame ratings are based on paints applied to a wood surface (fir) or a noncombustible surface (cement-asbestos board). A paint applied to a cement-asbestos board will have a lower flame rating than the same one applied in the same manner to the wood surface because of the difference in combustibility of the substrate materials.

Stains

Stains are pigments applied to bare or sealed wood and may be transparent or opaque, depending upon requirements. Medium to light hues enhance the wood surface. There are several different types of stains. Probably the most common for interior use is the oil-base type where the oil penetrates to a measurable depth, thereby giving a more durable colored base. The oil-based stains should be covered with a urethane varnish when used on doors, window sills, and cabinetry, in order to provide a protective, durable surface for the wood. Because of the higher cost of urethane varnish, other wood surfaces not subject to heavy traffic or abuse may be coated with an alkyd varnish.

Water-based stains have a water vehicle and have a tendency to penetrate the surface rapidly, but not always evenly. Because water raises the grain of the wood, sanding is necessary, whereas it is not needed with oil-based stains. Alcohol stains have an alcohol base and dry extremely quickly due to the rapid evaporation of the solvent. They are mainly used under lacquer and are applied by spraying.

Non–grain raising (NGR) stains are more of a surface type of stain, rather than a penetrating one, but they do not require sanding before application of the final coat. Both alcohol stains and NGRs are used industrially, because of ease of application and fast-drying qualities.

Stain waxes do the staining and waxing in one process, penetrating the pores of the wood and allowing the natural grain to show, while providing the protective finish of a wax. Real wood paneling may be finished with a stain wax provided the surface of the wood will not be soiled.

Varnish

Varnish is a transparent or pigmentless film applied to stained or unstained wood. Varnish dries and hardens by evaporation of the volatile solvents, oxidation of the oil, or both.

Where a hard, glossy finish that is impervious to moisture is desired, spar varnish is recommended for both outdoor and indoor use. In areas where moisture is not present, an alkyd varnish provides a slightly longer-lasting finish. Polyurethane is a synthetic resin used to make varnish resistant to water and alcohol, thus making it usable as a finish on wood floors and table tops. This type of varnish does not yellow or change color as much as conventional varnishes. The moisture-cured urethane varnishes are more durable but are also more expensive. **Humidity** must be rigidly controlled, because less than 30 percent humidity will cause too slow a curing time, and too high humidity will cause too fast a curing time, resulting in a bubbly surface.

Where a satin finish is desired, the gloss varnish surface may be rubbed down with steel wool, or a "satin" varnish may be used. Names of finishes do not seem to vary as much in opaque paints as they do in varnishes. One manufacturer will label varnish "dull" and another will call it "flat." Semigloss may also be called "satin" or "medium-rubbed-effect," and high gloss may simply be called "gloss." It should be remembered that the paired names are synonymous.

Varnish stains are pigmented and give a very superficial-colored protective surface to the wood. These are used when a cheap, fast finish is desired, but they never have the depth of color obtained with other stains. When the surface of a varnish stain is scratched, the natural wood color may show through.

Shellac

Shellac is a resinous substance secreted by the lac bug and dissolved in alcohol. It is available in clear, orange, and pigmented white. Shellac was the original glossy, transparent surface finish for furniture and was the finish used on what are now considered antiques. The urethane and oil varnishes have replaced shellac because they are not as quickly affected by heat and water. On a piece of furniture, shellac will turn white when exposed to water and/or heat. Shellac is an inexpensive finish and is very seldom used today. Old shellac should never be used, as the surface will not dry thoroughly. If there is any doubt about the age of a particular shellac, it should be tested before it is used on a project. If the surface remains tacky, the shellac should be discarded in the proper manner as it will never harden.

Lacquer

Lacquer is a paint that dries by solvent evaporation only and is applied by a spray gun. Lacquer may or may not contain pigments and is used commercially in the finishing of wood furniture and cabinets. A fine built-up finish may be achieved by many coats of lacquer, each of which is finely sanded before the subsequent coats.

Danish Oil

Danish oil finish is used on wood; there are two types—clear and stain. The clear gives a natural finish while the stained contains a wood stain to achieve the colored effect. Danish oil finish has as its main components tung oil and boiled linseed oil, and it gives the wood a rich, penetrating oil surface, while sealing the pores.

Novelty Finishes

Aquafleck® Acrylic Latex Multi-Color is a decorative, durable, seamless wall finish ideal for new or existing space. Aquafleck is virtually odorless, is water-based, requires no evacuation during application, is VOC/VOS compliant, generates no hazardous waste, and is easy to clean up with water. Available in 48 standard colors, Aquafleck also offers custom color-matching capabilities; an acrylic polyurethane clear glaze coat is available in a gloss or satin finish for maximum protection.

Duroplex® coatings are very tough finishes applied exclusively by factory-trained installers who are in the painting trade. Depending upon the desired finish, Duroplex can be applied by spray or roller methods and cures to a surface hardness that is 80 percent as hard as mild steel. It is as tough as concrete and provides an improved performance dimension to drywall.

APPLICATION METHODS

There are four methods of applying paints—brush, roller, pad, and airless spray. The pad and roller are do-it-yourself tools, although the roller may be used in remodeling where removal of furniture is impossible. The best available equipment should be used, since poor quality tools will result in a poor quality paint job.

Regardless of the material used for the bristles (hog hair or synthetic), brushes should have **flagged bristles,** which help load the brush with more paint while assisting the paint to flow more smoothly. Cheap brushes have little or no flagging, which causes the paint to flow unevenly. Brushes are used for woodwork and for uneven surfaces, while rollers are used for walls and flat areas.

Spraying is used to cover large areas such as walls and ceilings in new homes, but especially for commercial interiors. Airless spraying uses fluid pressure. Most airless spraying uses undiluted paint, which provides better coverage but also uses more paint. All surrounding areas must be covered or masked off to avoid overspray, and this masking time is always included in the painting contractor's estimates.

Spraying is eight to ten times faster than other methods of application. These figures refer to flat walls, but spraying is an easier and more economical method of coating uneven or irregular surfaces than brushing, since it enables the paint to penetrate into the crevices. When spraying walls, the use of a roller immediately after spraying does even out the coat of paint.

Spraying is also the method used for finishing furniture and kitchen cabinets. For a clear finish on furniture and cabinets, a heated lacquer is used, which dries quickly, cures to a very hard film with heat, and produces fewer toxic emissions. Heated lacquer is formulated to be used without **reduction,** thus giving a better finished surface.

Because OMNIPLEX® is sprayed, it is placed here in the paint chapter. It is a lightweight nonporous polyester material that is applied to simulate the colors and patterns of granite, onyx, and other natural stone. OMNIPLEX is available in 12 stone finishes and can be custom blended, textured or sanded smooth, matte-finished or polished to a glossy luster like real stone. A clear topcoat is available for added protection or higher gloss. It is EPA compliant and may be used on all surfaces, walls, counters, or furniture.

There are several companies that now manufacture multi-colored wall coatings that give the surface a **faux** finish—stone, fabric, or texture. The finish consists of separate and distinct pigmented enamel particles suspended in an aqueous solution, the vehicle being a modified acrylate. These nonflammable coatings are sprayed over a special basecoat, with a two-step final coat.

Other faux finishes are obtained by using paints, but applying them by methods other than those described previously—including stippling with a sponge, swirling that imitates marble, and other methods that will achieve the desired effect. Some even add sand to the paint to give a stucco appearance.

SURFACE PREPARATION

Surface preparation is the most important procedure in order to achieve a good paint finish.

Mildew is a major cause of paint failure. It is not

produced by the paint itself; it is a fungus whose spores will thrive in any damp, warm place—exterior or interior. There are several mildew-cleaning solutions available, the simplest of which is bleach and water. Other remedies have additional ingredients and may be purchased premixed, but caution should be used with these products as they are extremely irritating to the eyes and skin. Instructions should be read and followed very carefully.

Wood

Moisture is the major problem when painting wood. Five to 10 percent moisture content is the proper range. Today most wood is **kiln dried,** but exposure to high humidity may change that moisture content. While knots in the wood are not technically a moisture problem, they also cause difficulties when the surface is to be painted, as the resin in the knots may **bleed** through the surface of the paint; therefore, a special knot sealer must be used.

All cracks and nail holes must be filled with a suitable wood putty or filler. This may be applied before or after priming according to instructions on the can or in the paint guides. Some woods with open pores require the use of a paste wood filler (Table 2–3). If a natural or painted finish is desired, the filler is diluted with a thinner; if the surface is to be stained, the filler is diluted with the stain.

If coarse sanding is required, it may be done at an angle to the grain; medium or fine sanding grits should always be used with the grain. Awkward places should never be sanded across the grain because the sanding marks will show up when the surface is stained.

Plaster

When preparing a plaster wall for painting, it is necessary to be sure that the plaster is solid, has no cracks, and is smooth and level, since paint will only emphasize any problems. Badly cracked or loose plaster should be removed and repaired. ALL cracks, even if hairline, must be repaired, since they will only enlarge with time. To achieve a smooth and level wall, the surface must be sanded with a fine sandpaper and, before the paint is applied, the fine dust must be brushed from the wall surface. Plaster is extremely

TABLE 2–3
Wood Classification According
to Openness of Pores

NAME	SOFT	HARD	OPEN PORE	CLOSED PORE	NOTES
Ash		X	X		Needs filler
Alder	X			X	Stains well
Aspen		X		X	Paints well
Basswood		X		X	Paints well
Beech		X		X	Varnishes well, paints poorly
Birch		X		X	Paints and varnishes well
Cedar	X			X	Paints and varnishes well
Cherry		X		X	Varnishes well
Chestnut		X	X		Requires filler, paints poorly
Cottonwood		X		X	Paints well
Cypress		X		X	Paints well and varnishes well
Elm		X	X		Requires filler, paints poorly
Fir	X			X	Paints poorly
Gum		X		X	Varnishes well
Hemlock	X			X	Paints fairly well
Hickory		X	X		Needs filler
Mahogany		X	X		Needs filler
Maple		X		X	Varnishes well
Oak		X	X		Needs filler
Pine	X			X	Variable
Redwood	X			X	Paints well
Teak		X	X		Needs filler
Walnut		X	X		Needs filler

Source: Abel Banov, *Paintings and Coatings Handbook.* Torstar Corporation, 1973, p. 127.

porous, so a primer-sealer is required, which may be latex or alkyd.

Gypsum Board

On gypsum board, all seams must be taped, and nail or screw holes filled with spackling compound or joint cement; these filled areas should then be sanded. Care should be taken not to sand the paper areas too much as this causes the surface to be **abraded.** This may still be visible after the final coat has dried, particularly if the final coat has any gloss. Gypsum board may also have a texture applied, as described in Chapter 5, page 83, and the luster selected will be governed by the type of texture. Gypsum board must also be brushed clean of all fine dust particles before the primer is applied.

Metals

Metals must have all loose rust, **mill scale,** and loose paint removed before a primer is applied. There are many methods of accomplishing this removal. One of the most common and most effective is sandblasting, where fine silica particles are blown under pressure onto the surface of the metal. Small areas may be sanded by hand. The primer should be rust-inhibitive and specially formulated for that specific metal.

Masonry

Masonry usually has a porous surface and will not give a smooth top coat unless a block filler is used. The product analysis of a block filler shows a much larger percentage of calcium carbonate than titanium dioxide. A gallon of masonry paint does not cover as large an area as a gallon of other types of paint, because this heavier calcium carbonate content acts as a filler. One problem encountered with a masonry surface is **efflorescence,** which is a white powdery substance caused by an alkaline chemical reaction with water. An alkaline resistant primer is necessary if this condition is present. However, the efflorescence must be removed before the primer is applied.

WRITING PAINTING SPECIFICATIONS

The specifier should learn how to read the technical part of the product guide, or find the same information on the label of the can. Some manufacturers state in the product description that it is a short-, medium-, or long-oil coating. A long-oil paint has a longer drying period and is usually more expensive. One of the properties of a long-oil product is that it coats the surface better than a short-oil product because of its wetting ability. The volume of solids is expressed as a percentage per gallon of paint. This percentage can vary from the 40s to the high teens. If, for the sake of comparison, a uniform thickness of 1 1/2 **mils** is used, the higher percentage volume paint would cover 453 square feet and the lower percentage only 199 square feet. This, of course, means that more than twice as much paint of the lower volume would have to be purchased when compared to the higher volume. Thus, the paint that seems to be a bargain may turn out to cost more if the same result is to be achieved.

Painting specifications are a way of legally covering both parties in the contract between the client and the painting contractor. There will be no misunderstanding of responsibility if the scope of the paint job is clearly spelled out, and most major paint companies include in their catalogues sample painting specifications covering terms of the contract. Some of these are more detailed than others. Table 2–4, Coverage According to Method of Application, and Table 2–5, Average Coat Requirements for Interior Surfaces, will aid the designer in calculating the approximate time required to complete the painting contract.

A time limit and a penalty clause should be written into the contract. This time requirement is most important, as painting is the first finishing step in a project and, if it is delayed, the final completion date is in jeopardy. The penalty clause provides for a deduction of a specific amount or percentage for every day the contract is over the time limit.

Information on surface preparation may be obtained from the individual paint companies. The problems created by incorrect surface treatment, priming, and finishing are NEVER corrected by simply applying another coat of paint.

High-performance paints should be selected if

TABLE 2–4
Coverage According to Method of Application

METHOD	COVERAGE PER HOUR
Brush	50–200 sq ft
Roller	100–300 sq ft
Spray	300–500 sq ft

TABLE 2–5
Average Coat Requirements for Interior Surfaces

SURFACE	VEHICLE	NUMBER OF COATS
Woodwork	Oil gloss paint	2–3 coats
	Semigloss paint	2–3 coats
Plaster	Alkyd flat	2–3 coats
Drywall	Alkyd flat	2–3 coats
	Vinyl latex	3 coats
Masonry	Vinyl latex	3 coats
Wood floor	Enamel	3 coats

budget restrictions permit, as high-performance paints last several times longer than regular paints. This longer durability means business or commercial operations will not have to be shut down as frequently. Therefore, the increase in cost will more than offset the loss of business. The words "high performance" should be included in the product description.

Method of application should be specified: brush, roller, or spray. The specifier must be sure that the method suits the material to be covered and the type of paint to be used. Also, primers or base coats must be compatible with both the surface to be covered and the final or top coat. When writing painting specifications, items to be excluded are just as important as items to be included. If other contractors are present at the site, their work and materials must be protected from damage. One area should be designated as a storage for all paint and equipment, and this area should have a temperature at or near 70°F, the ideal temperature for application of paints. All combustible material should be removed from the premises by the painting subcontractor.

The specifier should make certain that inspections are made prior to the application of each coat, as these inspections will more properly cover both client and contractor. If some revisions or corrections are to be made, they should also be put in writing and an inspection should be made before proceeding.

Clean up is the responsibility of the painting contractor. This means that all windows and glass areas will be free of paint streaks or spatters. The area should be left ready for the succeeding contractor to begin work without any further cleaning.

Some states do not permit interior designers to sign a contract on behalf of clients, while other states do allow this. The designer will have to check state laws to see whether he/she or the client must be the contractual party.

USING THE MANUFACTURER'S PAINTING SPECIFICATION INFORMATION

All paint companies have slightly different methods of laying out their descriptive literature, but a designer with the background material of this chapter will soon be able to find the information needed.

First, the material to be covered is listed, then the use of that material, and then the finish desired. Let us use wood as an example: The material is wood, but is it going to be used for exterior or interior work? If interior, is it to be used on walls, ceilings, or floors? Each different use will require a product suitable for that purpose. Floors will obviously need a more durable finish than walls or ceilings.

Another category will be the final finish or luster—flat, semigloss, or gloss? Will you need an alkyd, a latex, or, for floor use, a urethane? This is sometimes classified as the vehicle or generic type. The schedule then tells you which primer or sealer is to be used in order to be compatible with the final coat. After the primer, the first coat is applied. This may also be used for the final coat or another product may be suggested. Drying time for the different methods of application may also be found in these catalogues. Two different times will be mentioned, one "dust-free" or "tack-free," meaning the length of time it takes before dust will not adhere to the freshly painted surface. In some cases, a quick-drying paint will have to be specified because of possible contaminants in the air. "Recoat" time may also be mentioned; this is important so that the application of the following coat can be scheduled.

The spreading rate per gallon will enable a specifier to calculate approximately how many gallons are needed for the job, thereby estimating material costs. Sometimes, in the more technical specifications, an analysis of the contents of the paint is included both by weight and by volume. However, the most important percentage is the volume amount, because weight of solids can be manipulated while volume cannot. This is the only way to compare one paint with another. It is the type and percentage of these ingredients that makes paints differ in durability, application, and coverage.

Some paint companies now have these percentages printed on the label of the paint cans, similar to the manner in which percentages of the daily requirements of vitamins and minerals are printed on food packages.

If paint is to be sprayed, there will be information on lowering the **viscosity** and, for other methods of application, the maximum reduction permitted without spoiling the paint job. Most catalogues also include a recommended thickness of film when dry, which is expressed as so many mils **DFT**. This film may be checked with specially made gauges. The DFT cannot be specified by the number of coats. The film thickness of the total paint system is the important factor and not the film thickness per coat.

PROBLEMS WITH PAINT AND VARNISH AND HOW TO SOLVE THEM

Temperature should ideally be around 70°F, but it can vary from 50°F up. Cold affects viscosity, causing slower evaporation of the solvents, which results in sags and runs. High temperature lowers viscosity, also causing runs and sags. High humidity may cause less evaporation of the solvent, giving lower gloss and allowing dirt and dust to settle and adhere to the film. Ventilation must be provided when paints are being applied, but strong drafts will affect the uniformity of luster.

Today, most paint starts out with a base and the pigments are added according to charts provided to the store by the manufacturer. Sometimes, it may be necessary to change the mixed paint in hue and this can be done by the judicious addition of certain pigments. Therefore, it is vital that the designer be aware of the changes made by these additions.

BIBLIOGRAPHY

Banov, Abel. *Paintings and Coatings Handbook.* Farmington, MI: Torstar Corporation, 1973.

"50,000 Years of Protection and Decoration," *History of Paint and Color.* Pittsburgh, PA: Pittsburgh Plate Glass Company.

Innes, Jacosta. *Paint Magic.* New York: Pantheon, 1986.

Morgans, W.M. *Outlines of Paint Technology.* Vol. 1: Materials, 2nd ed. London & High Wycombe: Charles Griffin & Co. Ltd., 1982.

Painting and Coating Systems for Specifiers and Applicators. Cleveland: Sherwin Williams, 1994.

Rose, A. R. "With Paint . . . It's the Dry Film That Counts." *Decorative Products World*, November 1981, pp. 58–59. New York: Time-Life Books, 1976.

GLOSSARY

Abrade. To scrape or rub off a surface layer.

Binder. The part of a paint that holds the pigment particles together, forms a film, and imparts certain properties to the paint. It is part of the solids and is also known as vehicle solids.

Bleed. Color penetrates up through another coat of paint.

Calcium carbonate. An extender pigment.

Coalescence. The merging into a single mass.

DFT. Dry film thickness. The mil thickness when coating has dried.

Efflorescence. A white alkaline powder deposited on the surface of stone, brick, plaster, or mortar caused by leaching.

Faux. French for fake or false. These include marbling or other imitation finishes.

Flagged bristles. Split ends.

Flatting. Lowering of the gloss.

Flexibility. Ability of paint film to withstand dimensional changes.

Gloss. Luster. The ability of a surface to reflect light. Measured by determining the percentage of light reflected from a surface at certain angles (see Table 2–1).

Gum. A solid resinous material that can be dissolved and that will form a film when the solution is spread on a surface and the solvent is allowed to evaporate. Usually a yellow, amber, or clear solid.

Gypsum board. Thin slabs of plaster covered with a heavyweight 100 percent recycled paper covering.

Hiding power. The ability of paint film to obscure the substrate to which it is applied. Measured by determining the minimum thickness at which film will completely obscure a black and white pattern.

Humidity. The amount of water vapor in the atmosphere.

Kiln dried. Controlled drying in an oven to a specific moisture content.

Luster. Same as gloss.

Mill scale. An almost invisible surface scale of oxide formed when iron is heated.

Mils. Measurement of thickness of film. One one-thousandth of an inch. One mil equals 25.4 microns (micrometers).

Oxidation. Chemical combination of oxygen and the vehicle of a paint that leads to drying.

Reduction. Lowering the viscosity of a paint by the addition of solvent or thinner.

Resin. A solid or semisolid material that deposits a film and is the actual film-forming ingredient in paint. May be natural or synthetic. See Gum.

Solvent. A liquid that will dissolve something, commonly resins or gums, or other binder constituents and evaporates in drying. Commonly an organic liquid.

Substrate. The piece or object that is to be painted.

Titanium dioxide. A white pigment providing the greatest hiding power of all white pigments. Nontoxic and nonreactive.

Tooth. The slight texture of a surface that provides good adhesion for subsequent coats of paint.

Vehicle. All of a paint except the pigment; the liquid portion of a paint.

Viscosity. The resistance to flow in a liquid. The fluidity of a liquid, i.e., water, has a low viscosity and molasses a very high viscosity.

0–25 flame spread. Lowest acceptable rating for commercial and public buildings.

_____ *Chapter 3*

Carpeting

HISTORY OF CARPETING

The origins of carpet weaving have been lost in antiquity. The first wool carpet may have been crudely handwoven in Ninevah or Babylon around 5000 B.C. An Egyptian fresco, depicting workers at a loom, provides concrete evidence of skillful weaving as far back as 3000 B.C. The most ancient records, including the Bible, mention the use of carpets. Nomadic tribes of central Asia were known to have woven hand-knotted rugs—not only to cover the cold ground in their tents, but for saddle blankets and tent flaps as well. As treasures were brought back from Eastern conquests by the Greeks and Romans, Persian rugs were among the most sought after and valued possessions. Exactly when hand-knotted Oriental rugs were first woven is uncertain. Marco Polo, however, brought the news of their incredible beauty with him on his return to Italy from the Orient in 1295. The Saracens had been weaving carpets in France as early as the 8th century. No royal support was given until Henry IV set up a workroom for weaving in the Louvre in 1604. Royal support not only meant the development of carpets that reflected courtly taste, but also ensured the protection and growth of the industry. Often credited with the "invention" of the weaving industry is Englishman Thomas Whitty of Axmin-

ster who developed the first machine loom that could weave carpets. The resulting product: Axminster carpets.

In Colonial America, the first floor coverings were herbs, rushes, or sand spread on the floor. Later, rag rugs made from clothing scraps, and hooked or braided mats were used. Affluent settlers, however, introduced America to prized Oriental rugs which they brought with them to the New World. Oriental rugs may have as many as 500–600 knots per square inch. It is interesting to note that while Europeans buy old Oriental rugs, Americans prefer to buy new ones.

The first U.S. carpet mill was started in Philadelphia in 1791. America's most important historic contribution to the industry was the invention of the power loom by Erastus Bigelow in 1839. Years later, the first Brussels-type carpet was made here, utilizing **Jacquard** method of color pattern control, and with further modification the first **Wilton** carpets were also woven in the United States. By the later 19th century, much machinery and skilled labor found its way to our shores, and the roots of many of today's major carpet manufacturing firms were firmly established.

For centuries, a hand-made wool rug has been a status symbol. The high price of a wool rug or carpet was probably due to the tremendous labor involved; an ancient weaver needed 900 days to complete an Oriental carpet![1]

As can be seen from this historical background, carpets were originally for the wealthy. Today, because of modern technology, carpeting is one product that gives more value for the money than in the past.

This chapter deals with carpet, defined as fabric used as a floor covering, rather than rugs (carpet cut into room or area dimensions and loose laid). Area rugs also include Oriental rugs, **Rya** rugs, **dhurries,** American Indian rugs, etc. Much of the information on weaves, pile, etc., may also apply to area rugs.

Area rugs are gaining in popularity because of the mobility of our population. Rugs can be used in many ways: as accents over existing carpet, to highlight a wood floor, or to spotlight area groupings.

Much of the following information is taken, with permission, from the Carpet and Rug Institute's *Specifier's Handbook,* a very detailed and informative book available from the CRI. All interior designers should have a copy in their design library.

FUNCTIONS OF CARPETING

Acoustical

Carpet absorbs ten times more airborne noise than any other flooring material and as much as most other types of standard acoustical materials. It virtually eliminates floor impact noises at the source. . . .

Beauty

Carpet provides a tremendous choice of colors, textures, and designs to suit every taste. Custom-designed carpet for commercial installation is also available at reasonable prices. Carpet has a way of framing the furnishings in a room or office, which makes them look more important and distinctive.

Atmosphere

Carpet dramatically enhances the feeling of quality in interior design—a major consideration in hotels and motels. Carpet also has the ability to "deinstitutionalize" a building—a significant factor in improved patient morale in hospitals, and in student attitudes in school.

Thermal Insulation

Physically, the pile construction of carpet is a highly efficient thermal insulator. Mechanical demonstrations have shown that over a cold cement slab, carpet's surface temperature is substantially higher than that of hard surface tile. Thus, carpet relieves coldness at foot and ankle levels [and lends a psychological warmth as well] . . .

Safety

The National Safety Council reports that falls cause most indoor injuries. . . . Carpet's ability to cushion falls and prevent serious injuries means savings in medical costs and man-hours to businessmen.

Comfort

Carpet reduces "floor fatigue." . . . This characteristic is important to salespeople, teachers, nurses, waiters—all those who spend many hours on their feet during the course of their work.[2]

The three Cs—Color, Comfort, and Cost—are probably the major factors in residential choice, whereas in commercial and institutional projects durability, traffic, cost, and ease of maintenance are more important features.

The properties considered in the selection of carpeting include type of fiber, density of pile, depth of pile, method of construction, and cleanability.

FIBERS

The fiber selected is the major decision. Each fiber has its own characteristics, and modern technology has greatly improved the features of synthetic fibers. The cost and characteristics of the fiber need to be considered together so that the final selection will fulfill the client's need.

The main natural fiber used in carpeting is wool, but in some rare instances silk, linen, and cotton may be used. Other natural fibers gaining popularity are sisal and coir. Synthetic fibers are always more color-fast than natural fibers because in order to produce colored fibers, the dye can be introduced while the fiber is in its liquid state. Wool, in its natural state, is limited to off-white, black/gray, and various shades in between.

Carpet manufacturers do not produce the actual fibers described below, but rather buy the fibers from the various chemical companies.

Nylon accounts for nearly 90 percent of all carpeting sold today.

There are numerous types of nylon; however the two used to produce carpet fibers are type 6,6 and type 6. . . . Since 1947, the carpet industry has moved through five generations of nylon carpet fibers; however, all, to some degree, are still found in carpet manufactured today. The generation can best be distinguished by technical advances in the performance of the nylon fiber.

The first generation nylon fibers were round, clear, and readily showed soil. Being round and clear, the fibers actually magnified the soil. Inherent **static** build-up was, and still is, a disadvantage of this type of fiber.

The second generation of nylon fibers effectively reduced soil magnification by changing the fiber shape or cross section from round to non-circular configuration. . . . These second generation nylon fibers are sometimes referred to as soil hiding types.

The third generation nylons are characterized by improved soil-hiding properties and built-in static protection. The soil-hiding characteristics were improved, in some cases, by further modifying the cross sections and by adding a delustering agent to the fiber. The anti-static properties can be brought about by the use of conductive **filaments** (metallic or carbon-based) incorporated within the nylon fibers.

The fourth generation nylons go one step further by adding carpet protectors to the fiber to make them *soil resistant.* Some fiber producers have also included anti-microbial treatments in or on the fiber.

Technical developments have provided improved stain release properties to some advanced generation nylon fibers; some of which are promoted as "fifth generation" nylons.[3]

Being a synthetic fiber, nylon absorbs little water and, therefore, stains remain on the surface rather than penetrate the fiber itself. Dirt and soil are trapped between the filaments and are removed by proper cleaning methods. Nylon has excellent abrasion resistance. The reason for worn or thin spots is that the yarn has been damaged physically by grit and soil ground into the carpet. This problem can be taken care of with proper maintenance.

Wool has, for many years, represented the standard of quality against which all other carpet fibers were measured, and it still does to some degree. Most important is wool's aesthetics and inherent resilience. The best wool for carpeting comes from sheep that are raised in the colder climates. Although wool has a propensity for high static generation, treatments are available to impart static-protection properties. Wool retains color for the life of the carpet despite wear and cleanings. Wool has good soil resistance because of its naturally high moisture content and has excellent pile resilience.

Wool gives good service. When price is no object, the best carpet fiber is wool. Wool blends, usually 80 percent wool and 20 percent nylon, have a larger market segment than a decade ago. However, wool will stain or bleach in reaction to some spills and is not as easy to clean as nylon: "Wool is naturally flame resistant, forming a char that will neither melt nor drip."[4]

Acrylic is the synthetic fiber that most feels like wool. Acrylic carpets have a low soiling rate, clean well, are highly static resistant, have very good to excellent abrasion resistance and excellent colorfastness. In properly constructed carpets, pile resilience is good. "Acrylics are always used in **staple** form, and sometimes can be found in blends with other fibers."[5]

In the 1960s and early 1970s, acrylic was a very popular fiber for commercial and residential carpeting because of its good performance. However, new dyeing processes introduced in the 1970s favored nylon due to its high dyeing rate and resistance to deformation under hot-wet conditions. Now, producer-dyed acrylic is being offered, which should again make acrylic a viable fiber for commercial and residential installations.

Polyester has excellent color clarity and retains its color and luster. It is resistant to water soluble stains, and is noted for a luxurious "hand" when used in thick cut pile textures. Polyester is offered for carpet in staple form only. Polyester is an important carpet fiber, but more in residential styles than for commercial carpet applications.[6]

Polyester is a soft fiber with good soil and wear resistance, but has a tendency to crush with wear.

Polypropylene is classified as an olefin . . . and is the lightest commercial carpet fiber, with a density of 0.905. It has excellent strength, toughness, and chemical resistance. The fiber is offered as both **continuous filament** and a staple. It is sold as a

Figure 3–1
*Linda Pettibone, a sisal painter, stenciled this Art Deco border on a
5 foot × 9 foot hall rug. Note the horizontal texture of the sisal in
the foreground. (Photograph courtesy of Linda Pettibone.)*

solution dyed fiber or yarn. Because of its very low moisture absorbency and the fact that the color is sealed into the fiber, olefins have excellent resistance to stains. They have resistance to sunlight fading, and generate low levels of static electricity.[7]

They do, however, have fair to poor resilience of pile. Polypropylene should not be used outdoors unless specifically recommended by the carpet manufacturer. Another use is in carpet backing. When working with golf-related areas, the Playfield® Country Club Collection™ may be used. This olefin floor covering is spike- and stain-resistant.

Cotton is an expensive natural fiber most often used for flat woven rugs such as Indian dhurries.

Sisal, the world's strongest natural fiber, is made from yarns spun from the sisal fibers extracted from the long, spike-shaped leaves of the tropical sisal plant. Coir is also a natural fiber taken from the tough fibrous husks that surround the coconut. Because sisal and coir are natural fibers, there will be color variations when left undyed; however, several companies are dyeing, painting, or stenciling these fibers, as shown in Figure 3–1.

Construction Methods

In the beginning, looms came only 27 inches wide. Although that width is still available, most carpeting is usually 12 feet wide. Some come in 15-foot widths and may be custom-sized for large installations.

Another method of production is the **carpet module,** which comes in 12-inch × 12-inch and 18-inch × 18-inch sizes, although the 24-inch × 24-inch size is occasionally used. Tiles 36 inches × 36 inches are rarely used. Should severe damage occur, modules are easier to remove and replace, as shown in Figure 3–2.

The main manufacturing processes in order of quantity of carpeting produced are tufting, weaving, needle-punch, and others, some of which are shown in Figure 3–3.

Tufting

In a tufted piece of carpet, the back is woven first and then the face is tufted into it and backed with additional material. It is a much faster process than the traditional weaving method and has greatly reduced the cost of carpeting, thereby making it available to more buyers. The technique is fast, efficient, and simple.

Figure 3–2
Installation and removal of carpet modules is very easy, as shown in this photograph. (Photograph courtesy of Interface)

More than 90 percent of all carpet sold in the United States is tufted.

Weaving

Weaving is a fabric formation process used for manufacturing carpet in which **yarns** are interlaced to form cloth. The weaving loom interlaces lengthwise (warp) and widthwise (filling) yarns. **Pitch** is measured by the number of lengthwise warp yarns, in a 27-inch width—the higher the number, the finer the weave. Carpet weaves are complex, often involving several sets of warps and filling yarns. The back and the face are produced simultaneously and as one unit. When describing an area rug, the term "tapestry weave" is sometimes used. Coir and sisal are always woven.

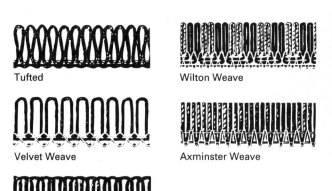

Tufted

Wilton Weave

Velvet Weave

Axminster Weave

Knitted

Figure 3–3
Construction methods.

Velvet carpets are the simplest of all to weave. They are made on a velvet loom that is not unlike the Wilton loom without the Jacquard unit. The rich appearance of velvets is due to their high-pile density. Velvets can be cut or looped pile.

Knitted

Knitted carpets were not made by machine until 1940. Their quality is generally high, depending on the yarns used and their density. Knitting a carpet involves at least three different facing yarns and perhaps a fourth for backing. Face yarns are knitted in with warp chains and weft-forming yarns in a simple knitting process. Variations of colors, yarns, and pile treatment (cut or looped, high or low) create design choices for knitted carpets. Knitting today is a speedy process that produces fine quality carpeting:

Most knitted carpet is solid colored or tweed, although some machines have pattern devices. Both loop and cut pile surfaces are available.

Needlepunching

Needlepunched carpet is a durable, felt-like product manufactured by entangling a fiber fleece with barbed needles. . . . A latex coating or attached cushion is applied to the back. . . . Technological advances in machinery now allow a diverse range of designs, including ribs, sculptured designs, and patterns. Needlepunched carpet is almost always glued down when installed.[8]

Aubusson

Aubussons are flatly woven tapestries and carpets in silk or wool, named for the French town where they originated (circa 1500). Tapestries bear narratives or portraits, while carpets feature architectural designs in rich colors or flowers in muted pastels.

Axminster and Wilton

While the appearance of the Axminster and Wilton may be similar, the construction is very different. In an Axminster, pile tufts are individually inserted from colored yarns arranged on spools, making possible an enormous variety of colors and patterns. The Wilton looms have Jacquard pattern mechanisms that use punched cards to select pile height and yarn color. In a Wilton, unwanted yarn colors are buried under the surface of the carpet, limiting the color selection to five or six colors. The carpets are often patterned or have multilevel surfaces. The traditional fiber in Axminster and Wilton construction is wool, but a blend of 80 percent wool and 20 percent nylon is sometimes used. One way to distinguish between the two types is to roll them across the warp and weft. A Wilton will fold in both directions, an Axminster only in one.

DYEING

Color is the most important aesthetic property of carpet. Designers should be familiar with the major methods of color application to carpet. This increases their ability to specify the most appropriate carpet for a given application.

Solution dyed yarns and fibers are pre-colored by the fiber manufacturer by introducing pigments into the molten polymer before extrusion into fiber. Solution dyed fibers have outstanding fade resistance and wet fastness. Stabilized with ultraviolet inhibitors, they are excellent for outdoor applications. The most common solution dyed carpet fiber is polypropylene, but polyester and nylon are also available.

Stock Dyeing

Stock dyeing is the application of color to fibers before conversion into **spun yarn.** This method of dyeing is probably the oldest method of coloring yarns and is still important today for dyeing wool. Other fibers, such as acrylic, polyester, and some nylon can also be dyed in this manner.

In stock dyeing, bulk staple fiber is placed in a large drum-like kettle where a prepared dye liquor is forced through the fiber. By controlling the temperature and, in some cases, the pressure, the dyeing is continued until the dyestuff has been completely exhausted from the bath onto the fiber. The kettle is then drained, and the fiber is rinsed, followed by centrifuging to remove excess water. It is then dried and ready for spinning.

Fiber blending during the spinning operation produces uniform color throughout the yarn lot.

Stock dyeing is a valuable styling device for contract carpet designers. Heather blends and **berber** effects are produced by combining stock-dyed fibers of various colors. . . .

TABLE 3-1
Contract Cushion Selection

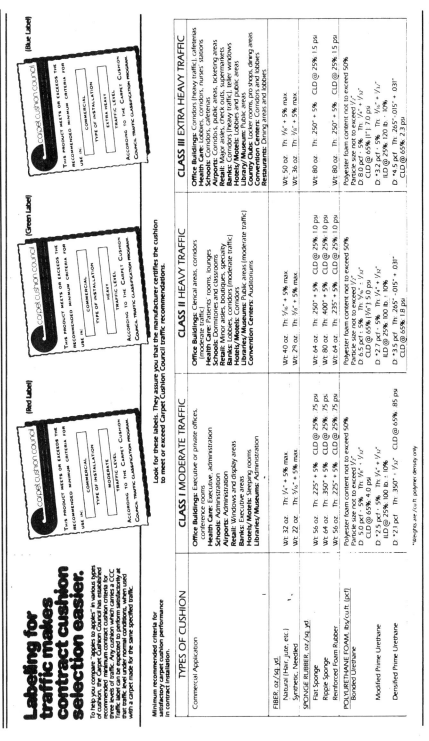

Labeling for traffic makes contract cushion selection easier.

To help you compare "apples to apples" in various types of cushion, the Carpet Cushion Council has established recommended minimum contract cushion criteria for three levels of traffic. Any cushion which carries a CCC Traffic label can be expected to perform satisfactorily at that traffic level under normal conditions, when used with a carpet made for the same specified traffic.

Minimum recommended criteria for satisfactory carpet cushion performance in contract installation.

Look for these labels. They assure you that the manufacturer certifies the cushion to meet or exceed Carpet Cushion Council traffic recommendations.

(Red Label)   (Green Label)   (Blue Label)

TYPES OF CUSHION	CLASS I MODERATE TRAFFIC	CLASS II HEAVY TRAFFIC	CLASS III EXTRA HEAVY TRAFFIC
Commercial Application	**Office Buildings:** Executive or private offices, conference rooms **Health Care:** Executive, administration **Schools:** Administration **Airports:** Administration **Retail:** Windows and display areas **Banks:** Executive areas **Hotels/Motels:** Sleeping rooms **Libraries/Museums:** Administration	**Office Buildings:** Clerical areas, corridors (moderate traffic) **Health Care:** Patients' rooms, lounges **Schools:** Dormitories and classrooms **Retail:** Minor aisles, boutiques, specialty **Banks:** Lobbies, corridors (moderate traffic) **Hotels/Motels:** Corridors **Libraries/Museums:** Public areas (moderate traffic) **Convention Centers:** Auditoriums	**Office Buildings:** Corridors (heavy traffic), cafeterias **Health Care:** Lobbies, corridors, nurses' stations **Schools:** Corridors, cafeterias **Airports:** Corridors, public areas, ticketing areas **Retail:** Major aisles, check outs, supermarkets **Banks:** Corridors (heavy traffic), teller windows **Hotels/Motels:** Lobbies and public areas **Library/Museum:** Public areas **Country Clubs:** Locker rooms, pro shops, dining areas **Convention Centers:** Corridors and lobbies **Restaurants:** Dining areas and lobbies
FIBER, oz/sq yd			
Natural (Hair, jute, etc.)	Wt: 32 oz Th: 1/4" + 5% max	Wt: 40 oz Th: 5/16" + 5% max	Wt: 50 oz Th: 3/8" + 5% max
Synthetic, Needled	Wt: 22 oz Th: 5/16" + 5% max	Wt: 29 oz Th: 3/8" + 5% max	Wt: 36 oz Th: 3/8" + 5% max
SPONGE RUBBER, oz/sq yd			
Flat Sponge	Wt: 56 oz Th: .225" + 5% CLD @ 25%: .75 psi	Wt: 64 oz Th: .250" + 5% CLD @ 25%: 1.0 psi	Wt: 80 oz Th: .250" + 5% CLD @ 25%: 1.5 psi
Ripple Sponge	Wt: 64 oz Th: .350" + 5% CLD @ 25%: .75 psi	Wt: 80 oz Th: .400" + 5% CLD @ 25%: 1.0 psi		
Reinforced Foam Rubber	Wt: 56 oz Th: .225" + 5% CLD @ 25%: .75 psi	Wt: 64 oz Th: .235" + 5% CLD @ 25%: 1.0 psi	Wt: 80 oz Th: .250" + 5% CLD @ 25%: 1.5 psi
POLYURETHANE FOAM, lbs/cu ft (pcf)			
Bonded Urethane	Polyester foam content not to exceed 50% Particle size not to exceed 1/2" D: 5.0 pcf + 5% Th: 3/8" + 1/32" CLD @ 65%: 4.0 psi	Polyester foam content not to exceed 50% Particle size not to exceed 1/2" D: 6.5 pcf + 5% Th: 3/8" + 1/32" CLD @ 65% [3/8"]: 5.0 psi	Polyester foam content not to exceed 50% Particle size not to exceed 1/2" D: 8.0 pcf + 5% Th: 1/4" + 1/32" CLD @ 65% (1"): 7.0 psi
Modified Prime Urethane	D: *2.5 pcf + 5% Th: 1/4" + 1/32" ILD @ 25% 100 lb. 10%	D: *2.7 pcf + 5% Th: 1/4" + 1/32" ILD @ 25% 100 lb. 10%	D: *3.2 pcf + 5% Th: 3/16" + 1/32" ILD @ 25% 120 lb. 10%
Densified Prime Urethane	D: *2.1 pcf Th: .350" - 1/32" CLD @ 65% .85 psi	D: *3.5 pcf Th: .265" -.015" + .031" CLD @ 65% 1.8 psi	D: *4.5 pcf Th: .265" -.015" + .031" CLD @ 65% 2.3 psi

*Weights are/cu ft. polymer density only

Used with permission of Carpet Cushion Council.

29

WRITING CARPET SPECIFICATIONS

Construction

Carpet construction specification prescribes how a carpet is to be manufactured without reference to its end-use or performance. There are many factors in construction which help define the finished quality of carpet. Those most frequently written into construction specifications are listed below:

1. Construction type (tufted, woven, knitted, etc.)
2. **Gauge** (pitch)
3. Stitches per inch (**wires** per inch)
4. Pile height (wire height)
5. Pile fiber (generic type-nylon, polypropylene, polyester, wool)
6. Yarn ply, count, and heat set
7. Pile yarn weight (ounces per square yard)
8. Backing materials
   a. In woven carpet—type and weight per square yard
   b. In tufted carpet—types and weights per square yard for both primary and secondary backs
9. Back coating—type and weight per square yard
10. Finished total weight per square yard

Construction specifications can be proprietary, identifying a specific carpet by grade, name, and manufacturer. An "or equal" specification could also identify a specific grade, listing its construction factors so that other manufacturers can bid for the order competitively. In this case, the usual procedure is to approve "or equals" in advance of the actual bidding. Full attention can then be given to price and delivery information when bid documents are analyzed.

Performance

To clarify the difference between performance and construction specifications, performance specifications define what characteristics the carpet must deliver in use. In other words, performance specifications tell the manufacturer what the carpet must do without detailing how it must be made. By contrast, a construction specification tells the manufac-turer, in very precise terms, how the carpet is to be manufactured without stipulating performance needs.

Specifying performance rather than construction can also take other important pressures off the specifier. For example, if the specifier does not regularly deal with carpet products, the latest technology and materials may be overlooked. The best, most economical product to ensure the desired performance may not be chosen.

Whether written for construction or performance, most carpet specifications also incorporate requirements governing the following items:

1. Type of installation (tackless or glue-down)
2. Cushion type and grade, if required
3. Installation procedures and accessories
4. Certification that materials meet federal, state, and local government ordinances*
5. Delivery and installation schedules
6. Carpet maintenance (Request maintenance instructions from the manufacturer.)

*Particularly for flammability. . . .

Special requirements for different types of installation sites can be very complex and technical. For example, in window-wall architecture, fade resistance could be a matter of primary concern. In a hospital medical dispensary, stain resistance might be placed high on the list of performance priorities. Special static protection properties may be necessary for computer and data-processing areas. . . .

The following concerns should be addressed:

1. Budget
2. Surface texture, pattern or design
3. Color—solid, tweed, figured
4. Traffic load—light, medium, heavy
5. Maintenance levels that will be sustained—good, better, best
6. Minimum life expectancy
7. Installation requirements . . .

Performance factors to consider:

1. Ease of maintenance
2. Stain resistance
3. Resistance to cigarette burns

4. Resistance to excessive wear
5. Very firm—for ease of rolling objects
6. Superior sound absorption
7. Superior impact insulation
8. Superior static control
9. Low moisture absorbency
10. Luxurious appearance
11. Superior dimensional stability
12. Superior resistance to sunlight
13. Flammability requirements.[15]

RECYCLING

Carpet manufacturers and the companies who make the chemicals from which the fibers are made have united in an effort to recycle both used fibers and factory waste. These two types of discards used to be added to the landfill in great quantities, but the manufacturers have become increasingly aware that dumping is not the responsible solution (see Chapter 1).

MEASURING

Before estimating the amount of carpet needed for a particular job, there are several points that the designer needs to remember. First of all, if carpet is available in other widths than the usual 12 feet, then all the carpet must be of that width. DO NOT COMBINE DIFFERENT WIDTHS because of differences in dye lots. Second, the **nap** or pile of the carpet needs to be considered and all pieces must have the nap running in the same direction, toward the entrance unless otherwise specified, or the seams will be obvious.

Third, seaming and nap direction must be shown on all carpet seaming plans. Placement of furniture will often decide where seams should be placed. Seams should never be in the middle of high-traffic areas such as at right angles to a doorway, across a hallway, or in front of often used office machines such as copiers and drinking fountains. In residential seaming layouts, do not place seams directly in front of seating areas.

Carpets that have to be seamed at right angles will also have an obvious seam; however, seams placed under a door are quite often necessary. The nap on stairs should run downwards. The warp (nap) should always run the longer direction.

The precise measuring of the carpet should be done by the installer on site, with a carpet seaming diagram submitted to the designer for approval. However, the designer should have an understanding of how it is done.

Carpeting usually comes in 12-foot widths, but 6-foot, 9-foot, and 15-foot widths are sometimes available. Whatever width is selected, it will be necessary to piece or seam the carpet. This may entail purchasing slightly more yardage, since the fewer the seams, the better the appearance will be.

Although carpet comes in widths measured in feet, the amount ordered is always square yards, so be sure to divide a square foot answer by 9 to arrive at the square yardage needed. (From experience, the author finds this is the most common error made by design students, resulting in ordering far too much carpeting when specifying during exams.)

All measurers seem to have their own method of calculation. Some suggest using templates; others have complicated formulas. Some answers are very close with little waste and others have few seams and much waste. The number of seams does depend on each job. A master bedroom may have a seam one foot in from a wall where a dresser, bed, or other piece of furniture is to be placed, because it will not be visible, but in an art gallery a one foot piece would be unacceptable. Whichever method is used, the installer is responsible for the accuracy of the measurements.

In today's computerized design offices, programs are available to assist the designer in producing an economical and yet viable plan. Some programs actually produce a floor plan with measurements, nap directions, and seam placements. The program can provide an estimate needed with the 12-foot width going across the room or at right angles. A pattern repeat can be programmed so that the repeat is taken into consideration. Some programs do the calculation but do not provide a line drawing of the seams and cuts, but rather a summary of how many pieces are needed.

Problems

Sprouting. Occasionally, a tuft will rise above the pile surface of a carpet. Just snip off these tufts level with other tufts. DO NOT PULL THEM OUT!

Ripples. Ripples in carpet are usually the result of improper stretching during installation, stretching of the back yarns after the carpet was installed, or elongation of the backing fibers from moisture. With a jute-backed carpet, it is not uncommon to have ripples during periods of high humidity that disappear during periods of low humidity. A de-humidifier may help to eliminate this problem. Using waffled sponge cushioning under a woven carpet will also cause this problem.

Mildew. Mildew can be a problem on carpet and rugs, but it does not have to be. If a carpet is going to be used where mildew or other bacteria-growing conditions are present some or all of the time, then a carpet with all synthetic fibers (both front and back) should be used.

Indentations. When a heavy object such as a piano, piece of furniture, etc., is allowed to remain for an extended period of time in one spot on a carpet, indentation or crush marks will develop. In most cases, the crushed areas can be either restored or greatly improved. The crushed pile can be lifted by working it gently with a coin. The yarn should be lifted to its original appearance without fuzzing or distorting the yarn. After the yarn has been raised, moisten the area with a steam iron, held at least 4 inches above the pile. The procedure can be repeated if the original appearance was not obtained the first time. Moving furniture a few inches will help to prevent permanent indentations. Moving the furniture will also help prevent damage to the back of the carpet from small furniture legs and rollers.

To help prevent matting, Monsanto Company has created Wear-dated® carpet. Its new Traffic Control™ fiber system employs a unique dual fiber design. By taking tough nylon fibers and interweaving them with acrylic fibers, Monsanto has built in a new type of resilience.

Corn Rowing. Corn rowing is a characteristic that should be expected in carpet with higher tufts and lower density pile. Corn rowing develops in the traffic areas or those areas subjected to mechanical action such as in front of chairs, television sets, etc. Vacuuming alone will not raise the fallen yarns. Specially designed carpet rakes will lift the yarns but will not keep them erect—the yarns will be crushed again when subjected to foot traffic.

Shedding or Fluffing. When a newly installed carpet is vacuumed, a large amount of fiber may be found in the vacuum. This is a normal process. A carpet made with staple fibers will not have all the fibers anchored into the back or tightly held in the yarns. Mechanical action will work some of the fibers loose. As the carpet is vacuumed, some of the loose fibers will be removed. Many styles of carpet are sheared as one of the final steps in manufacturing. Most fibers are removed at the factory, but some of these sheared fibers will fall into the carpet pile. The shorter the fiber and the longer the tuft, the greater the number of

loose fibers in the yarns will be. The yarns with less twist will not hold the loose fibers as tightly. Therefore, they are easier to remove. A deep brushing action produces the maximum removal.

Static Electricity. Static electricity is caused by the rubbing together of two different types of materials, which results in a transfer and a build-up of electrical charges. Most carpets have some type of treatments built into them that will eliminate the static electricity problem. Moisture in the air will help the problem but may produce condensation on window glass in colder climates.

Shading. Shading is a natural characteristic of plush carpet and should be expected to develop. It is not something that is due to neglect during manufacturing, nor is it something that the manufacturer can eliminate in a plush or velvet type of construction. Shading helps to break up the plainness or sameness in solid color, dense, cut pile carpet. It is a characteristic that occurs in good quality carpet, and it should be enjoyed; but the client should be made aware of this characteristic. When the carpet is manufactured and rolled, the ends of the face yarns will all lean toward the end of the roll. After the carpet is installed and vacuumed, the pile will have a uniform appearance. This uniformity is a result of light being reflected from a uniform surface.

Some changes can be expected after the carpet is used. The traffic areas will appear a little different from the adjacent, unwalked-on areas. This difference is because the carpet pile has been compressed by the pressure from footsteps. Vacuuming and brushing will help to raise the crushed pile. However, an occasional vacuuming cannot equalize the continual compressing of the carpet. The end-user will have to work to keep the pile erect. Sometimes these shaded spots will occur even in areas with little or no traffic and may be called shading, watermarking, pooling, highlighting, or pile reversal. Vacuuming and brushing the pile all in one direction, or professional cleaning, may temporarily improve the condition. However, this changes only the top portion of the pile, and shading will soon redevelop. With some plush carpet, vacuum cleaner marks and footsteps may show after the carpet has been freshly cleaned.

INSTALLATION

The International Certified Floorcovering Installers Association is an organization that certifies carpet installers. The certification covers five different categories:

Residential I (R-1)—Construct seam in entry-level carpet.

Residential II (R-2)—Construct seams in Berber-patterned and dense-cut pile carpets.

Commercial I (C-1)—Construct glue-direct seam in base-grade carpet.

Commercial II (C-2)—Construct seam in patterned carpet.

Master Installer—Handsewn seams to be constructed.

The test also covers written OSHA, EPA, and CRI-104 and CRI-105 knowledge. Oral tests are given concerning job layout, pattern matching, powerstretching, installation procedures, reading blueprints, and estimating jobs. Certification will assist the designer in choosing a qualified installer.

The Carpet and Rug Institute (CRI) provides the standard industry reference guides for the installation of both residential and commercial textile floorcovering materials. CRI-105 gives the residential installation standards, and CRI-104 gives the commercial installation standards. If there is a dispute or problem with a job, these documents will determine how an installation will be judged. Always use the best carpet installer available.

There are three principal methods of commercial carpet installation. These are stretch-in, direct glue-down (including attached cushion), and double glue-down. Stretch-in installations are stretched in over a separate cushion using **tackless strips** to hold the carpet in place. These installations are best suited to areas which must have maximum underfoot comfort and luxury.

The most important aspects of stretched-in tackless strip installations are: (1) sufficient stretching of carpet; (2) proper selection of cushion; (3) correct environmental conditions, before, during, and after installation.[16]

The tackless strips are narrow pieces of wood with two to four rows of pins, set at a 60 degree angle and long enough to penetrate the backing. The strips are nailed or glued down around the perimeter of the room a slight distance from the wall. When installing carpet over a cement floor, two rows are used. For stairs, the strips are placed at the base of the riser and the back of the tread. After the tackless strip is nailed down, the padding is cut to fit inside the strips. The principle of the tackless installation is that the carpet is stretched by means of a knee kicker or power stretcher so that it hooks over the pins in the wooden strip. Knee kickers are permissible only in areas so small that power stretchers do not fit, such as closets. The excess carpet is cut off and the small amount remaining is tucked into the slight gap between the strip and the wall. The base is then installed to cover this area.

The Carpet and Rug Institute finds that most complaints about wrinkling or buckling in stretch-in installations result from inadequate stretch during initial installation, or from cushion that does not provide adequate support for the carpet. Guidelines for proper stretch for various carpet constructions are contained in *CRI 104, Standards for Installation of Commercial Textile Floorcovering Materials*. Adequate stretch can only be obtained by the use of power stretchers. Additional information concerning the amount of stretch for each carpet can be obtained from either the carpet manufacturer or the secondary backing manufacturer.

Construction and density of the cushion are equal in importance to adequate stretch. Firm, low profile cushion with minimal deflections should be used in commercial traffic areas. Cushions that are too thick and soft will permit carpet backings to stretch and eventually wrinkle. Recommendations from both cushion and carpet manufacturers should be considered prior to [tackless] stretch-in installations.

Regardless of the method of installation chosen, seams are always of utmost importance for a quality installation. Most modern installations employ hot-melt tape seams, which are generally adequate. Follow the carpet manufacturer's recommendations for seaming. Woven carpet constructions may require hand sewing or other specialized seaming techniques. In all cases, cut edges must be buttered with appropriate seam sealer prior to seaming. . . .

Glue-down installations can be made with two types of carpet: carpet with attached cushion, or carpet without attached cushion. These installations are well suited to heavy traffic and to rolling traffic.

Double glue-down installations combine cushion and carpet in a floorcovering system by first glueing the cushion to the floor and then the carpet to the cushion. This method, often referred to as double-stick, has grown in popularity due to combining the stability of direct glue-down of carpet with the cushioning benefits of separate cushion. The cushion materials must be designed specifically for this method of installation in order to achieve a successful installation. Direct glue-down and double glue-down installations can be made on many subfloors including wood, concrete, metal, terrazzo, ceramic tile, and other suitable surfaces. Generally, most are on concrete; therefore, proper preparation of the subfloor is needed for adequate adhesion. Testing concrete for moisture and alkalinity is necessary for best results.

The specified amounts of adhesives must be applied to floors to obtain the required 100 percent adhesive transfer into the carpet back. The quantity applied is controlled by the size of the notches in the installers' floor adhesive trowels. If too little is used, carpet will not adequately adhere to the floor. Adequate open time for adhesives to develop **tack** (to partially set) prior to laying carpet into the adhesives is also very important for many of today's carpet backing systems. For the purposes of improved indoor air quality, low VOC adhesives are available from most adhesive manufacturers.

Carpet with an attached cushion, secondary, unitary or woven backings may be adhered to floors; whereas separate cushion stretch-in installations are usually limited to woven construction or tufted carpet with secondary backings. For heavy and rolling traffic, or other severe conditions, adhesive installation with either secondary, unitary, woven or attached cushion backing is recommended.[17]

The Carpet and Rug Institute finds that the major cause of separation from the floor in a glue-down installation is an insufficient amount of carpet floor adhesive.

The glue-down method may also be used for carpet modules. Because of the heavy backing, carpet tiles may also be loose laid. Carpet modules can be freely rotated and/or replaced without detracting from overall like-new appearance of the installation, particularly in the health care, institutional, retail, and hospitality areas with their heavy use and traffic. This type of installation also eliminates restretching problems, with no movement of pattern-type carpeting or bordering. It is also useful in furnishing the upper floors of tall buildings, where delivering heavy, cumbersome rolls of broadloom may present a problem. This is particularly true in the case of refurbishing when construction cranes and elevators used to lift the original carpets are no longer available.

Coir and sisal are highly absorbent and therefore they should be allowed to acclimate for at least 24 hours prior to installation to the humidity and temperature of the room in which they will be placed. The direct glue-down procedure is the best method of

wall-to-wall installation for coir and sisal, if there are no great fluctuations in humidity or temperature. If these conditions exist, then loose-laying is suggested.

The following should be included in installation contracts:

1. Scope, including description of area involved as well as details on measurements, seam locations, diagrams, etc.
2. Qualifications required of contractor and installation specialists and references for similar jobs. . . .
3. The installation contractor must perform work in strict compliance with all local, state, and federal regulations. The Occupational Safety and Health Administration (OSHA) Hazard Communication standard must also be followed where applicable.
4. Storage and delivery responsibilities.
5. Preparatory work responsibilities (installer, general contractor, or owner) including:
   a. inspection and cleaning of subfloors;
   b. vertical transportation;
   c. removal and replacement of furniture;
   d. removal and disposition of existing floorcovering.
6. Submittal and approval of materials to include moldings, base materials, cushions, adhesives, etc. *Note:* The selection of an appropriate adhesive is essential to a successful installation. The use of low VOC emitting adhesives should be considered for improved indoor air quality.
7. Method of installation:
   a. Stretch-in with separate cushion
   b. Direct glue-down
      without cushion
      with attached cushion
   c. Double glue-down.
8. Specify that installation should be in accordance with *CRI 104, Standard for Installation of Commercial Textile Floorcovering Materials* for all aspects not specifically covered by manufacturers' recommendations.
9. Adequate ventilation must be provided during and after the installation by the general contractor or owner to eliminate or minimize lingering odors.
10. Responsibility for cleanup.
11. Disposition of excess carpet.

12. Details of guarantee.
13. Time of installation, completion date, final acceptance inspection by specifier and installer prior to acceptance.[18]

MAINTENANCE

Carpet is the only textile product on which people walk. This is why carpet construction, or performance, and installation specifications are so critical. Also critical is the specification of maintenance. Specification of any one of these three elements without knowledge or consideration of the other two increases the risk that the carpet will not perform up to potential or expectation.

Even properly specified carpet can wear out or appear to be worn out if it is not maintained adequately. Dirt is unsightly but it can also be abrasive. As foot traffic deposits soil and causes the pile yarns to flex, embedded grit cuts the face fibers. The carpet begins to lose density and resilience. Threadbare spots appear and the carpet wears out. Moreover, allowing soil to build up and to spread may give the carpet a worn out appearance even if the face fibers are essentially intact.

If carpet is not vacuum cleaned regularly, the dirt builds up and begins to spread. To guard against build-up, a well-planned maintenance program is essential in commercial installations with their high traffic loads. Planned maintenance is the key to extending the life expectancy of carpet. The maintenance plan is no less important than the initial carpet specification and installation.

The maintenance plan should be developed as the carpet specifications are being considered. A plan should be prepared in case the carpet is installed prior to completion of construction.

When preparing the maintenance plan, keep in mind that one of the advantages of carpet compared to hard floors is that carpet localizes soil. Carpet tends to catch and hold soil and spills where they occur instead of allowing them to spread quickly. This feature of carpet suggests, then, that the best maintenance plan is to identify in advance the most likely areas for soiling and spilling. The plan will specify maintenance schedules and procedures for these areas as well as the remainder of the carpet.

Specifically, heavy traffic areas, like entrances and lobbies, will not only require the most substantial carpet, they will probably have to be vacuumed once a day. In some instances, greasy motor oil from parking lots should be anticipated.

Kitchen smoke in restaurants and cafeterias will contribute heavily to overall soiling. Stains and spills in restaurants and hospitals will be very common. Routine procedures for attending to these as quickly as possible are necessary.

Whatever the nature of the installation, it is wise to anticipate dealing with soil from the very first day the carpet is installed. Otherwise, abrasive dirt may build up faster than it can be handled.

Two elements essential to an efficient maintenance program include daily procedures encompassing both regular vacuuming and spot cleaning, and scheduled overall cleanings to remove discoloring grime and to refresh the pile.

Overall grime not only causes discoloration, it presents another undesirable quality. Carpet that is not cleaned and reconditioned regularly, no matter how faithfully it is vacuumed, will tend to permanently crush and mat down. As greases present in smoke, or pollutants in the air, settle on the carpet, pile yarns may become gummy enough to stick to each other and flatten in use. Matted carpet appears to be worn out, even if there is no real pile loss. Obviously, carpet which must be replaced because it **looks** worn out is no less costly than carpet which must be replaced because it is worn out!

The color of the carpet can contribute significantly to minimizing the appearance of dirt, particularly for entrances and lobbies, which get the bulk of tracked-in soil. If possible, colors that blend with the color of the dirt brought in from outside should be chosen.

Since the most common dirt colors are grays, beiges, browns, and reds, carpet colors for entrances should be chosen from these tones. The best choice would be a tweed coloration combining two or more of the colors.

Another choice might be a multicolored, patterned carpet which would add visual interest while helping camouflage dirt and spills until they can be removed. Such highly patterned carpet is a popular choice for hotel lobbies and restaurants.

Lighter, more delicate colors are best reserved for inside spaces—offices, guest rooms, lounges—where soiling rates are obviously lower and danger of accidental spills is more remote.

As a matter of preventative maintenance, **walk-off** mats should be installed in all entrances to collect dirt before it reaches the carpet inside. Walk-off mats can be constructed of stiff bristles; pieces of the inside carpet itself; or one of a variety of types specially made for commercial use. [Some have aluminum strips between the carpet. Sometimes pieces of carpet used as walk-off mats can, if the backing is rough enough, cause as much wear as walking on the carpet itself.]

Elevators should also be carpeted, even if the entrance lobby is not. It is wiser to have soil wiped off on the elevator carpets rather than having it tracked over the carpet elsewhere.

It is common to have two sets of walk-off mats and removable carpets available. Because they take such heavy abuse, one set is kept in place while the other is being cleaned.[19]

Another method of dirt control is to use a recessed mat or grating inside exterior doors. These gratings feature a system of self-cleaning recessed treads that are closely spaced to prevent the smallest heel from catching, yet allow dirt and sand to collect below the surface. The grate removes easily for cleaning.

Vacuuming Schedules

Of all the carpet maintenance procedures, vacuuming takes the most time and attention . . . yet is the most cost effective. The carpet should be inspected for spots during vacuuming. Spots should be removed as soon as possible. The longer they are allowed to set, the more permanent they may become.

The following is a normal vacuuming schedule:

High Traffic—Vacuum daily
Medium Traffic—Vacuum twice weekly
Light Traffic—Vacuum weekly

This broad guide recommends minimum schedules only. In order to reduce this general rule to specifics, some definitions will be useful:

TRACK-OFF AREA—The place where carpet collects foot soil tracked in from the outdoors or from hard surfaced floors indoors. . . .

FUNNEL AREAS—The place where foot traffic is squeezed into or through a concentrated area such as a doorway, stairwell, in front of a drinking fountain or vending machine, etc. . . .

These areas can be identified in advance of soiling. Planned vacuuming in these areas, EVEN WHEN SOIL IS NOT VISIBLE, will help prevent soil buildup. Also it will help focus maintenance attention on the places where it is known that soil will be tracked.

In the final analysis, an adequate schedule must be based on the individual installation and its own traffic load and soiling rate. For example, soil may accumulate so rapidly at entrances (track-off areas) that carpet at those locations will have to be vacuumed several times a day. In another instance, rooms may be entered directly from an uncarpeted corridor. Under those circumstances, even light traffic may cause heavy soiling, and the carpet may have to be vacuumed several times a week. Only experience will tell whether more frequent vacuuming is indicated.

Vacuum Cleaning Equipment

Vacuum cleaning equipment for implementing a maintenance program with the maximum efficiency is a basic necessity. Two types of machines may be required. The first of these, a heavy-duty wide track machine, is recommended for large open areas. Because of its size, maintenance time can be measurably reduced with commensurate savings in labor costs. Such large industrial vacuums should be equipped with a cylindrical brush, or a beater-bar, to whip embedded dirt to the surface, and also equipped with a powerful suction.

A second machine, an industrialized version of the domestic upright vacuum cleaner belongs in every maintenance program. It too should have a good brushing action or a beater-bar and powerful suction. If possible, it should also have a hose and wand attachment for cleaning under heavy furniture not normally moved. Otherwise, a canister vacuum, preferably with a power head, may also be needed for hard-to-reach places.

Stain Removal

Identification and immediate action are the keys to effective spot removal procedures. To minimize time and effort, it is helpful to know what causes a spot so that treatment can begin without guesswork. In most installations, spot identification may not be difficult because the possibilities are limited. In others, it could be a real problem.

A drug dispensing area in hospitals, for example, is susceptible to hundreds of spotting and staining agents. Employees must be instructed to report spills as they occur and to identify the spilled material.

It is also important to clean up spills as quickly as possible. The longer a spill sets, the more difficult it may be to remove. If it sets too long, it might react with the carpet dyes and cause permanent discoloration. Hence, an alert staff and a well stocked spot removal kit are important to a good carpet maintenance program. . . . Always test a cleaning agent to determine its effect upon the carpet dye, fibers, and the spot before applying larger amounts. . . .

Specifically, detergent solutions to be used on wool should have a neutral pH. Natural fibers absorb moisture and are apt to be somewhat more vulnerable to chemical damage from acids or alkalies.

Man-made fibers absorb less moisture. Detergents which are alkaline in nature, between 7.0 and 10.0 pH, cut grease and suspend soil better and can be used satisfactorily on man-made fibers but should be tested on each color.

Whether neutral or alkaline, some detergents may leave a sticky residue that will cause rapid resoiling on the face of the carpet. The better detergents will dry to a crisp flake, which can then be removed by vacuuming. . . .

There are many factors that will influence the frequency of cleaning, but a maintenance plan should be in effect before the traffic areas start to show discoloration. If the traffic areas are allowed to become excessively soiled, on-location cleaning may not remove sufficient soil to restore them to an acceptable level. The high use areas must be cleaned more frequently in order to maintain a satisfactory overall appearance.

Five major methods are used in the maintenance and cleaning of carpet. Those methods are absorbent compound; absorbent pad or bonnet (dry); dry foam cleaning; shampoo cleaning; and steam cleaning (hot water extraction). . . .

ABSORBENT COMPOUND is the lowest moisture system that can be used on carpet. In heavily soiled areas, a preconditioner may be applied prior to the application of the absorbent compound. . . .

ABSORBENT PAD or BONNET (DRY) is another minimum moisture system, which can be used on nearly all carpet. Deeply soiled traffic areas are normally treated prior to cleaning with a preconditioner. . . . The drying time is normally one to three hours, after which the carpet should be thoroughly vacuumed to further remove any cleaning agent and loosened soil.

DRY FOAM CLEANING uses a detergent solution, which can be aerated before it is applied to the carpet. This method adds only a minimum amount of moisture to the carpet and, therefore, this method can be used on most carpets. Normally, in the heavily soiled traffic areas, a preconditioner is used to loosen the soil before cleaning with the dry foam method. . . . Drying normally takes place within one to three hours, unless multiple passes have been made over the carpet.

SHAMPOO CLEANING can be employed on nearly all types of carpet, if properly used. Heavily soiled traffic areas are usually treated with a preconditioner prior to overall cleaning. . . . The drying time will be determined by the amount of moisture allowed to remain in the carpet and may vary from one to twelve hours, and, in extreme cases, as long as twenty-four hours.

STEAM CLEANING (HOT WATER EXTRACTION) applies the largest amount of cleaning solution, and when operated by a skilled operator, can be used on most carpets. In heavily soiled areas, a preconditioner may be applied as the first step. . . . The maximum drying time should not be longer than twenty-four hours.

The above methods illustrate the various systems available. They may be used separately or in combination. Some may be used for maintaining traffic areas, while others may be used for overall cleaning. Some methods may not be suitable for all types of carpet construction, such as certain cut pile construction; therefore, it is always advisable to obtain the carpet manufacturer's recommendations for the preferred methods to be used in order to prevent invalidation of applicable warranties. Again, the important points are to develop a regularly scheduled maintenance program and to have qualified, skilled individuals perform the cleaning.[20]

Beware of the bargain carpet cleaning companies who will clean a whole house for a ridiculously low price. They often hire untrained people and, in the case of water extraction, may soak the carpet so that it takes a long time to completely dry, especially in high humidity areas. The time invested in developing a plan for carpet maintenance will pay off in longer use from the carpet. CLEANING SHOULD BE DONE BEFORE THE CARPET SHOWS SIGNS OF SOIL. It is essential that the manufacturer's recommendations be followed, especially if guarantees and liabilities are involved.

BIBLIOGRAPHY

Bridgepoint Corp. "Protector Course," Salt Lake City, UT: Bridgepoint Corporation, 1990.

Burlington Industries, Inc. *Carpet Maintenance Guide for Hospitals and Health Care Facilities.* King of Prussia, PA: Burlington Industries Inc., Carpet Division, 1987.

The Carpet and Rug Institute. *Carpet Specifier's Handbook.* Dalton, GA: The Carpet and Rug Institute, 1987.

Monsanto Contract Fibers, *Concepts, Ideas for Specifiers.* Atlanta, GA: Monsanto Fiber and Intermediates Co.

Revere, Glen. *All About Carpets.* Blue Ridge Summit, PA: TAB Books Inc., 1988.

Reznikoff, C. S. *Specifications for Commercial Interiors.* New York, NY: Whitney Library of Design, an imprint of Watson-Guptil Publications, a division of Billboard Publications, 1989.

The Wool Bureau, New York, NY.

ENDNOTES

[1]Wool Bureau Library, Volume 6, Rugs and Carpets. (Emphasis added)

[2]The Carpet and Rug Institute. *Specifier's Handbook,* 5th ed. Dalton, GA: The Carpet and Rug Institute, 1992, pages 17–18. All quotes from *Specifier's Handbook* reproduced with permission.

[3]Ibid., page 50. (Emphasis added)

[4]Ibid., page 51.

[5]Ibid., page 49. (Emphasis added)

[6]Ibid., page 51.

[7]Ibid., page 51. (Emphasis added)

[8]Ibid., page 47.

[9]Ibid., pages 52–53. (Emphasis added)

[10]Ibid., page 53. (Emphasis added)

[11]Bridgepoint Corp., "Protector Course," Salt Lake City, UT: Bridgepoint Corporation, 1990.

[12]*Concepts, Ideas for Specifiers,* Monsanto Fiber and Intermediates Co., page 11.

[13]*Material Wealth, Living with Luxurious Fabrics* by Jack Lenor Larsen, published by Abbeville Press, New York, 1989, pages 195 and 197. Permission to reprint granted by John Calman & King Ltd., London, England. (Emphasis added)

[14]Carpet Cushion Council. *The Supporting Facts About Carpet Cushion,* Riverside, CT. (Emphasis added)

[15]The Carpet and Rug Institute. *Specifier's Handbook,* pages 60–62. (Emphasis added)

[16]Ibid., pages 56–57. (Emphasis added)

[17]Ibid., pages 56–57. (Emphasis added)

[18]Ibid., page 64.

[19]Ibid., pages 64–65. (Emphasis added)

[20]Ibid., pages 65–67. (Emphasis added)

GLOSSARY

Bulked Continuous Filament (BCF). The name given to continuous strands of synthetic fiber that are first spun into yarn and then texturized to increase bulk and cover.

Berber. A looped pile rug from North Africa. May be patterned or natural colored. Today Berbers are mostly textured natural earth tones.

Carpet modules. Carpeting precut into 18- or 24-inch squares, or other suitable dimensions.

Continuous filaments. Continuous strand of synthetic fiber extruded in yarn form without the need for spinning that all natural fibers require.

Corn rowing. A characteristic that should be expected in carpet with higher tufts and lower density pile, resulting in the pile laying flat.

CRF. Critical radiant flux.

Dhurrie. A reversible tapestry woven, flat rug with no pile. Originally from India, today comes mostly in pastel colors.

Face weight. Density of fiber in the pile.

Filaments. A single continuous strand of natural or synthetic fiber.

Gauge. The distance between needles in tufted carpets as measured in fractions of an inch. Gauge is also the number of yarn ends across the width of the carpet.

Indentations. Marks left in the carpet from heavy pieces of furniture remaining in one place.

Jacquard. An apparatus on a carpet weaving loom that produces patterns from colored yarns. The pattern information is contained on perforated cards. The holes in the cards activate the mechanism that selects the color to be raised to the pile surface.

Mildew. Discoloration caused by fungi.

Nap. Carpet or rug pile surface.

Noise Reduction Coefficient (NRC). The average percentage of sound reduction at various Hz levels.

Pitch. Number of lengthwise warp yarns in a 27-inch width.

Ripples. Waves caused by either improper stretching or humidity.

Rya. A Scandinavian handwoven rug with a deep resilient comparatively flat pile. Usually of abstract design.

Saxony. A cut-pile carpet texture consisting of heat-set plied yarns in a relatively dense, erect configuration, with well defined individual tuft tips. Their tip definition is more pronounced than in singles plush.

Sculpturing. A patterned carpet made by using high and low areas.

Set yarns. Straight yarns.

Shading. Apparent color difference between areas of the same carpet. The physical cause is the difference between cut end luster and side luster of fibers.

Shedding. Normal process of excess yarns coming to the surface in a freshly installed carpet.

Solution dyes. In synthetic fibers, the dye is part of the liquid chemical that forms the filament resulting in a colorfast fiber.

Sprouting. Protrusion of individual tuft or yarn ends above pile surface. May be clipped with scissors.

Spun yarn. Drawing out and twisting of numerous staple fibers into yarn.

Staple fiber. Short lengths of fiber that may be converted into spun yarns by textile yarn-spinning processes.

Static electricity. Shoe friction against carpet fiber causes production of electrostatic charge that is discharged from carpet to person to conductive ground (e. g., a doorknob).

Tack. Partially set.

Tackless Strip. Narrow lengths of wood or metal containing either two or three rows of angled pins on which carpet is stretched and secured in a stretch-in installation.

Unset yarns. Frizzy yarns.

Walk-off. Mats on which most of the exterior soil is deposited.

Wick. To carry moisture by capillary action.

Wilton. Carpet woven on a loom with a Jacquard mechanism, which utilizes a series of punched cards to select pile height and yarn color.

Wires. Stitches per inch.

Yarn. A continuous strand composed of fibers or filaments and used in the production of carpet and other fabrics.

_____ *Chapter 4*

Floors

WOOD

Wood was used in ancient times for flooring. According to the Bible, Solomon's Temple had a floor of fir, whereas the Romans used wood on only the upper floors of their buildings and used stone for the main floor. These stone floors persisted throughout the Dark Ages. In peasant homes, of course, a dirt floor was spread with straw; however, heavy, wide oak planks predominated in larger domestic structures.

The first wood floors were called puncheon floors. They were made of split logs, flat side up, fitted edge to edge, and smoothed with an ax or an adz. When saws became available to cut the wood into planks, white pine plank flooring of great widths was used in the Colonial period in the United States and was pegged in place.

In 18th- and early 19th-century America, sand was frequently spread over the wood floor to absorb dirt and moisture. Later, these floors were stained and then covered by Oriental rugs in wealthy homes; in more modest homes, they were either left bare or covered by homemade rugs. When renovating an old pine plank floor, the knots, which are much harder than the surrounding wood, have a tendency to protrude above the level of the worn floor and must be sanded to give a smoother surface. In some early floors that have not been renovated, it is actually pos-

sible to trip over these knots because they extend so far above the level of the floors.

In the early 19th century, **stenciling** was done directly on the floor in imitation of rugs, parquet floors, marble, and tile. Painted floors and **floorcloths** came to be highly regarded until the carpet industry spelled the decline of floorcloths in the 1830s and 1840s. These floorcloths are now making a comeback. From the early 1700s in France, **parquetry** and **marquetry** were used. One of the most famous examples of this period is the beautiful parquet floor at the Palace of Versailles.

In 1885, the invention of a machine capable of making a **tongue-and-groove** in the edge of the wood, plus the use of **kilns**, combined to produce a draft-proof hardwood floor.

In the Victorian era, inlaid border patterns using contrasting light and dark wood were put together in a very intricate manner (see Color Plate Figure 2).

End-grain wood was even used to pave streets at the beginning of the 20th century. In the early 1920s, unit block flooring was introduced, making parquet floors more reasonably priced because each piece did not have to be laid down individually, but rather in a block.

Wood as a material for floors has definitely made a comeback in recent years, particularly in contemporary homes. This is due in part to the use of polyurethane and urethane varnishes, which give an almost maintenance-free finish. Previously, a wood

41

floor had to be kept waxed, then frequently stripped of wax build-up, resanded, and refinished. Also contributing to the popularity of wood floors are the warranties, anywhere from 5 to 25 years.

Wood is divided into two broad categories: the hard woods from the deciduous trees that lose their leaves in the winter, and the soft woods that come from the conifers or evergreens. Actually, there is an overlapping of hardness because some woods from the evergreens are harder than those from the broad-leafed trees.

The harder woods will, of course, be more durable and this durability, together with color and texture, must be considered in both flooring and furniture construction. Ease of finish should also be considered when the wood will have an applied finish.

Weight is usually a good indicator of the relative strength of wood. Because wood is a natural material, it absorbs or eliminates moisture depending upon the humidity to which it is exposed. Most shrinkage or swelling occurs in the width of the wood; the amount depends on the manner of the cut. **Quartersawn** woods are the least troublesome.

Warping is the tendency of wood to twist or bend when drying. This may be in the form of a **bow**, **crook**, **twist**, or **cup,** and, as these terms are frequently referred to in construction, they are illustrated in Figure 4–1. The moisture problem can be reduced to a minimum by using kiln-dried lumber, where wood is stacked in an oven in such a manner that heated air can circulate around the whole plank in order to obtain a uniform moisture content. Seven to 8 percent is

acceptable in flooring and furniture making, and 12 to 19 percent is acceptable for construction grades.

Wood is composed of many cells that run vertically, thus giving wood its straight **grain**. At frequent intervals, **medullary rays** thread their way between and at right angles to the vertical cells. They are most noticeable in plain oak and beech.

We have all seen pictures or drawings of the circular rings of trees. Some of the giant sequoias of California and the ancient oaks of Great Britain have been dated by rings showing hundreds of years of growth. These rings show the seasonal growth and are comprised of spring wood—formed early in the growing season—and summer wood or late wood. In some trees, the different time of growth is very obvious, such as in ash or oak, while in others, such as birch and maple, the seasonal growth is more blended. When there is an obvious difference in growth time, there is also a difference in weight and hardness. The faster-growing trees, usually those in more moderate climates, are softer than the same trees grown in northern areas where the growing season is shorter. Next to the bark is the sapwood, containing the food cells, and this is usually lighter in color. Heartwood contains the now-inactive cells and is slightly darker because of chemical substances that are part of the cell walls.

Figure is the pattern of the wood fibers, and the wood grain is determined by the arrangement of the cells and fibers. Some are straight and others are very patterned; this is enhanced by the method of cutting the boards.

Warp

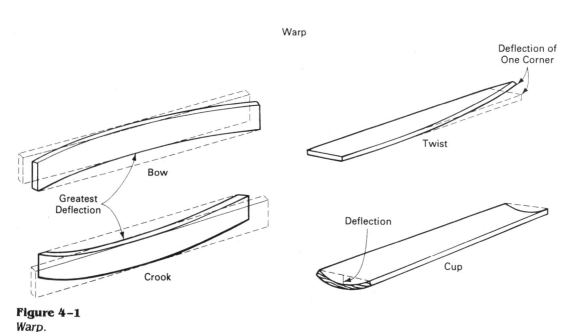

Figure 4–1
Warp.

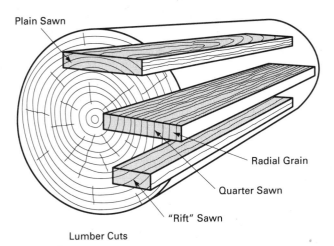

Plain Sawn

Radial Grain

Quarter Sawn

"Rift" Sawn

Lumber Cuts

Figure 4–2
Methods of sawing. (Adapted with permission from Architectural Quality Standards)

There are two principal methods of cutting lumber. One is called plain sawed for hardwoods and flat grained for softwoods. The second is quarter sawed for hardwoods or edge grained for softwoods. When referring to maple as a flooring material, the words "edge grained" are used, even though maple is a hardwood. Oak is quarter sawn, but fir cut in the same manner is called "vertical grain." As interior designers will probably be dealing mainly with hardwoods, the terms "plain sawed" and "quarter sawed" will be used from now on, with the exceptions mentioned above. Each method has its own advantages: Plain sawed is the cheapest, easiest, and most economical use of wood, while quarter sawing gives less distortion of wood from shrinkage or warping.

Each method of cutting gives a different appearance to the wood. Plain sawing gives a cathedral or pointed-arch effect, while quarter sawing gives more of a straight-line appearance. Saw mills cut logs into boards, producing 80 percent plain to 20 percent quartered lumber. Quartered oak flooring, therefore, is extremely hard to find and is expensive. Most production is mixed cuts (Figure 4–2).

Veneer is a very thin sheet of wood varying in thickness from 1/8 to 1/100 of an inch. Wood over 1/4-inch thick is no longer considered veneer. The manner in which the veneer is cut also gives different patterns. The three methods are rotary sliced, flat sliced, and quarter sliced. (These will be discussed in more detail in Chapter 5.) **Laminated** wood is used for some floors and is a sandwich with an uneven number of sheets of veneer, layered at right angles to prevent warping, with the better veneers on the face. Water-resistant glue should be used for bonding the layers together, and the sandwich is placed in a hot press where pressure of 150 to 300 pounds per square inch (**psi**) is applied. Heat around 250° permanently sets the adhesive and bonds the layers together into a single strong panel. Laminated prefinished floors are less affected by humidity and are therefore considered more stable.

Grades of oak are determined by appearance alone. Flooring generally free of defects is known as Clear, although it still may contain **burls,** streaks, and pinworm holes. Select is almost clear, but this grade contains more of the natural characteristics including knots and other marks. The Common grades have more marking than either of the other two grades and are often specified because of these natural features and the character they bring to the flooring.

The three different types of wood flooring are strip, random plank, and parquet (Figure 4–3).

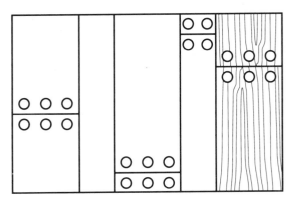 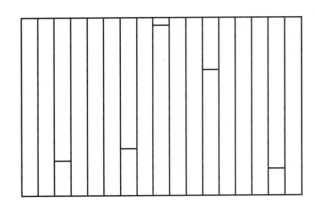

Figure 4–3
Types of flooring: random plank and strip.

TYPES OF WOOD FLOORING

Strip

Strip flooring comes in narrow widths, 2 1/4 inches or narrower, and is tongue-and-grooved on both sides and ends. This type of flooring is most commonly made of oak, although some other woods may be used, such as teak and maple. The strip flooring may be laid parallel to the wall, or diagonally. Gymnasium floors are always constructed of maple but require a special type of installation that provides a slight "give" to the floor.

Harris-Tarkett features Maple Natural in its Perennial Plank and Strip Collection. It is available with either square edge or the standard eased-edge design. This is a **prefinished** laminated product with UltraBrite™ no-wax finish. Board dimensions are 2 1/4 inches or 3 inches wide, 7/16 inches thick, and 46 1/2 inches long.

For residential installations, Mannington Wood Floors has a Lifetime Structural Guarantee, as long as you own your house, on the following: separation of bonded parts; unsightly cupping of planks; buckling due to expansion; and warping or twisting. In addition, if you do not like the appearance of any plank before installation, the company will replace it free of charge. There is a full five-year warranty against sub-floor moisture problems.

Regular strip flooring is sold by the board foot and 5 percent waste allowance is added to the total ordered.

Plank

Plank floors are considered to be any wood wider than 2 1/4 inches, and they come in random widths from 3 to 8 inches. Most installations are comprised of three different sizes; however, Figure 4–4 shows two widths only. The widths selected should correspond to the dimensions of the room in order to keep the flooring in proper scale: the narrower ones for small rooms and wider ones for larger rooms. Random plank comes with a **square** or **beveled edge** and may be factory finished or finished after installation.

Plank floors also have a tongue-and-groove side. The prefinished tongue-and-groove installation does disguise any shrinkage, as the V-joint becomes a fraction wider; with a square edge, the crack caused by shrinkage is more obvious. This is why it is important that all wood be stored in the climatic conditions that will prevail at the installation site. This will allow the wood to absorb or dissipate moisture and reach a sta-

ble moisture content. A white finish will also emphasize any shrinkage.

In the past, some plank floors were installed using wooden pegs or plugs. A hole (or several holes in the case of a wide plank) was drilled about 1 1/2 to 2 inches from the end of the plank and a dowel was pounded into the floor joist and glued into place. Any excess dowel was cut and sanded flush with the floor. Many times, these plugs were constructed of a contrasting wood and became a decorative feature of plank flooring. In later years, screws were countersunk and short dowels of walnut, other contrasting woods, or even brass were glued in to cover the screws for decorative purposes only. Today, unfortunately, some prefinished floors may even have plugs made of plastic, which seem incongruous in a wood floor. Another decorative joining procedure was the butterfly or key, where a dovetail-shaped piece of wood was used at the end joint of two boards.

The Timeless® Series II from PermaGrain® Products is an acrylic-impregnated plank flooring for high traffic areas, available in five types of wood: northern red oak, clear maple, tupelo, lindenwood, and American cherry. Timeless Series II is covered by a lifetime full replacement wear warranty, meets or exceeds all current requirements for slip resistance as set forth by the Americans With Disabilities Act (ADA) of 1991, and was named a winner in the Institute of Business Designers' 1991 Product Design Competition. This type of flooring has been treated with a liquid acrylic that has been forced under pressure into the porous structure of the wood. The wood is then subjected to irradiation, which causes the liquid acrylic to harden and thus to impart to the wood/plastic an extremely abrasion-resistant finish, which exists throughout its thickness.

Dyes and fire retardants may be added to the acrylic, if required. The stain penetrates throughout the wood so that worn areas need only be retouched with a topcoat. The floor never needs sanding, staining, or refinishing. With all these impregnated woods, it must be remembered that the color cannot be changed, as it has penetrated the whole depth of the wood. This can be an asset or a liability, depending upon your requirements.

Bruce® WearMaster® acrylic-impregnated floors are designed for use in heavy and light commercial applications as well as residential use. Bruce offers an exclusive 25-year engineered wood wear surface warranty on all WearMaster floors.

Plank flooring is sold by the square foot and a 5 percent waste allowance is generally added to the total square footage.

Figure 4–4
Chickasaw Mission Plank Oak flooring provides contemporary styling with the aura of Early American homes, but without pegs as in Colonial floors. The 3-inch and 4-inch alternating width planks are a full 3/4 of an inch thick and come sanded, prefinished and waxed, or unfinished but presanded for a job-site finish of the owner's choice of stain and seal or finish coating. Distinct 3/32 of an inch side bevels accentuate the full widths. Shown here prefinished. (Photograph courtesy of Memphis Hardwood Flooring Company)

Parquet

Parquet is comprised of individual pieces of wood, generally oak, from 3/8 to 3/4 of an inch thick, joined together to form a variety of patterns. These small pieces are held together by various methods: a **metal spline**, gluing to a mesh of paper, or gluing to a form of cheesecloth.

There are many patterns, as shown in Figure 4–5, and most manufacturers make a similar variety of patterns, but the names may vary. One company will name a pattern Jeffersonian, another Monticello or even Mt. Vernon, but they are basically variations of the same pattern. This particular design is made with a central block surrounded by **pickets** on all four sides (see Figure 4–5). The center may be made of solid wood or a laminated block; it may contain five or six strips going in the same direction, or there may be a standard unit of four **sets** in the center.

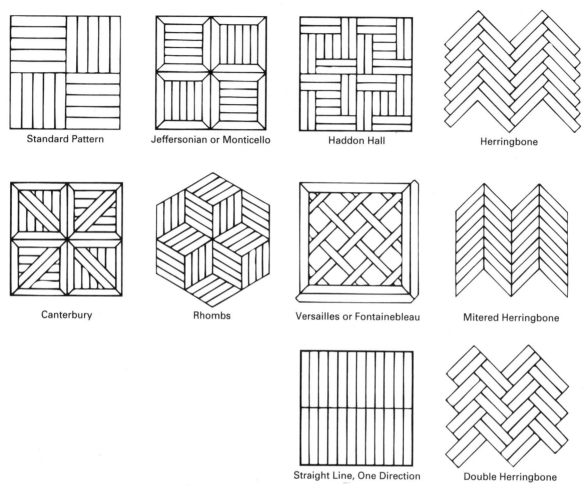

Standard Pattern Jeffersonian or Monticello Haddon Hall Herringbone

Canterbury Rhombs Versailles or Fontainebleau Mitered Herringbone

Straight Line, One Direction Double Herringbone

Figure 4–5
Common parquet patterns.

Designers need a word of warning about using some of the parquet patterns. Some parquets have direction, for example, the herringbone pattern. Depending on whether the pieces are laid parallel to the wall or at an angle, your client may see "Ls," "zig-zags," or arrows. The important thing is the client's expectations.

To minimize the expansion problems caused by moisture, the oak flooring industry has developed several types of parquets. PermaGrain offers the Paragon® Series, a solid red oak, acrylic-impregnated parquet floor.

The laminated or engineered block is a product that displays far less expansion and contraction with moisture changes and, therefore, can be successfully installed below grade (see Figure 4–6) in basements and in humid climates. It can even fit tight to vertical obstructions. The blocks can be glued directly to the concrete with several types of adhesive, which the in-

dustry is making VOC compliant. One of the concerns in the past has been the ability of a laminated block to be sanded and refinished. Because the face layer is oak, with proper maintenance the initial service life can be expected to be 20 to 30 years. Any of the laminated products on the market today can be sanded and refinished (at least twice) using proper techniques and equipment, so the expected life of a laminated block floor is 60 to 90 years.

Special custom-designed borders are available for use in a Victorian setting or for a contemporary custom look. These borders are made of contrasting woods and vary in width from 4 inches up to 20 inches. Thin strips of semiprecious stones or metals such as brass or aluminum may also be incorporated into the design.

Custom Borders from Kentucky Wood Floors are preassembled modules that can be glued down flush with 5/16-inch thick flooring or on top of underlay-

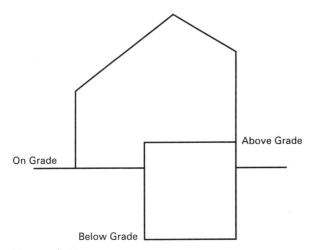

Figure 4–6
Grade levels.

ment with 3/4-inch thick flooring. Corner blocks are also available. Matching architectural millwork is available, such as quarter-round, baseboard, nosing, and **reducer strips** (see Color Plate Figure 2).

Parquet floor comes packed in cartons with a specific number of square feet. When ordering parquet flooring, only whole cartons are shipped, so the allowance for cutting may be taken care of with the balance of the carton.

All the woods mentioned before are quarter sawed or plain sawed, but some species are cut across the growth rings (end-grained).

End-grain patterns are formed by small cross-cut pieces that are attached together into blocks or strips with the end grain exposed. The thickness may vary from 1 to 4 inches, depending upon the manufacturer. One and a half inches of end-grain block have insulating qualities equal to 23 inches of concrete. Some end-grain block floors are still in place after more than 40 years of heavy industrial use. These blocks absorb noise and vibration and have been installed in museums and libraries.

Grade Levels

Figure 4–6 illustrates the difference between on, above, and below grade. Above grade is not a problem for installation of wood floors, because no moisture is present. As mentioned earlier, moisture is the major cause of problems with wood. On grade means that the concrete floor is in contact with the ground. The floor usually has drainage gravel as a base, covered by a polyethylene film to prevent moisture from

migrating to the surface. The concrete is then poured on top of this polyethylene sheet.

Below grade means a basement floor where the presence of moisture is an even greater problem. All freshly poured concrete should be allowed to **cure** for 30 to 60 days. The rubber mat test will show if moisture is present. A rubber mat is placed on the cement surface and left for 24 hours. When removed, if the concrete surface is dry, there is no moisture present. This test should be done even if the slab has been in place over two years. Only laminated wood floors may be installed below grade, but the manufacturer's installation procedures must be followed exactly. Laminated products expand very little so may fit to a vertical surface.

It is predicted that laminated wood flooring sales will more than double in the next five years, because strong environmental trends are leading consumers to these products.

Particleboard is a product used widely as a substrate for floors. Particleboard as defined by the National Particleboard Association (NPA) is a wood panel product consisting of discrete wood particles of various sizes that are bonded together with a synthetic resin or binder under heat and pressure. Particle geometry, resin levels, board density, and manufacturing processes may be modified to produce products suitable for specific end uses. At the time of manufacture, additives can be incorporated to provide greater dimensional stability or better fire resistance or to improve other properties. (See Chapter 1 for environmental information pertaining to particleboard.)

Installation Procedures. Substrates must be clean (free of dust, grease, or oil stains), dry, and level. As was stressed in Chapter 3 and will be repeated throughout this book, SURFACE PREPARATION IS EXTREMELY IMPORTANT. The completed floor is only as good as the subfloor. Any high spots should be ground down and low spots filled in using the correct leveling compound. One floor installer related a story about a client who complained of a loose wood floor installed over a slab. When the loose wood was removed, not only did the wood come up, but attached to it was the material used as a filler for the low spots. The person who leveled the floor had used the wrong leveling compound. Solid strip products are nailed down and parquet products are glued down with such products as Hydroment® Ultra-Set Hardwood Adhesive. This adhesive is a one-part trowel applied, light gray, elastomeric water-proof setting adhesive. Once cured, it is not affected by

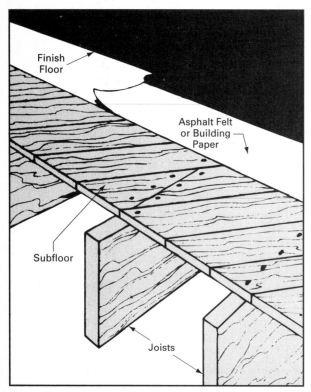

(a) Wood joist construction using square-edge board subfloor.

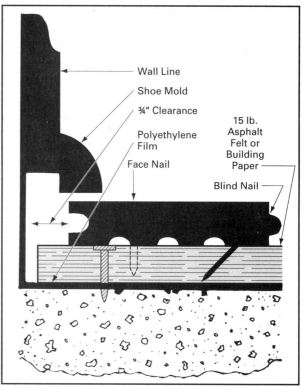

(b) Plywood-on-slab method of installing strip oak flooring.

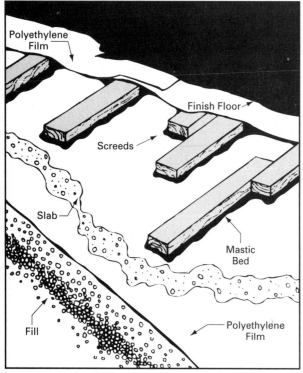

(c) Screeds method of installing strip oak flooring on slab.

(d) Use of power nailer for installing strip flooring.

Figure 4–7
Installation methods for wood floors.

water. Laminated plank is the only product that can be either nailed or glued.

The National Oak Flooring Manufacturers Association (NOFMA) suggests that several factors may contribute to an unsatisfactory installation. First, the wood floor installation should be scheduled at the very end of construction. Since most other work is completed, the floors will not be abused. The building should now be dry, with any moisture introduced during construction gone. Second, a subfloor of 5/8 of an inch or thicker plywood or 1 × 6-inch edge boards is preferred. The thicker, well-fastened subfloor gives the better installation. Third, the wood flooring should be well nailed; there should be no skimping on the number of nails per strip, plank, etc. The photographs in Figure 4–7 are taken from NOFMA's Hardwood Flooring Installation Manual and show correct installation procedures.

Walls are not used as a starting point because they are never truly square. Wood parquet must always be installed in a pyramid or stair step sequence, rather than in rows, to avoid a misaligned pattern (Figure 4–8). Parquet may also be laid either parallel or at a 45° angle to the wall.

Reducer strips may be used at the doorway if there is a difference in level between two areas, and they are available to match the wood floor. Most wood floor **mastics** take about 24 hours to dry, so do not walk or place furniture in the room during that period. Laminated planks must be rolled with a 150-pound roller before the adhesive sets. An unfinished wood floor is sanded with the grain using progressively finer grits until the floor is smooth and has an almost shiny appearance. After vacuuming to eliminate any dust particles, finishing materials specifically manufactured for use on wood floors are applied. For open-grained wood such as oak, a filler with or without stain may be used after sanding to provide a more highly reflective surface. There is a preference for natural-color hardwood floors, but stain may be used to bring out the grain or produce a darker tone. When a very light finish is desired, the wood may be bleached or pickled.

There are two main types of finish applied to wood floors: polyurethane and Swedish finish. A polyurethane finish will yellow with time, while the Swedish finish will not. Glitsa, a brand-name Swedish finish, is now VOC compliant.

Maintenance. It is the general housekeeping type of cleaning that prolongs the life of a wood floor. THE MAIN PROBLEM WITH MAINTENANCE OF ANY FLOOR IS GRIT. This can be removed by dust mop, broom, or vacuum. Another problem is the indentations caused by heels, especially ladies' high heels. A 125-pound woman with high heels exerts as much pressure as an elephant; therefore, indentations should be expected. If the floor is the type that may be waxed (very few are), a thin coat of wax should be allowed to dry and harden. Then an electric bristle brush buffer is used. Because old wax holds dirt and grease and a buildup of "scuffs," it should be removed periodically by means of a solvent type of wax remover specifically designed for wood floors. Food spills may be wiped up with a damp cloth.

Custom finishes such as polyurethane and Swedish should not be waxed. Manufacturers of acrylic wood provide special cleaning materials for their products.

MARBLE

Marble is a **metamorphic** rock derived from limestone. Pressure and/or heat created the metamorphic change that turned limestone debris into marble. Today all rocks that are capable of taking a polish come under the heading of marble. Dolomitic limestone ("hard" limestone), although technically limestone, is known commercially as marble. Travertine and onyx are related stones, travertine being the more important for flooring purposes because it is easier to work. Onyx is brittle and is mostly relegated to deco-

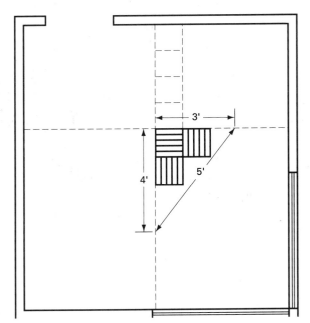

Figure 4–8
Method of laying parquet floor.

rative uses. Serpentine is of a different chemical make-up, but because it can be polished, it is classified as marble.

The colors of marble are as varied and numerous as the areas from which it is quarried. One of the famous kinds, Carrara marble, is pure white. Michaelangelo used this marble for many of his sculptures. Other Carrara marble may have black, gray, or brownish veinings. The name "verd antiques" is applied to marbles of prevailing green color, consisting chiefly of serpentine, a hydrous magnesium silicate. Verd antiques are highly decorative stones, the green being interspersed at times with streaks or veins of red and white. The pinks, reds, yellows, and browns are caused by the presence of iron oxides, whereas the blacks, grays, and blue-grays result from bituminous deposits. Silicate, chlorite, and mica provide the green colors.

Marble is the most ancient of all finished materials currently in use today. Some authorities believe that the onyx marble of Algeria was employed by the Egyptians as early as 475 B.C. Biblical references indicate that marble was used in King Solomon's Temple at Jerusalem, and in the palace of Sushun more than one thousand years before Christ. Parian marble from the Aegean Sea was found in the ruins of ancient Troy.

Pentelic marble was used in the Parthenon in Athens, and is still available today. Phidias used this same marble for the frieze of the Parthenon, and portions of this frieze known as the **Elgin Marbles** are intact today and greatly treasured by the British Museum. Makrana marble, a white marble, was used in the Taj Mahal in India. Inside, the sunlight filters through marble screens as delicate as lace and the white marble walls are richly decorated with floral designs in onyx, jasper, carnelian, and other semiprecious stones.

Knoxville, Tennessee, was known at the turn of this century as the "marble capital." Marble is found in many states from Vermont to Georgia and in some of the western states. The Georgia Marble Company ranks as the world's largest producer of marble products. Dolomitic marble is quarried in Tennessee and Missouri. The famous Yule Quarry in Marble, Colorado (from which came the columns of the Lincoln Memorial and the massive block forming the Tomb of the Unknown Soldier) has just been reopened. The white from this quarry may be the "purest" marble in the world.

Marble floors were used in the Baroque and Rococo periods in Europe. During the French empire, black and white marble squares were used, and they remain a popular pattern for marble floors today. In the formal halls of Georgian homes, the marble floors were appropriate for the mahogany tables and chairs. In his Barcelona Pavilion, Mies Van der Rohe used great slabs of marble as free-standing partitions. Today, marble is used for furniture, floors, and both interior and exterior walls (see Color Plate Figure 4).

Marble does not come in sheets and must be quarried with care by drilling holes outlining the block. Then wedges are driven into the holes and the blocks are split from the surrounding rock. Diamond blades are used to cut the blocks into the sizes required. Marble chips are used in the production of **terrazzo, agglomerated** marble tiles, and cast polymer products.

Marble is a relatively heavy and expensive material for use on floors because of the necessity of using the conventional, thick-bed installation method. One method of cutting down weight and cost is to use a layer of fiberglass and/or epoxy resins as a backing for thin layers of marble. Another method uses a 1/4-inch thick layer of marble backed by a 1-inch thick piece of styrofoam. This latter method also provides a marble floor that is warmer to the touch than one made of thicker marble.

The agglomerated marble tiles consist of 90 to 95 percent marble chips, combined with 5 to 10 percent resins and formed into blocks in a vacuum chamber, and are available as floor tile or marble wall veneers. Agglomerated marble may be classified as cast marble, but the term "cast" is also used to describe a polyester product containing ground marble.

The following properties need to be considered for marble floors:

Density. Averages 0.1 pound per cubic inch. This figure may be used to calculate the weight of the marble.

Water absorption. Measured by total immersion of a 2-inch cube for 48 hours and varies from 0.1 to 0.2 percent, which is less than other natural stones. The maximum absorption as established by ASTM C503 is 0.20 percent.

Abrasion resistance. Measured by a scuffing method that removes surface particles in a manner somewhat similar to the action of foot traffic. Abrasion resistance for commercial flooring should be at least a hardness value of 10 as measured by ASTM C241. The Marble Institute of America (MIA) recommends a hardness value of 12. This value is not necessary for single-family homes.

Marble is also classified A through C, according to what methods of fabrication are considered necessary and acceptable in each instance, as based on standard trade practice.

A polished or glossy finish may be used in a residential installation but is not used for commercial installations. Smooth satin or honed (a velvety, smooth surface with little or no gloss) or sand-rubbed (a flat nonreflective surface with little or no gloss) should be specified for commercial floors (see Color Plate Figure 4). The biggest problem with a polished floor is that the shine is removed in the traffic area and the edges still retain the shine, emphasizing the difference in the two areas.

When using marble or any other natural stone, it is necessary to calculate the weight of these materials and be sure the subfloor is strong enough to support the extra weight. This, of course, is where the 3/8-inch materials come into use, especially for remodeling, where the floor was probably not constructed to bear these heavy stones. Any deflection in the floor will result in cracking of the marble.

One of the materials used to help provide rigidity to a stable subfloor is HARDIBACKER® board, a lightweight, dimensionally stable cement-based board that is water resistant for residential or commercial construction. Because this board is only 1/4 of an inch thick, it reduces the height variations where different types of flooring materials meet, such as ceramic tile and carpeting. Other backerboards vary in composition, thickness, weight, and compressive strength. The subfloor suggested is a 1/3-inch minimum thickness plywood firmly fastened to 16-inch **o.c.**, floor joists, with nails and Type I mastic or latex modified thin-set adhesive. The backerboard is nailed in place every 6 inches, using suggested mechanical fasteners, which penetrate through to the floor joists. The subfloor is now ready for the installation of materials requiring the thin-set method.

Installation Methods. Several associations are responsible for codes and standards based on the consensus of their membership. The natural stones such as marble, travertine, and slate use the specifications and test methods contained in the American Society for Testing and Materials (ASTM) manual, Section 4 Construction; volume 04.08 Soil and Rock; Building Stones. The ceramic tile industry uses the American National Standards Institute (ANSI) A108 for installation specifications. A copy of these specifications and test methods may be obtained from the respective organizations (see Appendix B.)

As this is the first hard surface material covered in

this book, installation methods will be detailed. Basically, the same methods are used for all natural stones, ceramic tile, quarry tile, and other types of flooring.

Setting materials account for only 10 percent of the installation cost, but 90 percent of the problems, so proper specification and a professional installation will eliminate most problems. Skinning, a film that forms on the surface of the setting materials and causes improper bonding, is a common cause of installation failure for all setting materials. To cure this problem, the application tool should be used again to break up this skin.

The Tile Council of America provided the following information:

> Portland cement mortar is suitable for most surfaces and ordinary types of installation. A mortar bed, up to 2 inches in thickness, facilitates accurate slopes or planes in the finished tile work on floors and walls.
>
> There are two equivalent methods recognized for installing ceramic tile with a portland cement **mortar** bed on walls, ceilings and floors. They are (1) the method covered by ANSI A108.1A, which requires that the tile be set on a mortar bed while it is still workable, and (2) the method covered by ANSI A108.1B, which requires the tile to be set on a cured mortar bed with dry-set or latex-portland cement mortar. Absorptive ceramic tile must be soaked before setting on a mortar bed that is still workable when using a neat portland cement bond coat.
>
> Portland cement mortars can be reinforced with metal lath or mesh, can be backed with membranes, and can be applied on metal lath over open studding on walls, or on rough floors. They are structurally strong, are not affected by prolonged contact with water, and can be used to plumb and square surfaces installed by others. . . . Complete installation and material specifications are contained in ANSI A108.1A, A108.1B, and A108.1C.[1]

Thick-set or thick-bed MUST be used for setting materials of uneven thickness such as flagstone and slate. It may also be used for hard-surfaced materials of uniform thickness. Tiles are placed on the mortar and tapped into place until the surface is level. The mortar used on floors is a mixture of portland cement and sand, roughly in proportions of 1:6.

Dry-set mortar is suitable for thin-set installations of ceramic tile over a variety of surfaces. It is used in one layer, as thin as 3/32 of an inch, and after tiles are beat in, has excellent water and impact resistance; is water-cleanable, nonflammable, good for exterior work; and does not require soaking of tile:

Dry-set mortar is available as a factory-sanded mortar to which only water need be added. Cured dry-set mortar is not affected by prolonged contact with water but does not form a water barrier. It is not a setting bed and is not intended to be used in truing or leveling the work of others.

Complete installation specifications and material specifications are contained in ANSI A108.5 and ANSI A118.1. For conductive dry-set mortar see ANSI A108.7 and ANSI 118.2.[2]

Another thin-set method is to use an adhesive that is spread with a trowel, first using the flat edge for continuous coverage and then the notched edge for uniform thickness. Oil-based adhesives should be avoided when installing marble as they stain the marble. Again it must be repeated that thin-bed should be used only where the substrate is solid and level.

There are differences between a marble setter and a tile setter. One is that the former **butts** tiles together, resulting in a 1/16-inch wide space that may be filled in with portland cement if desired or left unfilled. A tile setter, however, is accustomed to working with **cushion-edged** tile and will leave a wider space between the tiles. It is necessary to state the spacing of the marble tile and whether or not **grout** is to be used. Another difference is that marble setters prefer a stiffer 1:3 ratio for the mortar mix.

Normal Maintenance. The following information is taken from the booklet "How to Keep Your Marble Lovely," which is available from the Marble Institute of America, Inc. (see Appendix B). Marble floors should be washed with clean lukewarm water, and if badly soiled, a mild detergent can be used. The floor is rinsed thoroughly with clean water. Any residue left could make the floor slippery. All stones and many synthetic hard-surfaced materials are to some degree porous and should, therefore, be protected from oil and water-borne stains.

Most old stains require the use of a poultice that consists of molding plaster, untreated white flour, white chalk, or white tissue paper soaked to form a paste. The poultice should be soaked in the proper solution depending on the type of stain and covered with a sheet of plastic that has been taped down around the edges to keep the moisture from evaporating while the stain is drawn out of the marble—this may take up to 48 hours, depending upon the type of stain.

To remove organic stains such as tea or coffee, or leached colors from paper or textiles, the surface is washed with clean water and a poultice is applied that has been soaked in either hydrogen peroxide (20 percent volume) or household ammonia (full commercial strength). Oil stains and mustard are soaked in Amyl Acetate or Acetone. (Caution: Amyl Acetate and Acetone are highly flammable and should be used only in a well-ventilated area and kept away from flame or sparks.) For rust stains, the poultice is soaked in commercial rust remover.

TRAVERTINE

Travertine is a porous limestone formed from the precipitation of mineral springs and has holes in it as a result of escaping gas. When it is to be used on the floor, travertine should be filled with an epoxy resin. As travertine is creamy colored, this resin may be opaque (of a creamy color) or transparent. The opaque filler does not reflect the light as well as the surrounding polished travertine, whereas the clear epoxy gives a three-dimensional appearance to the holes and takes on the shine of the travertine.

Maintenance. The maintenance of travertine is the same as for marble.

GRANITE

Granite is technically an igneous rock having crystals or grains of visible size. These grains are classified as fine, medium, or coarse.

Colors are white, gray, buff, beige, pink, red, blue, green, and black; but within these colors, the variegations run from light to dark. The color gray, for example, may be light, medium, or dark, or vary between dark and purplish gray, or dark and greenish gray. It is important to see an actual sample of the type of granite to be used. The National Building Granite Quarries Association (NBGQA) recommends submitting duplicate 12 × 12-inch samples to show the full range of color, texture, and finish, with the designer retaining one set and the other being returned to the granite supplier for reference.

In addition to color, finish is important. The following definitions were established by the NBGQA:

Polished: Mirror gloss, with sharp reflections.
Honed: Dull sheen, without reflections.

Fine rubbed: Smooth and free from scratches; no sheen.

Rubbed Plane: Surface with occasional slight "trails" or scratches.

Thermal: Plane surface with flame finish applied by mechanically controlled means to insure uniformity. Surface coarseness varies, depending upon grain structure of the granite.

As with other stones, polished granite should not be used for floors because the mirror gloss and color will eventually be dulled by the abrasion of feet. Where water may be present, flamed or thermal textures are used to create a nonslip surface. The same method of veneered construction used to make thinner and lighter weight marble squares is also used with granite, and for the same reasons. When a feeling of permanence and stability is needed, granite is a good choice; hence, the use of granite in banking institutions.

Installation. Granite is installed using the same methods as for marble, especially for the honed-face stones. When some of the more textured finishes are specified, and when the granite has not been cut to a definite size, a mortar joint is used.

Maintenance. Granite floors, particularly those with rougher surfaces, require ordinary maintenance by means of a brush or vacuum cleaner. The more highly finished granite surfaces should be maintained in a manner similar to marble.

GROUT

Grout is the material used to fill the joints between tiles. The type of grout employed, if any, depends on which variety of tile is being used. Therefore, not only is the type of grout important, but also the spacing of the tile. Proper joint placement is very important so that both sides of the room have equal-size pieces. The use of crack isolation membranes in thin-bed installations is necessary to prevent cracks in the substrate from cracking marble or ceramic tile installed over them.

The Tile Council of America states that

portland cement is the base of most grouts and is modified to provide specific qualities such as whiteness, mildew resistance, uniformity, hardness, flexibility, and water retentivity. Non-cement based grouts such as epoxies, furans, and silicone rubber offer properties not possible with cement grouts. However, *special skills on the part of the tile setter are required.* These materials can be appreciably greater in cost than cement-based grouts. Complete installation and material specifications are contained in ANSI A108.10 and ANSI A118.6.[3]

The commercial portland cement grout for floors is usually gray (but colors are available) and is designed for use with ceramic **mosaics**, quarry and paver tile. Damp curing is required, which is the process of keeping the grout moist and covered for several days, resulting in a much stronger grout. For areas that must be opened for traffic as quickly as possible, there are quick-set grout additives (Table 4–1).

Grouts with sand are not used with highly reflective tiles, as the roughness of the grout is not compatible with the high gloss. For glazed tiles, use unsanded grout or mastic grout. There are special grouts available that are chemical resistant, while some are fungus and mildew resistant, and others of a latex composition are used when any movement is anticipated. Intersept is incorporated into Portersept's grout sealer, which protects the grout against mold, mildew, and bacteria.

FLAGSTONE

Flagstone was used on the floors in Tudor England (1485–1603). Flagstone is defined as thin slabs of stone used for paving walks, driveways, patios, etc. It is generally fine-grained **sandstone**, **bluestone**, **quartzite**, or slate, but thin slabs of other stones may be used. One-inch thick bluestone flagging in a random multiple pattern compares very favorably in price to premium vinyl tiles.

The stone may be irregularly shaped as it was quarried, varying in size from 1 to 4 square feet, or the edges may be sawed to give a more formal appearance. Thickness may vary from 1/2 to 4 inches; therefore, the flagstone must be set in a thick mortar base in order to produce a level surface.

The extra thickness of the flagstone must be taken into consideration when positioning the floor joists. One client had flagstone drawn and specified on her blueprints, but the carpenter misread the plans and assumed that it was to be a flagstone-patterned floor and not the real thing. The client arrived at the house one day to discover that the entry way did not have the lowered floor necessary to accommodate the extra thickness of the stone. The contractor had to cut all the floor joists for the hall area, lower them 4 inches, and

TABLE 4–1
Grout Guide

Printed through the courtesy of the Materials & Methods Standards Association

A rubber faced trowel should be used when grouting glazed tile with sanded grout.

		Grout Type								
		Commercial Portland Cement		Sand-Portland Cement	Dry-set	Latex Portland Cement (3)	Epoxy (1)(6)(3)	Furan (1)(6)(3)	Silicone or Urethane (2)	Modified Epoxy Emulation (3)(6)
		Wall Use	Floor Use	Wall-Floor Use	Wall-Floor Use					
TILE TYPE	GLAZED WALL TILE (More than 7% absorption)	•			•	•	•		•	
	CERAMIC MOSAICS	•	•	•	•	•	•		•	•
	QUARRY, PAVER & PACKING HOUSE TILE	•	•	•		•	•	•		•
AREAS OF USE	Dry or limited water exposure	•	•	•	•	•	•	•	•	•
	Wet areas	•	•	•	•	•	•	•	•	•
	Exteriors	•	•	•	•	•(4)	•(4)	•(4)		•(4)
PERFORMANCE	Stain Resistance (5)	D	D	E	D	C	A	A	A	C
	Crack Resistance (5)	D	D	E	D	C	B	C	A Flexible	C
	Colorability (5)	B	B	D	B	B	B	Black Only	Restricted	B

(1) Mainly used for chemical resistant properties.
(2) Special tools needed for proper application. Silicone, urethane and modified polyvinylchloride used in pregrouted ceramic tile sheets. Silicone grout should not be used on kitchen countertops or other food preparation surfaces unless it meets the requirements of FDA Regulation No. 21, CFE 177.2600.
(3) Special cleaning procedures and materials recommended.
(4) Follow manufacturer's directions.
(5) Five performance ratings—Best to Minimal (A B C D E).
(6) Epoxies are recommended for prolonged temperatures up to 140F, high temperature resistant epoxies and furans up to 350F.

Source: 1994 Handbook for Ceramic Tile Installation. Copyright © Tile Council of America, Inc. Reprinted with permission.

then put in additional bracing and supports in the basement—a very costly error.

Another point to remember with flagstone is that the surface is usually slightly uneven because it comes from naturally cleaved rock; therefore, flagstone is not suitable for use under tables and chairs as the legs may rock. An entrance hall of flagstone is very durable but the stone needs to be protected from grease.

The grout used is a sand-portland cement type and fills all areas where flagstones adjoin.

Maintenance. There are sealing compounds on the market that make flagstone **impervious** to any staining and wear. These compounds are available in gloss and matte finishes and protect the treated surface against the deteriorating effects of weathering, salts, acids, alkalis, oil, and grease. The gloss finish does seem to give a rather unnatural shiny appearance to the stone, but where the impervious quality rather than the aesthetic quality is of prime importance, these sealers may be used. Vacuuming will remove dust and siliceous material from the surface and a damp mop will remove any other soil from the sealed surface.

SLATE

Slate was also used as a flooring material in Tudor England (1585–1603), and in 17th-century France, slate was combined with bands of wood. Slate is a very fine-grained metamorphic rock cleaved from sedimentary rock shale. One of the characteristics of slate is that this cleavage allows the rock to be split easily into relatively thin slabs. The most common colors for slate range from gray to black, but green, brown, and red are also available. In areas of heavy traffic, the honed black slate does have a tendency to show the natural scuffing of shoes, and the scratches give the black slate a slightly grayish appearance. All stones will eventually show this scuffing and, therefore, highly polished stones should be avoided as a flooring material.

Different finishes are available in slate, as in other stones. The Structural Slate Company describes the following finishes:

Natural cleft: The natural split or cleaved face. It is moderately rough with some textural variations. Thickness will have a plus or minus tolerance of 1/8 of an inch.

Sand-rubbed: This has a slight grain or stipple in an even plane. No natural cleft texture remains.

Finish is equivalent to **60-grit** and is obtained by wet sand on a rubbing bed.

Honed: This finish is equivalent to approximately **120-grit** in smoothness. It is semipolished, without excessive sheen.

The standard thickness of sawed flooring slate is 1/2 inch. Also available are 3/4- and 1-inch thicknesses, and these are suitable for both interior and exterior use.

American Olean has two patterns and two color ranges of slate. Pattern 1 has sizes that range from 6 × 6 inches to 12 × 12 inches, and Pattern 5 ranges from 6 × 9 inches to 15 × 18 inches. The two color selections are mottled purple with predominantly green mottling to darker purple with slight green mottling, and black ranging from gray black to blue black. The patterns each cover 15 square feet (Figure 4–9).

One half-inch slate weighs 7 1/2 pounds per square foot, 3/4 inch weighs 11 1/4 pounds, and 1 inch weighs 15 pounds. The absorption rate of slate is 0.23 percent. One-quarter-inch slate is used for interior foyers in homes and commercial buildings using the thin-set method. This thickness is an excellent remodel item over wood or slab and gives a rug level effect when it adjoins carpet. One-quarter-inch slate weighs only 3 3/4 pounds per square foot.

The thicker slate is available in rectangles and squares in sizes from 6 × 6 inches to 24 × 24 inches in multiples of 3 inches, whereas the sizes for 1/4-inch slate are 6 × 6 inches to 12 × 12 inches, also in multiples of 3 inches.

As can be seen from the above types, slate is avail-

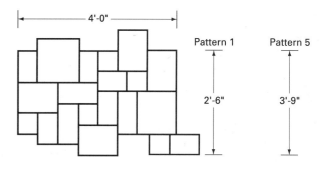

- Sizes include a 3/8" (1.0 cm) joint.
  Example: 6" × 6" (15.2 cm × 15.2 cm) is 5-5/8" × 5-5/8"
- 1/4" (0.6 cm) gauged thickness; other thicknesses available special order
- May be specified in single colors or a combination of colors

Figure 4–9
The two sizes of slate in Pattern 1 and Pattern 5 are shown in this illustration from American Olean. (Courtesy of American Olean)

able for both thin-set and thick-set applications. When thin-set mastic or adhesive is used, a $1/4 \times 1/4$ inch notched trowel held at a 45° angle is suggested.

There are, however, several points to remember with both types of installations. If grout is used with slate (the spacing varies from 1/4 to 1/2 of an inch), it is important that any excess be cleaned off immediately, because grout that has dried on the slate surface will probably never come off. If grout is not used, the slate tiles are butted against each other. Joint lines are staggered so no lines are more than 2 to 3 feet long in a straight line.

Thick-bed installation is similar to flagstone. All joints should be 1/2-inch wide flush joints and should be **pointed** with 1:2 cement mix the same day the floor is laid to make joints and setting bed **monolithic**.

Maintenance. A slate floor is easily maintained with mild soap and water. While waxing is not harmful, it detracts from the natural beauty of the stone, turns the floor a darker shade, and may yellow the grout.

CERAMIC TILE

Because ceramic tile was one of the most durable materials used by ancient civilizations, archaeologists have been able to ascertain that thin slabs of fired clay, decorated and glazed, originated in Egypt about 4700 B.C. Tile was, and frequently is, used in Spanish architecture to such a degree that a Spanish expression for poverty is "to have a house without tiles." The Spanish also use decorative ceramic tile on the **risers** of stairs.

In England, many abbeys had mosaic tile floors and the European cathedrals of the 12th century also had tile floors. The ancient tiles were used to make pictures on the walls, with the pattern covering many tiles. A good example is the bulls and dragons in the Ishtar Gate from Babylon now in the Pergamon Museum in Berlin. Later, each tile was decorated with very intricate patterns, or four tiles were used to form a complete pattern. Eighteenth- and 19th-century tiles used a combination of these two types.

Tiles were named after the city where they originated—Faience from Faenza in Italy, Majolica from Majorca, and Delft tiles from the town of Delft in Holland. Delft tiles, with their blue and white designs, are known worldwide. Tiles are made as follows:

Most glazed ceramic tiles for interior use are produced by the dust-press process. A mixture of damp, white-burning clays and other ceramic materials are forced into steel dies under heavy pres-

sure. After pressing, the tile is inspected for smoothness, size, and imperfections. It may then be fired at a high temperature to form a **bisque**, a tile ready to be glazed. A glaze of ceramic materials and mineral pigments is sprayed on the bisque and a second firing at a lower temperature fuses the glaze to the bisque. Some glazed tiles are produced with a single firing. In this process, the tile is pressed, allowed to cure, given a coat of glaze, and then fired in the kiln.

Tiles are also made by extrusion, a slush-mold process, or a ram-press process. In the extrusion process, the clay is mixed the consistency of thick mud and forced through a die. The machine cuts the clay to proper lengths as it comes from the die. In the slush-mold process, a wet mixture of clay is poured into molds and allowed to set. The tiles are then removed from the molds, glazed, and fired in a kiln. In the ram-press process, tiles are formed between two steel dies. This method produces larger tiles of any shape or surface texture. The tiles are glazed and fired in the same manner as dust-pressed tiles.[4]

It is the temperature and the proportions of the ingredients that dictate the use: walls, floors, interior or exterior, and residential or commercial.

The water absorption test can also be used as a good indicator to predict the stain resistance of the unglazed tile. The lower the water absorption is, the greater the stain resistance will be.

Porcelain tiles are inherently impervious and are used frequently in heavy-use commercial and retail areas (Table 4–2). These can be used in light colors that give an airy and spacious feeling to the installation. One problem may be that light-colored tile often means light-colored grout and, therefore, stain-resistant grout should be specified. Because of the low absorption rate of porcelain tiles, bond-promoting additives are added to the mortars and grouts.

There are many types of finishes and patterns available in ceramic tile, ranging from a very shiny, highly reflective glaze to a dull matte finish and even an unglazed impervious tile (Figure 4–10). Tile may be solid color or hand painted with designs.

TABLE 4–2
Porosity Variances

TYPE	WATER ABSORPTION RATE
Impervious	0.5% or less
Vitreous	More than 0.5% but less than 3%
Semivitreous	More than 3% but less than 7%
Nonvitreous	More than 7%

Figure 4–10
*A combination of textures creates this interesting entrance to The Stratford
Apartments, Atlanta, Georgia. Dal Porcelana is used throughout. The foreground is
absolute Black Slate Finish, with the light border of Grey Granite Natural Finish
Slate Finish and the center is Charcoal Granite Polished Finish. Designer: Nancy
Whitaker. Developer: Worthing Southeast Builders. Contractor: S & S Tile, Dallas.
(Photograph courtesy of Dal Tile®.)*

Highly glazed tile is not recommended for floor use for two reasons. First, the surface can become extremely slippery when wet; second, some wearing and scratching can occur over a period of time, depending on type of use. Of course, if moisture and wear are not a problem, then glazed tile may be used.

To arrive at a comparative number for how slippery a floor may be, there is now a test that measures the coefficient of friction. The static coefficient of friction is a term used in physics to describe the amount of force required to cause an object (shoe sole material) to start moving across a flooring material. By measuring the coefficient of friction, a quantitative number can be used to express the degree of slip resistance. A 50-pound weight is placed on a Neolite shoe heel, which was previously placed flat on the tile surface. The heel and weight assembly is pulled across the tile with a spring or electronic scale. The maximum amount of force (pounds) needed to start the assembly in motion is then recorded. The measurement is divided by the amount of weight (50 pounds) and referred to as the coefficient of friction value. Although there is no current ANSI requirement, a coefficient of friction of 0.5 and above is the recognized industry standard for a slip-resistant flooring surface. The ADA recommends a coefficient of friction of 0.6 or above.

The ASTM procedure states that the measurement made by this apparatus is believed to be one important factor relative to slip resistance. Other factors can affect slip resistance, such as the degree of wear on the shoe and flooring material; presence of foreign matter such as water, oil, and dirt; the length of the human stride at the time of the slip; type of floor finish; and the physical and mental condition of the person. Therefore this test method should be used for the purpose of developing a property of the flooring surface under laboratory conditions and should not be used to determine slip resistance under field conditions unless those conditions are fully described. The coefficient of friction can, however, vary with each production run.

The surface texture of the tile also has a great deal to do with the reflectance qualities. For example, a perfectly smooth tile will have a much higher reflectance rate than a rough surface tile, even though they may have identical glazes. Ceramic tiles are available in many different shapes and sizes. Instead of the 4 1/4 × 4 1/4-inch tile, the 8 × 8-inch tile is more widely used, as are 12-inch-square tiles.

Most ceramic tile companies produce a raised dome surface tile that can be detected underfoot and by cane contact (which meets the guidelines set by the ADA). Its yellow color serves as a caution for platform and curb edges.

When ceramic or quarry tile is used on the floor, it is usually finished with a **base** or combination trim tile having a **bullnose** at the top and a **cove** at the bottom in the same material as the floor tile (Figure 4–11). If ceramic tile is to be continued onto the wall surface, a cove base is used.

CERAMIC MOSAIC TILE

Ceramic mosaic tile is usually formed by the dust-pressed method, 1/4 to 3/8 of an inch thick, with a facial area of less than 6 square inches. Pigments and, if required, abrasives, are added to the porcelain or clay mixture and therefore the color is dispersed throughout the tile. Ceramic mosaic tile is fired in kilns with temperatures reaching 2,150 °F. It is impervious, stainproof, dentproof, and frostproof. Because of a mosaic tile's small size, the individual tiles are mounted on a sheet to facilitate setting. Back-mounted material may be perforated paper or a fibermesh. Face-mounted tiles have paper with a water-soluble adhesive applied to the face of the tile, which is removed prior to grouting.

Ceramic mosaic tile lends itself to murals and corporate logos (Figure 4–12; see also text cover photo).

A paver tile has the same composition and physical properties as a mosaic tile, but it is thicker and has a facial area of more than 6 square inches.

Ceramic Tile. The *Handbook for Ceramic Tile Installation* is published by the Tile Council of America, Inc., each year and contains Table 4–3, which will help the designer to choose the correct tile installation for every type of floor use and specify a Handbook Method Number, grout, and setting method. This handbook is also a guide in developing job specifications. As can be seen from Table 4–3, ceramic tile for floor use may be installed by both thick- and thin-set methods.

Other Types of Tiles

Conductive tile is made from a special body composition by adding carbon black or by methods resulting in specific properties of electrical conductivity, while retaining other normal physical properties of tile. These tiles are used in hospital operating rooms, certain laboratories, or wherever the presence of oxygen

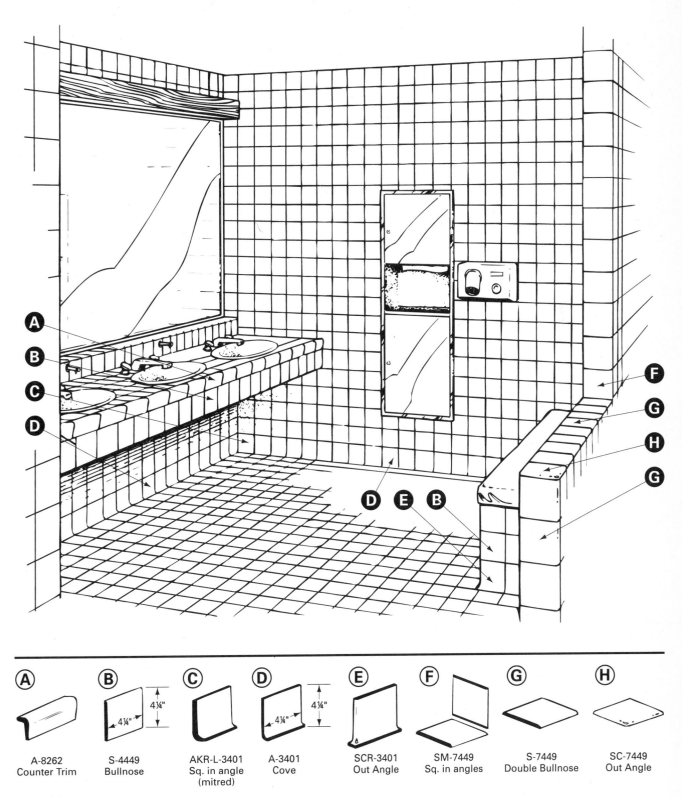

Ⓐ	Ⓑ	Ⓒ	Ⓓ	Ⓔ	Ⓕ	Ⓖ	Ⓗ
A-8262 Counter Trim	S-4449 Bullnose	AKR-L-3401 Sq. in angle (mitred)	A-3401 Cove	SCR-3401 Out Angle	SM-7449 Sq. in angles	S-7449 Double Bullnose	SC-7449 Out Angle

Figure 4–11
Ceramic tile trim. (Tile trim reprinted with permission of American Olean)

Figure 4–12
*Dal-Keystone 1-inch by 1-inch Custom Design in assorted colors
was used for the floor and walls at Wizards, Universal City,
California. Architects: BTS Co. Inc. Designer: Pacific Tile.
(Photograph courtesy of Dal Tile)*

and sparks from static electricity could cause an explosion. Conductive tile should be installed using a conductive dry-set mortar with an epoxy grout.

Pregrouted tiles usually come in sheets of up to 2.14 square feet that have already been grouted with silicone rubber. Pregrouted tiles save on labor costs because the only grouting necessary is between the sheets, rather than between individual tiles.

Slip-resistant tiles contain abrasive particles. Other methods of slip-resistance may be achieved by grooves or patterns on the face of the tile.

Some tiles are self-spacing because they are molded with **lugs**. Other means of spacing are achieved by using plastic spacers to ensure alignment of tiles and an even grout area.

When ordering any tile, add 2 percent extra of each color and size for the owner's use. This will allow immediate replacement of damaged tiles and the color will match exactly.

QUARRY TILE

Quarry tile is strong, hard-body tile made from carefully graded shale and fine clays, with the color throughout the body. Depending upon the geographic area where the clays are mined, the colors will vary from the warm brown-reds to warm beiges. The face of quarry tile may be solid colored, variegated with lights and darks within the same tile, or flashed where the edges of the tile are a darker color than the center. Quarry tile is extruded in a 1/2-inch thick ribbon and then cut to size. The quality of the clays and temperatures at which they are fired (up to 2,000 °F) provide a wide variety of finished products. Quarry tile is generally considered stain resistant but not stain proof.

The rugged, unglazed surface of quarry tile develops an attractive **patina** with wear. An abrasive grit

TABLE 4–3
Floor Tiling Installation Guide

Performance-Level Requirement Guide and Selection Table
Based on results from ASTM Test Method C-627 "Standard Method for Evaluating Ceramic Floor Tile Installation Systems."

SERVICE REQUIREMENTS Find required performance level and choose installation method that meets or exceeds it.	FLOOR TYPE—Numbers Refer to Handbook Method Numbers			
	CONCRETE	PAGE	WOOD	PAGE
EXTRA HEAVY: Extra heavy and high impact use in food plants, dairies, breweries and kitchens. Requires quarry tile or packing house tile. (Passes ASTM C627 cycles 1 thru 14.)	F101, F102 F111, F112, F113 F114, F115 F121[b] F131, F132, F133 F134	12 13 14 15 16 17		
HEAVY: Shopping malls, stores, commercial kitchens, work areas, laboratories, auto showrooms and service areas, shipping/receiving and exterior decks. Heavy tile except where noted. (Passes ASTM C627 cycles 1 thru 12.)	F103[b] F111 (ceramic mosaic) F112 (ceramic mosaic) F113 (ceramic mosaic) F121[b] (ceramic mosaic) F125 RF918[c]	12 13 13 13 15 15 34	RF913, RF915[c] F143[a]	34 18
MODERATE: Normal commercial and light institutional use in public space of restaurants and hospitals. Ceramic mosaic or heavier tile. (Passes ASTM C627 cycles 1 thru 10.)	F112 (cured bed) F115 F122[d] (quarry tile) RF914, RF916[c]	13 14 15 34		
LIGHT: Light commercial use in office space, reception areas, kitchens, bathrooms. Ceramic mosaic or heavier tile. (Passes ASTM C627 cycles 1 thru 6.)	F122[d] RF912, RF917[c]	15 34	F121[b] F141 F143[a], F144 RF911	15 17 18 34
RESIDENTIAL: Kitchens, bathrooms, foyers. Ceramic mosaic or heavier tile. (Passes ASTM C627 cycles 1 thru 3.)	F116　　(ceramic mosaic or TR711[e]　glazed floor tile)	14 30	F142	17

Notes:
   Consideration must also be given to (1) wear properties of surface of tile selected, (2) fire resistance properties of installation and backing, (3) slip-resistance.
   Tile used in installation tests listed in Selection Table were unglazed ceramic mosaic and 1/2″ thick quarry tile unless otherwise noted. Unglazed Standard Grade tile will give satisfactory wear, or abrasion resistance in installations listed. Glazed tile or soft body decorative unglazed tile should have the manufacturer's approval for intended use. Color, pattern, surface texture and glaze hardness must be considered in determining tile acceptability on a particular floor.
   Selection Table Notes:
   Tests to determine Performance Levels utilized representative products meeting recognized industry standards:
   a. ANSI A118.3 epoxy mortar and grout.
   b. Rating extrapolated from other test data.
   c. Data in Selection Table based on tests conducted by Tile Council of America, except data for F144 and RF900 Methods, which are based on test results from an independent laboratory through Ceramic Tile Institute.
   d. ANSI A118.1 latex portland cement mortar and grout.
   e. Tile bonded to existing resilient flooring with epoxy adhesive.

Source: 1994 Handbook for Ceramic Tile Installation. Copyright © Tile Council of America Inc. Reprinted with permission.

surface is available where slip resistance is important. Most quarry tile is manufactured unglazed in order to retain the natural quality of the tile, but some quarry tile is available glazed.

Quarry tile may be installed by either thick- or thin-set methods. The grout is either a sanded portland cement mix or an epoxy grout with a silica filler.

Maintenance. Ceramic or quarry tile may be cleaned with a damp mop if the soil is light, or with water and a detergent if the soil is heavier. It must be remembered that tile and grout are two different materials, with grout being the more porous. Any soil that is likely to stain the grout should be removed as soon as possible.

It is the responsibility of the tile installer to remove all excess grout as part of the installation contract.

MEXICAN TILE

Clay, taken directly from the ground, is shaped by hand into forms. Mexican tile differs from ceramic and quarry tile in that the proportion of ingredients in the clay are not measured. It is allowed to dry in the sun until it is firm enough to be transported to the kiln. As Mexican tile is a product of families working together, it is not uncommon to find a child's handprint or a dog or cat paw imprinted in the surface of the tile. Leaf prints may also be noticed where they drifted down when the tile was drying. These slight imperfections are part of the charm of using Mexican tile. Mexican tile is often named for the town in which it is made. Today, factories are producing more consistent quality tile.

Because of the relatively uneven thickness of Mexican tile, it should be installed using the thick-set method (Figue 4–13). If used in a greenhouse or similar area where drainage is possible, Mexican tile may be laid in a bed of sand, which will accommodate any unevenness of the tile. All cracks or joints are then filled in with sand.

Mexican tile is extremely porous—the most porous of all tile—because of its natural qualities. If the tile is not sealed from the factory, and most are not, use a "grout release" product. This is sponged, sprayed, or rolled on.

It is recommended that one of the many new sealer/finish products that allow the combination of linseed oil and wax into one process application be used. Additional coats can be applied to provide a matte or a gloss finish. The more coats applied, the

Figure 4–13
Mexican tile.

higher the gloss will appear. The benefits are cost, labor, and an environmentally friendly finish. Plaza® from Johnson Wax is such a product.

Maintenance. Keep the floor free of dust and dirt by sweeping or vacuuming and, when the floor shows signs of wear, apply another coat of wax or sealer/finish and buff. Traffic areas may need to be touched up.

GLASS BLOCK

The glass block for floors may be DELPHI® Paver Units, 6-inches square of solid glass that are 1-inch thick, with a prismatic pattern and raised nonskid surface, also available in a sandblasted finish. VISTABRIK® units are 8-inches square and either 3-inches or 1 1/2-inches thick. The latter units provide excellent light transmission and good visibility, with high-impact strength. These blocks may also be used as covers for light fixtures recessed in floors. This material is also used where special lighting effects are required.

Maintenance. Simple cleaning with clean water and a sponge or mop should suffice. Any oily deposits should be removed by using soap and water and then rinsing with clean water.

CONCRETE

Concrete is basically a mixture of two parts: **aggregates** and paste. The paste, comprised of portland cement and water, binds the aggregates (sand and gravel or crushed stone) into a rocklike mass as the paste hardens because of the chemical reaction of the cement and water.

Aggregates are generally divided into two groups: fine and coarse. . . . Since aggregates make up about 60 percent to 75 percent of the concrete, their selection is important. Aggregates should consist of particles with adequate strength and resistance to exposure conditions and should not contain materials that will cause deterioration of the concrete. . . . In properly made concrete, each particle of aggregate is completely coated with paste (portland cement and water), and all the space between aggregate particles is completely filled with paste.[5]

A concrete floor is low in cost as compared to other materials and is very durable. However, it is difficult to maintain for interiors unless the surface has been treated with a floor sealer specially manufactured to produce a dust-free floor. Color may be added when the concrete is mixed, or dusted on the surface during the finishing operation. A concrete floor looks less like an unfinished floor or subfloor if it is stamped and/or colored into squares. Also, any cracking is more likely to occur in these grooves and be less visible. There are several products on the market today that are patterns to mark the surface of the **plastic** concrete, so that it imitates the shapes and patterns of brick or natural stone.

Dark-colored concrete floors are used in passive solar homes because the large mass absorbs the rays of the sun during the day and radiates the heat back at night.

Concrete floors may be painted with an epoxy, polyurethane, or acrylic paint. Generally, epoxy paints are the best for adhesion.

Maintenance. Because cured concrete can absorb moisture, which in some cases can be harmful chemicals, prewetting must be done before using any cleaning solution. Synthetic detergent should be used, since soap will react with the lime and cause a scum.

TERRAZZO

Terrazzo was used as a flooring material during the Italian Renaissance. However, terrazzo as we know it today was not produced until after the development of portland cement in the 18th century. Terrazzo is a composite material, poured in place or precast, consisting of marble chips, **seeded** or unseeded with a binder that is cementitious, noncementitious (epoxy, polyester, or resin), or a combination of both.

The National Terrazzo and Mosaic Association explains that the chips are mixed with the **matrix** in a ratio of two parts aggregate to one part matrix before pouring. After the terrazzo topping is poured in place (in a monolithic installation), additional chips are sprinkled or seeded and troweled into the terrazzo topping to achieve the proper consistency.

Terrazzo that is poured into forms should be cured for at least three days and then ground on a water-coated surface, first with a coarse grit and then with successively finer grits.

The NTMA gives the following sizes for aggregates:

Standard—1/16- to 3/8-inch chips.

Venetian—1/4- to 1 1/16-inch chips.

Palladian—3/8-inch thick **spalls** up to 5 inches in breadth.

The binder may be gray or white portland cement, or it may be colored to blend or contrast with the marble chips. General Polymers Corporation's thin-set terrazzo is a monolithic installation that uses a binder of epoxy, polyester, or polyacrylate, with epoxy being the most durable. It is recommended for heavily used public areas such as airports, malls, and arenas (Figure 4–14). Divider strips of brass, zinc, or plastic are attached to the subfloor and are used for several purposes—as expansion joints to take care of any minor movement, as dividers when different colors are poured in adjacent areas, and as a means of enhancing a design motif, logo, or trademark.

Because of the labor involved in a monolithic in-

Figure 4–14
At Nike Town, Chicago, Illinois, this 24-color, 5,600 square foot epoxy terrazzo installation demonstrates the ultimate in design versatility. Patterns range from a tennis court to a globe to a graduating color spiral connecting various sales areas. This highly visible corporate flagship store is visited by thousands of people each day and the ease of maintenance make epoxy terrazzo the perfect choice for this six-month, five-phase thin-set job. Contractor: John Caretti & Co. Architects: Carmen Farnum Igonda Design with Designer/Artist Gordon Thompson III. (Photograph courtesy of General Polymer)

stallation, terrazzo tiles consisting of portland cement with an aggregate of marble chips may be used. The size of the chips may be large or small, or a mixture of sizes. The finish may be polished or slip-resistant. Tiles are usually 12-inches square with a thickness varying between 3/16 inches to 7/8 inches.

Maintenance. The National Terrazzo and Mosaic Association specifically warns that soaps and scrubbing powders containing water-soluble inorganic salts or crystallizing salts should never be used in the maintenance of terrazzo. Alkaline solutions will sink into the pores and, as they dry, will expand and break the cells of the marble chips and matrix, causing **spalling**. (This is similar to the problem with cement floors.)

After the initial cleaning, the floor should be allowed to dry and then sealed as soon as possible. This sealing is for the cement portion of the floor. The cleaning program for terrazzo is as follows:

1. Daily sweeping
2. Regular damp-mopping to prevent dirt accumulation

3. Machine buffing to remove traffic marks and restore luster
4. Sealing as needed in high traffic areas
5. Periodic machine scrubbing to remove heavy accumulation of dirt

Stain removal for terrazzo is the same as for marble.

EXPOSED AGGREGATE

When an exposed aggregate floor is specified, the type of aggregate to be used is extremely important, since this is the material visible on the finished floor. River stone gives a smooth rounded texture. Today, the river stone effect may be achieved by tumbling the stones in a drum to remove the sharp edges.

Installation. While the concrete is still plastic, the selected aggregate is pressed or rolled into the surface. Removal of the cement paste, by means of water from a hose when the concrete is partially hardened, will expose the aggregate and display the decorative surface. For interior use, most of the aggregate should be approximately the same size and color, but other values within that hue may also be used, with a scattering of white and black stones.

One drawback to the use of exposed aggregate is that, like any other hard-surfaced material, exposed aggregate is not sound absorbent and is hard on the feet for prolonged standing.

A clear polyurethane finish specially formulated for masonry surfaces can be applied. This gives a finish that brings out the natural color of the stone, similar to the way a wet stone has more depth than a dry one. The coated exposed aggregate seldom seems to become soiled. A vacuum brush used for wood floors will pick up any loose dirt from between the stones.

BRICK

Prehistoric man made brick from dried mud but soon discovered that when mixed with straw, the shaped brick was able to withstand the elements. Sun-dried brick, or **adobe,** dates from around 5000 B.C. and is still a method used in some areas of the Southwest United States, but with some modern-day materials added. Fired bricks and kilns first appeared between 2500 B.C. and 2000 B.C. in Mesopotamia and India, but the art was lost around 1700 B.C. and fired brick was not used again until 300 B.C.

The earliest recorded use of brick is in the Bible

when the Egyptians made the Israelites work "in mortar and in brick" (Exodus 1:14). Burnt brick was used in the Tower of Babel and also in the wall surrounding the city of Babylon.

The Chinese used brick in the 3rd century B.C. for building part of the Great Wall. The Romans used sun-dried bricks until about A.D. 14 when they started using bricks burnt in kilns. The Romans took this knowledge of brickmaking to Europe and Britain but after they left in A.D. 410, the art died out and was not restored until the 11th and 13th centuries.

The first brick buildings in the United States were built in Virginia around Jamestown by British settlers, and on Manhattan Island by the Dutch. The bricks used in Virginia were probably made locally, as there are records of brick being exported in 1621. Of course, the Aztecs of Mexico and Central America also used adobe bricks for building purposes.

Until about the mid-1850s, brick was molded by hand; but from then on it was made using mechanical means. Bricks are made by mixing clays and shales with water and are formed, while plastic, into rectangular shapes with either solid or hollow cores.

During the process of heating the bricks, the clay loses its moisture content and becomes rigid, but it is not chemically changed. It is during the higher temperatures used in burning of the brick that it undergoes a molecular change. When the temperature is raised further the grains fuse together, closing all pores, and the brick becomes vitrified or impervious.

The color of the brick depends on three factors: chemical composition of the clay, method of firing control, and temperature of the kiln. The red color comes from the oxidizing of iron to form iron oxide. The lighter colors (the salmon colors) are the result of underburning. If a higher, longer heat is applied, the brick will be harder. The harder bricks have lower absorptions and higher compressive strengths than the softer ones. Generally, the denser the brick and the lower the absorption, the easier it is to clean and maintain.

Installation. For areas where spilled liquids are likely, such as in a kitchen or bathroom, a mortared installation is appropriate. When installing over a wood frame floor, a relatively thin brick paver may be selected to minimize the additional dead weight of the floor assembly. Brick pavers weigh approximately 10 pounds per square foot (psf) per inch of thickness.

Installation methods are shown in Figure 4–15. Pavers are laid in a conventional manner in a 1/2-inch wet mortar bed with mortar joints. When the joints are thumbprint hard, they are **tooled**, compacting the mortar into a tight water-resistant joint.

Where moisture is not a problem, a mortarless method may be used.

Maintenance. Brick may be vacuumed, swept, damp-mopped, or spray-buffed.

LINOLEUM

Linoleum was first invented more than a hundred years ago and was the only resilient flooring material available for many years. Modern technology has now produced vinyl sheet flooring, and linoleum has not been manufactured in the United States since 1974. However, many people still persist in calling sheet vinyls "linoleum" out of habit. And although the components of the two products are very different, the end results do appear similar.

For the environmentally conscious user, Forbo does import a linoleum from Europe (Scotland and Holland). Its product Marmoleum Fresco won a 1993 Interior Design Product Award. The all-natural floor covering is made from raw materials that include linseed oil, jute, pine resins, wood flour, cork, and pigments and come in an array of marbleized colors. The judges praised the floor covering's resilience, said it came in an exceptional color range, and applauded its environmental materials. Because linoleum is made from natural materials, it is biodegradable. Forbo also produces Marmoleum Dual in both sheet and tile formats.

ASPHALT TILE

Like linoleum, asphalt tile is another flooring material that has gradually been phased out as a result of advanced technology. Actually, at the moment, there is very little asphalt in this tile. Asphalt tile is very inexpensive but does not have resistance to stains and can be softened by mineral oils or animal fats. The individual tiles are brittle and have poor recovery from indentation. Solvents will permanently damage the surface. Nine × 9-inch squares are available in the darker shades in a marbleized pattern.

Installation of Resilient Tile. Asphalt, vinyl-composition, vinyl, cork, and other resilient tiles are all installed using the thin-set method. The most important step in this installation procedure is to be sure the subfloor is smooth and level. Because of the thin nature of these tiles, any discrepancies in the subfloor will be visible on the surface of the tile. One friend was extremely disturbed to find that her newly in-

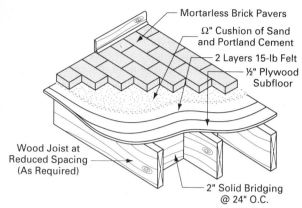

Mortarless Brick Pavers
Ω" Cushion of Sand and Portland Cement
2 Layers 15-lb Felt
½" Plywood Subfloor
Wood Joist at Reduced Spacing (As Required)
2" Solid Bridging @ 24" O.C.

Brick Paving Over Wood Joists

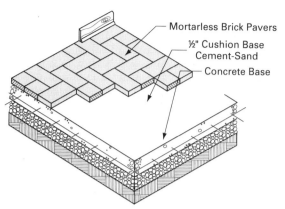

Mortarless Brick Pavers
½" Cushion Base Cement-Sand
Concrete Base

Brick Paving Over Concrete Slab

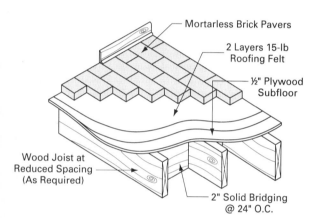

Mortarless Brick Pavers
2 Layers 15-lb Roofing Felt
½" Plywood Subfloor
Wood Joist at Reduced Spacing (As Required)
2" Solid Bridging @ 24" O.C.

Brick Paving Over Wood Joists

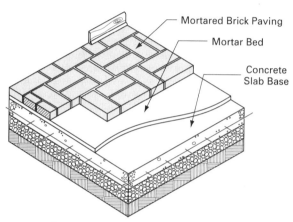

Mortared Brick Paving
Mortar Bed
Concrete Slab Base

Brick Paving Over Concrete Slab

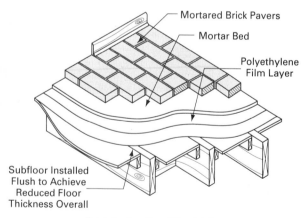

Mortared Brick Pavers
Mortar Bed
Polyethylene Film Layer
Subfloor Installed Flush to Achieve Reduced Floor Thickness Overall

Brick Paving Over Wood Joists

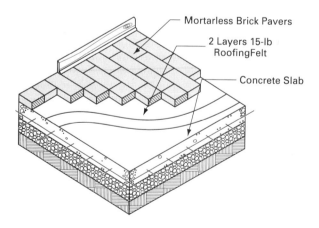

Mortarless Brick Pavers
2 Layers 15-lb RoofingFelt
Concrete Slab

Brick Paving Over Concrete Slab

Figure 4–15
Methods of installing brick.

stalled floor had developed a wavy and bumpy appearance after only several weeks because the wood subfloor had not been sanded.

The subfloor is troweled with the suggested adhesive and, as with the installation of parquet floors, the walls should not be used as a starting point (see Figure 4–8).

Maintenance. All resilient tile floors should be washed using only a damp mop, as an excess of water is likely to cause raised or uneven tiles due to moisture penetrating through the joints to the subfloor. Asphalt tile may have a factory coating for protection during shipping and installation. If this is present, it should be removed before further treatment. There are many liquid waxes on the market that may be used for residential use, but the solvent types of paste waxes should never be used on asphalt tile. For commercial installations, Hillyard Chemical Company makes cleaners and waxes that may or may not require buffing. This company specializes in floor treatments and supplies finishing and maintenance information for every type of flooring discussed in this book. Many janitorial supply companies also produce suitable maintenance cleaners and waxes for commercial installations.

Vinyl composition and vinyl tile floors are all maintained in the same manner as asphalt tile.

VINYL COMPOSITION

Vinyl composition, or reinforced vinyl, is the most commonly used floor tile for less expensive installations. Vinyl composition consists of PVC resins, plasticizers, fillers such as gypsum and clays, and color pigments, formed into thin sheets under heat and pressure. The thin sheets, without backing, are then cut into tiles, as seen in Figure 4–16.

In recent years, asbestos has proven to have adverse health effects. As vinyl composition tiles are no longer made with asbestos fibers, there are no health hazards now. Note: If you are removing an old vinyl asbestos floor, OSHA has extremely rigid rules as to the manner in which they may be removed and the safety precautions that must be taken (see Chapter 1 and Appendix A).

The thickness, or **gauge**, as it is sometimes called, is 1/16, 3/32, or 1/8 of an inch. For commercial and better residential installations, the 1/8-inch gauge is the best choice. The advantages of vinyl composition tile are that it (1) is inexpensive, (2) is easy to install and maintain, (3) may be installed on any grade, (4)

Figure 4–16
Vinyl composition tile from Kentile utilizes three different colors to create a custom flooring design. (Photograph courtesy of Kentile Inc.)

resists acids and alkalis, and (5) withstands strong cleaning compounds. The disadvantages are that it (1) has low impact resistance, (2) has poor noise absorption, and (3) is semiporous as compared to solid vinyls and solid rubber.

FIRM-STEP® slip-resistant tile from Kentile combines a textured surface with special slip-resistant particles embedded throughout the tile to provide a firm footing with rugged wearability.

Maintenance. See Asphalt Tile.

SOLID VINYL

This type of tile is actually not all vinyl. It has a lower percentage of fillers and a higher percentage of PVC than vinyl composition tiles. It usually consists of a fiberglass-reinforced backing, on which the pattern is printed. The final coat may be either clear vinyl or vinyl with urethane. The latter is tougher and wears longer.

Maintenance. Maintenance is the same as for vinyl composition.

PURE VINYL TILE

Pure vinyl tiles are homogeneous or, in other words, pure vinyl with few, if any, fillers, with the color throughout the tile. They are available in faux-stone finishes, marble, travertine, brick, and slate. Pure vinyl tiles are also used as feature strips or for borders. Borders should be of approximately the same width at all walls.

Several companies manufacture a vinyl floor with real wood veneer literally sealed between solid vinyl. The top layer is made of a transparent 1/5-inch thick pure vinyl that permits the natural color and texture of the wood grain to be visible yet protected.

A conductive tile is required in environments where static electricity poses danger to sensitive electronic devices, as well as in areas where flammable gases or explosives may be present. If higher voltages are used in the working environment, then a static dissipative vinyl tile should be used.

Flexco combines conductive or static dissipative vinyl tile with a specially formulated conductive adhesive. This creates a moderately conductive pathway for static charges—following through the tile and along the conductive adhesive to ground.

Vinyl wall base effectively trims off a resilient floor installation and also helps hide minor wall and floor irregularities. Its distinctive profile consists of a reclining curvature at the top and a descending thin-toe line that conforms snugly with wall and floor. Some vinyl coves can be hand-formed to make the corners, while others come with both inside and outside corners preformed. The cove wall base comes either in 20-foot rolls or 48-inch strips in 2 1/4-inch or 4-inch heights (Figure 4–17).

Installation. Tiles are installed with a specified adhesive in a pyramid fashion (see Figure 4–8).

Maintenance. The new tile floor should not be washed, only damp-mopped for a week to allow the adhesive to set. Spots of adhesive can be removed with a clean white cloth dampened with paste wax or lighter fluid. Periodic sweeping with a soft broom or vacuum will prevent buildup of dust and dirt. Spills should be cleaned immediately. Damp-mopping with a mild detergent is sufficient for slightly soiled floors, or scrubbing with a brush or machine for heavy soil. Soap-based cleaners should not be used because they can leave a dulling film. The floor should then be rinsed with clean water. The floor should never be flooded, and excess dirty water should be removed with a mop or vacuum. No-wax floors can be damaged by intense heat, lighted cigarettes, and rubber or foam-backed mats or rugs. If stubborn stains persist, try rubbing the spot with alcohol or lighter fluid.

RUBBER

Rubber flooring is now made of 100 percent synthetic rubber. Although available with a smooth surface, the multi-level rubber flooring (raised discs or pastilles, solid or duo-colored squares, or even rhythmic curves) has become increasingly popular where excessive dirt or excessive moisture is likely to be tracked

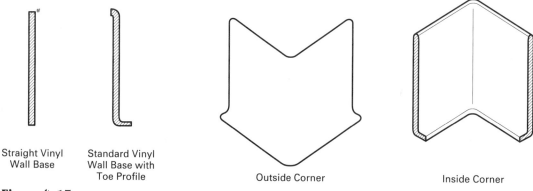

Straight Vinyl
Wall Base

Standard Vinyl
Wall Base with
Toe Profile

Outside Corner

Inside Corner

Figure 4–17
Bases.

inside. The raised portions have beveled edges, causing the dirt to drop down below the wear surface, which lowers the abrasion on the wear surface. The same thing happens with water; most of it flows below the wear surface. While the original purpose of this tile was as stated above, many installations today are done purely for aesthetic rather than utilitarian reasons.

Rubber tiles are available in 9-, 12-, 20- and 39-inch squares, with a thickness of 3/32, 1/8, or 3/16 inch. The tiles are usually marble or travertine patterned, laid at right angles to each other. They may be laid below grade and are extremely sound absorbent.

Johnsonite® has a new generation rubber flooring system, ComfortTech™, featuring an exclusive fused cushion core providing enhanced walking comfort, sound absorption, and thermal insulation with a slip-resistant surface that meets ADA recommendations.

The explosion at the World Trade Center in New York accelerated Johnsonite's process of developing a supplemental evacuation solution. Johnsonite's Permalight™ system integrates color with fire retardant flooring products and a new self-illuminating technology in vinyl or rubber flooring products and accessories for low-level escape routing, while enhancing present building safety systems. Johnsonite received a 1994 ROSCOE award in the category Hard Surfacing Materials, and the first place award in the Hard Surface category from ASID, for innovation and fine craftsmanship. Johnsonite's Permalight system has also been awarded 1994 Newsmaker of the Year Award by the Canadian chapters of the International Facility Managers Association (IFMA), and the Best Product of 1994 by the Institute of Business Designers (IBD) in its annual product design competition (Figure 4–18).

Figure 4–18
Johnsonite's Permalight® Safe-T-System is visible in light and sudden darkness as can be seen in these two photographs. (Photographs courtesy of Johnsonite Inc.)

Maintenance. New rubber flooring should be thoroughly machine stripped and scrubbed with black stripping pad and stripper. The floor should be thoroughly cleaned with a good grade of mild detergent cleaner. The stripper or detergent solution should be vacuumed, mopped, or squeezed from floors. The floor should be rinsed with a solution of 10 percent Clorox® in warm water. When the floor is dry, an ultra-high-speed buffer can be used. New floors will require more frequent buffing until a high sheen is acquired. For further maintenance, dry dust or mop floors (but do not use mops treated with mineral oil or other petroleum products). Periodically, repeat the cleaning procedure and rebuff as needed.

Sheet Vinyl

The sheet vinyl manufacturers have greatly improved not only the quality but also the designs of their products. Precise information as to construction is a trade secret but the following information is generic to the industry.

Sheet vinyl comes in 6-, 9-, or 12-foot widths and is manufactured by two methods—inlaid or rotogravure. Most inlaid sheet vinyls are made of thousands of tiny vinyl granules built up layer by layer, then fused together with heat and pressure. The result is a soft, hefty flooring with a noticeable depth of color and a crafted look. Some have extra layers of foam cushioning to provide comfort underfoot and muffle footsteps and other noises. Color and pattern go all the way through the vinyl layer. A fiberglass backing will produce a light flexible flooring that virtually eliminates tearing and creasing as well as the telegraphing of irregularities from the old flooring to the new.

Rotovinyls, also called rotogravure vinyls, are made by a rotogravure process that combines photography and printing. Almost any image that can be photographed can be reproduced on a rotovinyl floor. The printed layer is protected by a topping (called the wear layer) of vinyl resin (**PVC**) either alone or in combination with urethane. The vinyl resin composition produces a gloss surface, whereas urethane creates a high-sheen result. A mechanical buffer with a lamb's wool pad will bring back the satin gloss of the vinyl resin composition wear layers (Figure 4–19). All rotovinyls are made with an inner core of foamed or expanded vinyl, which means they are cushioned to some extent. But at the lower end of the price scale,

Figure 4–19
Congoleum's Highlight "Stonegate"/Discover "Stonegate II" sheet vinyl floor is a foil for this contemporary kitchen. (Photograph courtesy of Congoleum Corporation)

cushioning may be quite thin. Most sheet vinyls are flexible enough to be coved up the **toe space** to form their own base (check manufacturer's specifications).

The trend in the 1990s is a high-gloss finish with manufacturers providing 5-year and, in the case of Mannington Gold Floors, a 10-year warranty that the floor will not wear out. For those customers wishing an alternative to the high-gloss products, Mannington has the mid-priced Silver series with SoftShine wearlayer.

For commercial or institutional installations where the floor must be slip resistant, Altro Safety Flooring has aluminum oxide grains and quartz crystals distributed throughout the entire thickness to ensure consistent slip resistance, even after many years of wear.

Installation. Seaming methods vary from manufacturer to manufacturer, but all result in an almost invisible seam. Installation may be a perimeter-bond system that is stretched over the floor and secured only at the edges. The other—a full-adhered system—is set in a full bed of mastic. All sheet vinyls should be rolled with a 100-pound roller to eliminate air pockets and form a good bond between the backing and the adhesive.

It is preferable to install new flooring over an existing resilient floor, particularly if it is known that the existing floor contains asbestos. As has been mentioned in Chapter 1 and previously in the vinyl asbestos section of this chapter, removal of old floor coverings that might contain asbestos requires, in some states, a trained asbestos abatement contractor, whether or not it is friable.

The old floor must be fully adhered. Do not cover a perimeter-bonded system. When covering over a textured or embossed surface, use a manufacturer-recommended embossing leveler. Do not cover asphalt tiles or asphalt adhesive, as asphalt eats through vinyl.

Furniture should be equipped with the proper loadbearing devices; otherwise, indentations will mar the vinyl surface. Most manufacturers recommend limiting the static load to 75 psi (Figure 4–20).

Heavy refrigerators and kitchen or office equipment must not be dragged across the floor, as this will damage and tear the surface. These items should be "walked" across the floor on a piece of wood or on Masonite® runways. Runways must be used even if using an appliance dolly or if the heavy objects are equipped with wheels or rollers.

Maintenance. Maintenance is the same as that for vinyl tiles, bearing in mind that no-wax does not mean no maintenance.

CORK

Ipocork® is the largest manufacturer of cork flooring in the world and has furnished the following information:

Cork is actually the wood skin of the cork oak tree. Every nine years the bark loosens and the cork can be harvested without harm to the tree. The cork oak, grown in Portugal, then grows its bark back completely, therefore, cork is one of the most environmentally friendly flooring systems on the market today. Frank Lloyd Wright was one of the first Americans to use cork as a decorative durable flooring material in his renowned Falling Waters house in Pennsylvania.

Ipocork® flooring features a unique lamination process, which incorporates a vinyl backing, a cork cushion layer, a decorative cork veneer, and a clear

TYPE OF LOAD	KENTILE FLOORS INC. RECOMMENDS	KENTILE FLOORS INC. DOES NOT RECOMMEND	TYPE
HEAVY FURNITURE, more or less permanently located, should have composition furniture cups under the legs to prevent them from cutting the floor.	Right 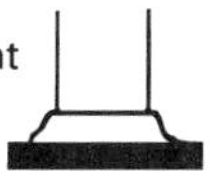 Wide Bearing Surfaces Save Floors	Wrong 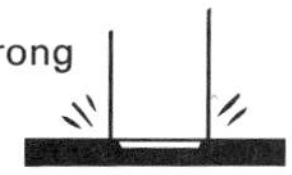 Small Bearing Surfaces Dent Floors	Composition Furniture Cups 
FREQUENTLY MOVED FURNITURE requires casters. Desk chairs are a good example. Casters should be 2" in diameter with soft rubber treads at least ¾" wide and with easy swiveling ball bearing action. For heavier items that must be moved frequently, consult the caster manufacturers as to the suitable size of equipment that should be used.	Right 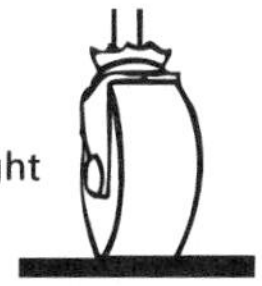 Rubber Rollers Save Floors	Wrong 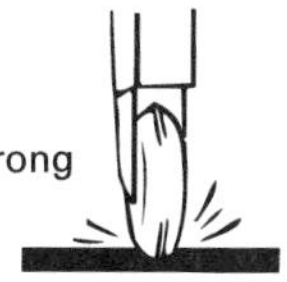 Hard Rollers Mark Floors	Rubber Wheel Casters 
LIGHT FURNITURE should be equipped with glides having a smooth, flat base with rounded edges and a flexible pin to maintain flat contact with the floor. They should be from 1¼" to 1½" dia., depending upon weight of load they must carry. For furniture with slanted legs apply glides parallel to the floor rather than slanted ends of legs.	Right 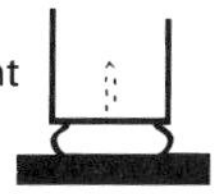 Use Flat Bearing Surfaces	Wrong  Remove Small Metal Domes	Flat Glides With Flexible Shank 

Figure 4–20
Static load for furniture. (Courtesy Kentile Floors)

heavy vinyl surface. Ipocork® tiles are 12 × 12 inches (30 cm nominal).

Installation. Because cork is a wood product, the floor tiles should be acclimatized to the installation site for 72 hours before installation. Because of its natural qualities, no two tiles are identical in pattern or color. Pieces may vary slightly in color, tone, and grain configuration. It is the installer's or client's responsibility to mix colors and patterns in an acceptable manner. Be sure to "shuffle" the tiles to acquire the desired aesthetic mix. Use only those subfloor materials and adhesives that are specified by the manufacturer of the cork flooring. Expansion and contraction, resulting from climatic conditions, will occur, so allow for an approximate 1/8- to 1/4-inch space around the perimeter of the room for this condition. The space is covered by a base.

Maintenance. Use walk-off mats, provided they do not have a rubber back, which may cause permanent discoloration. Use furniture guards as shown in Figure 4–19. Spills should be picked up immediately; never allow wet spills or water to stand on the cork floor. Regular maintenance should include frequent or daily sweeping, vacuuming and damp-mopping as required to keep the floor free of dust, dirt, grease, etc. NEVER use a wet mop, because this could cause delamination. For long-term maintenance, once or twice a year a no-wax vinyl treatment may be used.

FORMED-IN-PLACE OR POURED FLOORS

Formed-in-place floors come in cans and are applied at the site in a seamless installation. The basis of the "canned floors" may be urethane, epoxy, polyester, or vinyl, but they are all applied in a similar manner. First, as with all other floor installations, the surface must be clean, dry, and level. Second, a base coat of one of the above materials is applied to the substrate according to directions. Third, colored plastic chips are sprinkled or sprayed on the base and several coats of the base material are applied for the wearlayer.

This flooring seems to be popular in veterinary offices, where a nonskid and easily cleaned surface is desirable. It can also be coved up a base like sheet vinyl, eliminating cracks between floor and base. Of course, this type of flooring may be used in any area where cleanliness is paramount.

Maintenance. Maintenance is the same as that for sheet vinyl.

BIBLIOGRAPHY

American Institute of Maintenance. *Floor Care Guide.* New York, NY: The Institute, 1982.

Berendsen, Anne. *Tiles: A General History.* New York: Viking Press, 1967.

Dezettel, Louis M. *Masons & Builders Library*, Vols. 1 & 2. Indianapolis, IN: Theodore Audel, division of Howard W. Sams & Co. Inc., 1984.

Ellis, Robert Y. *The Complete Book of Floor Coverings.* New York: Charles Scribner & Sons, 1980.

The Everything Book of Floors, Walls and Ceilings. New York: Reston, 1980.

Feirer, John L. *Woodworking for Industry.* Peoria, IL: Charles A. Bennett, 1979.

Oak Flooring Institute. *Hardwood Flooring Finishing/Refinishing Manual.* Memphis, TN: 1986.

Oak Flooring Institute. *Wood Floor Care Guide.* Memphis, TN: 1986.

Plumridge, Andrew and Wlm. Meulenkamp. *Brickwork, Architecture and Design.* New York: Harry N. Abrams, Inc., 1993.

Watson, Don A. *Construction Materials & Processes,* 2nd ed. New York: McGraw-Hill, Gregg Division, 1978.

ENDNOTES

[1]*Handbook for Ceramic Tile Installation,* Tile Council of America, 1994, 32nd Edition, page 6.
[2]Ibid., page 5.
[3]Watson, Don A. *Construction Materials and Processes.* New York: McGraw-Hill, 1971, page 271. Reprinted, with minor changes, by permission of the publisher.
[4]*Handbook for Ceramic Tile Installation,* Tile Council of America, 1994, 32nd Edition, page 6.
[5]*Design and Control of Concrete Mixtures,* Portland Cement Association, 13th Edition, page 1.

GLOSSARY

Adobe. Unburnt, sun-dried brick.

Agglomerate. Marble chips and spalls of various sizes, bonded together with a resin.

Aggregate. The solid material in concrete, mortar, or grout.

Base. A board or moulding at the base of a wall that comes in contact with the floor; protects the wall from damage (see Figures 4–11, 4–17, and 7–1).

Beveled. In wood flooring, the top edge is cut at a 45° angle.

Bisque. Once-fired clay.

Bluestone. A hard sandstone of characteristic blue, gray, and buff colors, quarried in New York and Pennsylvania.

Bow. Longitudinal curvature of lumber (see Figure 4–1).

Bullnose. A convex rounded edge on tile (see Figure 4–11).

Burl. An abnormal growth or protuberance on a tree.

Butts. Close together, leaving no space.

Cove. A concave rounded edge on tile (see Figure 4–11).

Crook. The warp of a board edge from the straight line drawn between the two ends (see Figure 4–1).

Cup. Deviation of the face of a board from a plane (see Figure 4–1).

Cure. Maintaining the humidity and temperature of freshly poured concrete for a period of time to keep water present so it hydrates or hardens properly.

Cushion-edged. Tiles with a slightly rounded edge.

Elgin Marbles. (Pronounced with a hard "g".) Lord Elgin, the British Ambassador to Turkey from 1799–1802, persuaded the Turkish Government in Athens to allow him to remove the frieze of the Parthenon to the British Museum in London to prevent further damage.

Figure. The pattern of the wood fibers.

Floorcloths. Painted canvas used in the early 1800s.

Gauge. Thickness of tile.

Grain. Arrangement of the fibers of the wood.

Grout. Material used to fill in the spaces between the tiles.

Impervious. Less than 0.5 percent absorption rate.

Kiln. An oven for controlled drying of lumber or firing of tile.

Laminated. Bonding of two or more layers of material.

Lug. A projection attached to the edges of a ceramic tile to provide equal spacing of the tiles.

Marquetry. Veneered inlaid material in wood flooring that has been fitted in various patterns and glued to a common background.

Mastic. An adhesive compound.

Matrix. The mortar part of the mix.

Medullary rays. Ribbons of tissue extending from the pitch to the bark of a tree, particularly noticeable in oak.

Metal spline. Thin metal wire holding the strips of parquet together.

Metamorphic. Changes occurring in appearance and structure of rock caused by heat and/or pressure.

Monolithic. Grout and mortar base become one mass.

Mortar. A plastic mixture of cementitious materials, with water and fine aggregates.

Mosaic. A small size tile, ceramic or marble, usually 1-inch or 2-inch square used to form patterns.

o.c. Abbreviation for on center; for example, measurement from the center of one joist to the center of an adjacent joist.

120-grit. A medium-fine grade of sandpaper.

Parquetry. Inlaid solid wood flooring, usually set in simple geometric patterns.

Patina. Soft sheen achieved by continuous use.

Pickets. Wood strips pointed at both ends, used in parquet floors in patterns such as Monticello.

Plane. Flat and level surface.

Plastic. Still pliable and soft, not hardened.

Pointing. Act of filling the joints with mortar.

PVC. Polyvinyl chloride. A water insoluble thermoplastic resin used as a coating on sheet vinyl floors.

psi. Pounds per square inch.

Prefinished. Factory finished when referring to wood floors.

Quartersawn. Wood sliced in quarters lengthwise, which shows the grain of the wood to best advantage (see Figure 4–2).

Quartzite. A compact granular rock, composed of quartzite crystals usually so firmly cemented as to make the mass homogeneous. Color range is wide.

Reducer strip. A tapered piece of wood used at the joining of two dissimilar materials to compensate for difference of thickness.

Riser. The vertical part of a stair.

Sandstone. Sedimentary rock composed of sand-sized grains naturally cemented from mineral materials.

Screeds. 2 × 4s between 18 and 48 inches in length,

laid flat side down and randomly placed to support subfloor (see Figure 4–7).

Seeded. Sprinkling of marble chips on top of a base.

Semivitreous. 3 percent but not more than 7 percent moisture absorption.

Sets. Groups of parquet set at right angles to each other, usually four in a set.

60-grit. A medium sandpaper.

Spall. A fragment or chip, in this case of marble.

Spalling. Flaking of floor due to expansion of components.

Square. Edges cut at right angles to each other.

Stenciling. Method of decorating or printing a design by painting through a cut-out pattern.

Terrazzo. Marble chips, of similar size, combined with a binder that holds the marble chips together. This binder may be cementitious or noncementitious (epoxy resin).

Toe space. Area at base of furniture or cabinets that is inset to accommodate the toes.

Tongue-and-groove. A wood joint providing a positive alignment (see Figure 7–2).

Tooled. A mortar joint that has been finished by a shaped tool while the mortar is plastic.

Twist. A spiral distortion of lumber (see Figure 4–1).

Veneer. A very thin sheet of wood varying in thickness from 1/8 to 1/100 of an inch.

Vitreous. 0.5 percent, but less than 3 percent, moisture absorption.

Chapter 5

Walls

In floors, the weight of the flooring material was spread over a large area; however, when these same materials are used on walls, they create a heavy dead load. Thus walls, whether constructed or veneered with granite, stone, or brick, must have a foundation prepared to withstand this additional weight. **Compressive strength** is also important for wall installation materials.

There are two types of walls: loadbearing and nonbearing. The interior designer needs to know the difference. Loadbearing walls are those that support an imposed load in addition to their own weight; a nonbearing wall is just for utilitarian or aesthetic purposes. The architect deals with both, but the interior designer probably deals more with nonbearing walls. A load-bearing wall should never be removed or altered without consulting an architect or engineer.

STONE

This type of wall is usually a veneer and may be constructed of any type of stone. **Rubble** is uncut stone or stone that has not been cut into a rectangular shape. **Ashlar** is stone that is precut to provide enough uniformity to allow some regularity in assembly. The rubble masonry is less formal, requires the use of more mortar, and is not as strong as the

other types of bonds because of the irregularly shaped bonds. Uniform mortar joints are a mark of a skilled worker. **Fieldstone** or **cobble** has a more rounded feeling than does ashlar or rubble (Figure 5–1).

    Maintenance. Stonework should be cleaned with a stiff brush and clean water. If stains are difficult to remove, soapy water may be used, followed by a clean-water rinse. Stonework should be cleaned by sponging during construction, which facilitates final cleaning. The acids used to clean brick should never be used on stone walls.

Regular maintenance consists of brushing or vacuuming to remove dust. It is important to remember that, generally, igneous types are impervious, but sedimentary and metamorphic stones are more susceptible to stains. Stone walls should not be installed where grease or any substance that may stain the stone is present.

GRANITE

Granite is used wherever a feeling of stability and permanence is desired. This is probably why one sees so much granite in banks and similar institutions. The properties of granite were mentioned in the previous chapter. The only difference is that granite for walls

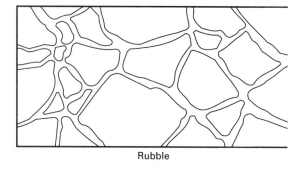

Rubble

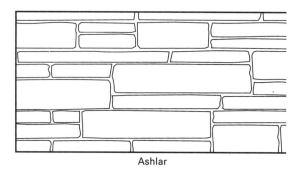

Ashlar

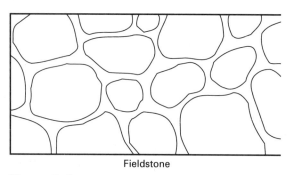

Fieldstone

Figure 5–1
Types of stonework.

may be polished or honed as abrasion is not a problem with walls.

Installation. Anchors, **cramps,** dowels, and other anchoring devices should be type 304 stainless steel or suitable **nonferrous** metal. A portland cement sand mortar is used and, where applicable, a sealant is used for pointing the joints.

Maintenance. If required, the granite wall may be washed with a weak detergent solution and rinsed with clear water. To restore the shine, buff it with a lamb's wool pad.

MARBLE

Marble has the same elegant and formal properties whether used for walls or for floors. According to the Marble Institute of America, interior marble wall facing may be installed by either mechanical fastening devices utilizing nonstaining anchors, angles, dowels, pins, cramps, and plaster spots, or in a mortar setting bed to secure smaller units to interior vertical surfaces. The overall dimensions of the marble determine the setting method. Resilient cushions are used to maintain joint widths, which are then pointed with white cement or other approved material.

In addition to the traditional sizes, new thin marble veneers that are backed with lighter weight materials have less weight per square foot and, depending on job conditions, may be set in either a conventional full mortar bed or by any of the several newer thin-bed systems.

Maintenance. Maintenance is the same as that for marble floors, see page 128.

TRAVERTINE

When travertine is used in wall applications, it is not necessary to fill the voids. Unfilled travertine gives an interesting texture to the wall surface but, for a perfectly smooth installation, filling is required. Like flooring, wall applications of travertine may be filled with a clear, translucent epoxy or an opaque epoxy matching the color of the travertine. Filled travertine does tend to have less sheen on the opaque filled area than on the solid area. The surface of the travertine may be left in its rough state, providing texture, or it may be cut and sanded or ground smooth.

Installation. Installation methods of travertine are the same as for marble.

BRICK

Brick is used for both exterior and interior, and the surface of the brick may be smooth, rough, or grooved. Bricks with these surface textures create interesting wall designs with interesting shadows. Bricks are obtainable in whites, yellows, grays, reds, and browns and may be ordered in special sizes or shapes.

The standard brick size is 3 5/8 inches wide by 8 inches long and 2 1/4 inches high. Those laid so as to expose the long side in a horizontal position are called **stretchers**; vertically they are called soldiers. When the end of the bricks show horizontally, they are called **headers,** but vertically they are called rowlocks (Figure 5–2). The bond is the arrangement of brick in rows or courses. A common bond is defined as bricks placed end to end in a stretcher course with vertical joints of one course centered on the bricks in the next course. Every sixth or seventh course is made up of headers. These headers provide structural bonding as well as pattern. A bond without headers is called a running bond. It is interesting to note that in some historical digs of buildings dating around the 1880s, it was possible to discover the nationality of the builders of brick walls by the type of bond used—not only English and Flemish, but also several other European nationalities (see Figure 5–2 for types of brick bonds).

Masonry walls may be hollow masonry, where both sides of the wall are visible, or they may be veneered. When both sides are visible, the **header course** ties the two sides together. A veneered wall is attached to the backing by means of metal ties (Figure 5–3).

The joints in a wall installation are extremely important as they create shadows and special design effects. The joints of a brick wall are normally 3/8-inch thick. The mortar for these joints consists of a mixture of portland cement, hydrated lime, and sand. The mortar serves four functions:

1. It bonds the units together and seals the spaces between.

2. It compensates for dimensional variations in the units.

3. It bonds to and therefore causes reinforcing steel to act as an integral part of the wall.

4. It provides a decorative effect on the wall surface by creating shadow or color lines.

Mortar joint finishes fall into two classes: troweled and tooled joints. In the troweled joint, the excess

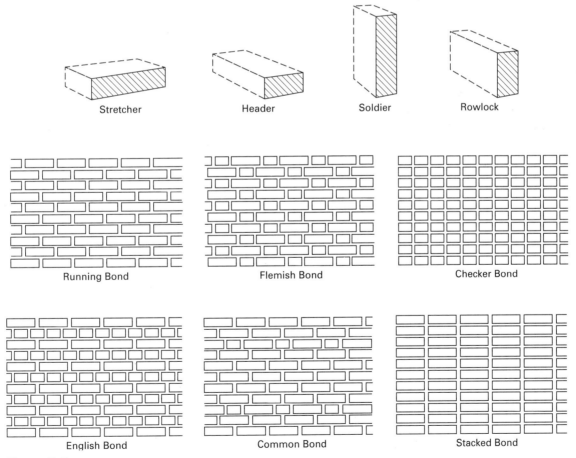

Figure 5–2

Stretchers, headers, and brick bonds.

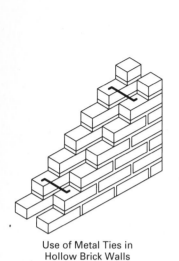
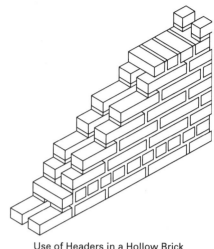

Use of Metal Ties in
Hollow Brick Walls

Use of Metal Ties in a
Brick Veneer Wall

Use of Headers in a Hollow Brick
Wall Visible from Both Sides

Figure 5–3
Brick wall construction.

mortar is simply cut off (**struck**) with a trowel and finished with the trowel. For the tooled joint, a special tool other than the trowel is used to compress and shape the mortar in the joint.

Installation. Brick and concrete block are both installed by masons. Bricks are placed in a bed of mortar and mortar is laid on the top surface of the previous course, or row, so as to cover all edges. The mortar joint may be any of the types shown in Figure 5–4.

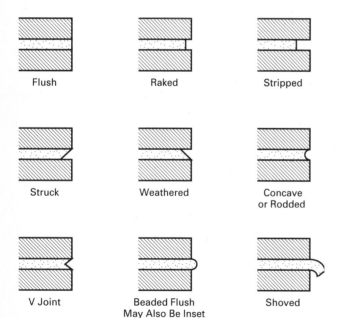

Flush

Raked

Stripped

Struck

Weathered

Concave
or Rodded

V Joint

Beaded Flush
May Also Be Inset

Shoved

Figure 5–4
Mortar joints for brick wall.

Maintenance. The major problem with finishing brick walls is the **mortar stain,** which occurs even if the mason is skilled and careful. To remove mortar stain, the walls are cleaned of surplus mortar and dirt, then scrubbed with a solution of trisodium phosphate, household detergent, and water, then rinsed with water under pressure. If stains are not removed with this treatment, a solution of muriatic acid and water is used. The acid should be poured into the water, and not vice versa, to avoid a dangerous reaction. Just the bricks themselves should be scrubbed. The solution should not be allowed to dry but should be rinsed immediately with clean water. For cleaning light-colored bricks, a more diluted solution of muriatic acid and water should be used to prevent burning.

Regular maintenance for bricks includes brushing and vacuuming to remove dust that may have adhered to the rough surface. Masonry walls that may come in contact with grease, such as in kitchens, should either be impervious or sealed to prevent penetration of the grease.

CONCRETE

Currently, many architects of contemporary buildings, particularly in the commercial, industrial, and educational fields, are leaving poured concrete walls exposed on the interior. The forms used for these walls may be patterned or smooth, and this texture is reflected on the interior surface. The fractured fin texture can be seen in Figure 5–5. The ties that hold the

Figure 5–5
Countless texture and color combinations make concrete a cost-effective and popular material for many interior designers. Here, selected concrete walls throughout the Palm Springs Desert Museum radiate with a fractured fin texture and a warm beige hue. The textures were created through the use of L. M. Scofield Company's LITHOTEX® Elastomeric Formliners. The color was created with the company's CHROMIX® Admixture, a coloring component that is integrally mixed into the concrete. (Photograph courtesy of L. M. Scofield Company)

forms together may leave holes that, if properly placed, may provide a grid design.

From the interior designer's point of view, a poured concrete wall is a fait accompli. The surface may be left with the outline of the forms showing, patterned or plain, or it may be treated by the following methods to give a different surface appearance: bush hammering, acid etching, and sandblasting. Bush hammering is done with a power tool that provides an exposed aggregate face by removing the sand-cement matrix and exposing the aggregate. Sandblasting provides a textured surface. Bush hammering produces the heaviest texture, while the texture from sandblasting depends on the amount and coarseness of sand used. Acid etching just removes the surface.

If left in its natural poured concrete state, the main problem facing the designer is using materials and accessories that will be compatible with cast concrete. Obviously, they need to imply weight and a substantial feeling, rather than any delicacy or formality. However, this massive feeling can be overcome by plastering over the concrete.

CONCRETE BLOCK

Concrete block is a hollow concrete masonry unit composed of portland cement and suitable aggregates. Walls of this type are found in homes, but they are more frequently used in commercial and educational interiors. There are several problems with concrete block: It has extremely poor insulating qualities if used on an exterior wall; if used on an outside wall and moisture is present, efflorescence will form; and it has a fairly rough surface that is difficult to paint, although this may be accomplished by using a specially formulated paint and a long-nap roller.

Installation. The mason erects a concrete block wall in a similar manner to a brick one except that, while a brick wall is viewed only from one side, a concrete block is often visible from both sides; therefore, the joints need to be finished on both sides of the block. Concrete block may be erected in either a running bond pattern or stacked, running bond being the stronger.

Maintenance. Acid is not used to remove mortar smears or droppings, as with brick. Excess mortar should be allowed to dry and then chipped off. Rubbing the wall with a small piece of concrete block will remove practically all the mortar. For painting instructions, see Chapter 3.

GLASS BLOCK

In the 1920s and 1930s the use of glass block seemed to be limited to the side of the front door and bathrooms, but it is now one of the revived materials for use in the 1990s. This is due to modern technology and the innovativeness of today's architects and designers. The use of glass block is only for nonload-bearing installations. This, however, should not be a limiting factor in the utilization of glass block.

Glass block, by definition, is composed of two halves of pressed glass fused together. The hollow in the center is partially **evacuated,** which provides a partial vacuum with good insulating qualities. The construction of the block is such that designs may be imprinted on both the inside and the outside of the glass surfaces. In all of their applications, glass blocks permit the control of light—natural or artificial, day or night—for function and drama. Thermal transmission, noise, dust, and drafts may also be controlled (see Figures 5–6 and 5–11).

Pittsburgh Corning Corporation, the only American manufacturer of glass block, produces a variety of styles that may be used for both exterior and interior purposes. The range of privacy varies from the VUE® pattern, which is clear for the greatest combination of light transmission and visibility, to the DELPHI® pattern, a multiple diamond design that lends a prismatic effect to the light it transmits, providing a combination of the greatest light transmission and privacy.

For finishing a free-standing glass block wall the choice may be EndBlock™ finishing units, a rounded finished surface on one edge, which makes them virtually disappear when used vertically or horizontally on the edges of panels, walls, or dividers. Also avail-

Figure 5–6
The VUE® pattern was used for a wall at AT&T Information Systems. Designer: Hugh Stubbins & Associates, Photographer: Nick Wheeler. (Photograph courtesy of Pittsburgh Corning Corporation)

Figure 1
Inspired by the Bayeaux Tapestry (the story of the Norman conquest), Grey Dun Studio painted this floorcloth/wallhanging. (Photograph courtesy of Grey Dun Studio)

Figure 2
This reception area has quartered oak and Brazilian cherry Buckingham Custom Border, with walnut feature strips, surrounded by burl walnut and Brazilian cherry Monticello. (Photograph courtesy of Kentucky Wood Floors Inc.)

Figure 3
Versatile scored Dal Semi Gloss 4 1/4 inch by 4 1/4 inch tiles were used to create this bathtub surround for the Holiday Inn Express, Abingdon, Virginia.
Owner/Developer: Impact Management; Supervisor: Sam Davis (Photograph courtesy of DalTile®)

Figure 4
Marble from Georgia Marble Company was used for the Registration and Office Area of the Key Largo Bay Beach Resort, Key Largo, Florida. The floor is Etowah Fleuri and Verde Oriental. Countertop is Etowah Fleuri. Photographer Paul G. Beswick. (Photograph courtesy of Georgia Marble Company)

Figure 1
Inspired by the Bayeaux Tapestry (the story of the Norman conquest), Grey Dun Studio painted this floorcloth/wallhanging. (Photograph courtesy of Grey Dun Studio)

Figure 2
This reception area has quartered oak and Brazilian cherry Buckingham Custom Border, with walnut feature strips, surrounded by burl walnut and Brazilian cherry Monticello. (Photograph courtesy of Kentucky Wood Floors Inc.)

Figure 3
Versatile scored Dal Semi Gloss 4 1/4 inch by 4 1/4 inch tiles were used to create this bathtub surround for the Holiday Inn Express, Abingdon, Virginia.
Owner/Developer: Impact Management; Supervisor: Sam Davis (Photograph courtesy of DalTile®)

Figure 4
Marble from Georgia Marble Company was used for the Registration and Office Area of the Key Largo Bay Beach Resort, Key Largo, Florida. The floor is Etowah Fleuri and Verde Oriental. Countertop is Etowah Fleuri. Photographer Paul G. Beswick. (Photograph courtesy of Georgia Marble Company)

able is HEDRON® I corner block, a hexagonal shaped corner block, perfect for turning 90-degree corners in projects such as partition walls. TRIDRON® 45° BLOCK units have a 45-degree angle and can be used for angles or in combination for right radius. A new product is Encurve™ finishing unit with a 3 7/8-inch radius at one corner. This block can be used to finish off glass block partitions in offices and residences.

Standard glass block is 3 7/8 inches thick, with the Thinline Series PC GlassBlock® units being 3 1/8 inches thick. Glass block is obtainable in 6-, 8-, and 12-inch squares, and some styles come in 4 × 8-inch and 6 × 8-inch rectangular blocks. The Thinline block has the additional advantage of 20 percent less weight.

Specialty blocks such as VISTABRIK® units are solid glass and provide maximum protection from vandalism and forcible entry. "LX" inserts, of fibrous glass sheet, are sealed into the PC GlassBlock® unit to provide significant light and thermal control by tempering glare, brightness, light transmission, and solar heat gain. For a one-of-a-kind design, PC® Signature block can be custom-manufactured with a corporate logo or design.

Glass block may also be of curved panel construction. It is suggested that the curved areas be separated from the flat areas by intermediate expansion joints and supports (Table 5–1).

Installation. The mortar-bearing surfaces of glass block have a coating that acts as a bond between the block and the mortar. Additionally, the coating acts as an expansion-contraction mechanism for each block. An optimum mortar mix is 1 part portland cement, 1/2 part lime, and 4 parts sand. Panel reinforcing strips are used in horizontal joints every 16 to 24 inches of height, depending on which thickness of block is used. Expansion strips are used adjacent to

jambs and **heads.** Joints are **struck** while plastic, and excess mortar is removed immediately. Mortar should be removed from the face of the block with a damp cloth before final set occurs.

For an all-glass look, blocks may be installed using Pittsburgh Corning's KWiK'N EZ® system, clear plastic spacer strips, silicone sealant, and a perimeter channel in place of mortar.

Maintenance. Ease of maintenance is one of the attractive features of glass block. Mortar or dirt on the face of glass block may be removed by the use of water, but not with abrasives (steel wool, wire brush, or acid).

PLASTER

The Egyptians and ancient Greeks used plaster walls that were then painted with murals. The frescoes of early times were painted on wet plaster, which absorbed the pigment and dried as an integral part of the plaster. The frescoes of Michelangelo's Sistine Chapel still retain their original brilliant color even after 400 years. Plaster was also used for very intricate mouldings and decorations. Today, plaster-covered walls are used only in commercial installations and the more expensive custom-built homes, because applications run as high as $2 per square foot, compared to about 50 cents per square foot for drywall. The process is also extremely labor intensive, involving three coats over gypsum or metal lath.

On the market are surface finishes called veneer plaster. This creates the upscale look of solid plaster at lower cost, about 25 percent more than gypsum board. Veneer plaster provides the hardness of plaster and the crack resistance of gypsum board. Veneer

TABLE 5–1
Radius Minimums for Curved Panel Construction

BLOCK SIZE	OUTSIDE RADIUS IN INCHES	NUMBER BLOCKS IN 90° ARC	JOINT THICKNESS IN INCHES	
			Inside	*Outside*
6 × 6	52½	13	⅛	⅝
4 × 8	36	13	⅛	⅝
8 × 8	69	13	⅛	⅝
12 × 12	102½	13	⅛	⅝

Courtesy of Pittsburgh Corning Corporation.

plaster is applied over a veneer plaster base, sometimes called blueboard, not to be confused with the water-resistant board used as a substrate for ceramic tile around the shower and bath area.

Joints are reinforced with a fiberglass webbing; steel corners and casing beads protect corners. A base and then a finish coat are applied to form a hard-surfaced, 1/8-inch total thickness. An alkali-resistant primer formulated for use over new plaster should be used if the surface is to be painted.

If a gypsum board wall is already installed, a plaster bonding agent must be applied before using the veneer plaster, which is then applied in two coats.

Lath is the foundation of a plaster wall. In the Pyramids in Egypt, the lath was made of intertwined reeds. The construction of the half-timbered homes of the English Tudor period is often referred to as daub and wattle (the daub being the plaster and the wattle the lath), this time a woven framework of saplings and reeds. When any restoration work is done on houses built prior to the 1930s, the lath will probably be found to be thin wood strips nailed to the studs about 3/8 of an inch apart.

Modern lath is either gypsum board, metal, or masonry block. The gypsum lath consists of a core of gypsum plaster between two layers of specially formulated, absorbent, 100 percent recycled paper. The gypsum lath is 3/8- or 1/2-inch thick, 16 inches wide by 48 inches long, and is applied horizontally with the joints staggered between courses. Other sizes are also available. Special types of gypsum lath may have holes drilled in them for extra adhesion or have a sheet of aluminum foil on one side for insulating purposes.

Metal lath is used not only for flat areas but also for curved surfaces and forms. Metal lath is expanded metal that is nailed to the studs. The **scratch coat** is troweled on and some plaster is squeezed through the mesh to form the mechanical bond, whereas the bond with gypsum board is formed by means of **suction. Beads** or formed pieces of metal are placed at exterior corners and around **casings** to provide a hard edge that will not be damaged by traffic.

Plaster used to be troweled on the lath in three different coats. The first coat bonded to the lath; the second was the brown coat; and the third, the finish coat, was very smooth. The first two coats were left with a texture to provide tooth. A three-coat plaster job is still done sometimes, but two coats or even one may be used to complete the finished surface.

As mentioned in Chapter 3, because of its extreme porosity, plaster must be sealed before proceeding with other finishes.

GYPSUM BOARD

Gypsum board has the same construction as the gypsum board lath. Sheets are normally 4 feet wide and 8 feet long, but they may be obtained in lengths up to 16 feet. The edges are usually tapered; some styles have the taper along the length and some types are tapered on all four edges. This allows for a tape and joint treatment to be applied, resulting in a finish that will be flat, smooth, and monolithic. Width of the taper is 2 inches. Square edge was designed to be a base for a fabric covering or wallpaper, paneling, or tile. The square edge also can be used where an exposed joint is desired for a paneled effect. Tapered with round edge can be used for walls and ceilings in both new construction and remodeling. It is designed to reduce the beading and ridging problems commonly associated with standard type gypsum board.

In some areas the term **drywall** is often synonymous with gypsum board. The term "dry wall" originated to differentiate between plaster or "wet wall" construction and any dry material such as gypsum board, plywood, or other prefabricated materials, without the use of plaster or mortar.

Another term mistakenly used is Sheetrock®, a registered trademark of the U.S. Gypsum Company for its brand of gypsum board. The term "gypsum wallboard" should not be used either, because most gypsum board companies now produce a type of reinforced gypsum board specially for ceilings, which can withstand the deflection.

All gypsum board companies produce their product with 100 percent recycled paper on both the face and the back.

Gypsum board is also obtainable with a foil back that serves as a vapor barrier on exterior walls. Another method of vapor barrier preparation is the use of a polyethylene sheet stapled to the studs before erecting the gypsum board.

In new construction, 1/2-inch thickness is recommended for single-layer application, or for laminated two-ply applications, two 3/8-inch thick sheets are used.

A fire resistant gypsum board has incombustible fibers added to provide greater resistance to heat transfer.

The horizontal method of application is best adapted to rooms in which full-length sheets can be used, as it minimizes the number of vertical joints. Today, screws are usually used rather than nails, as they can be installed by mechanical means and will not pull loose, or "pop." They are placed 6 to 8 inches o.c. with the heads slightly below the surface. The ceilings are done first and then the walls. A very good dry wall installation may also have an adhesive applied to the studs before installing the panels, in which case screws may be farther apart.

A thorough inspection of the studs should be made before application of the gypsum board to ensure that all warped studs are replaced. If this is not done, the final appearance of the plaster board will be rippled. Of course, this problem is not present when metal studs are used, as in commercial construction.

After all the sheets have been installed, outside corners are protected by a metal corner or bead. The normal bead is right-angled, but Softforms® extruded aluminum profiles come in 90° inside and outside corners and create an effect of softened space. Trim strips are available for a reveal effect.

Joint cement, spackling compound—or as it is called in the trade, "mud"—is applied to all joints with a 5-inch wide spackling knife. Then the perforated tape is placed to cover the joint and is pressed into the mud. Another layer of compound is applied, **feathering** the outer edges. After drying, the compound is sanded and a second or even a third coat is applied, the feathering extending beyond the previous coats. All screw holes are filled with joint cement and sanded smooth. Care must be taken to sand only the area that has been coated with joint cement, because sanding the paper layer will result in a roughness that will be visible, particularly when a painted semigloss or gloss finish is applied. In fact, the Gypsum Association suggests a thin skim coat of joint compound be applied over the entire surface to provide a uniform surface for these paints. The dry-wall installer should be informed of the final finish so that attention can be paid to special finishing.

ALL seams or joints must be taped regardless of length; otherwise, cracks will soon appear. The outside beads have joint cement feathered to meet the edge.

The surface of the gypsum board may be left smooth, ready for painting or a wallcovering, or it may have some type of texture applied. The latter is done for several reasons. Aesthetically, a texture may be more desirable to eliminate glare and is also more likely to hide any surface discrepancies caused by warping studs and/or finishing of joints. The lightest texture available is called an orange peel, with the surface appearing just as the name suggests. Another finish is a skip-troweled surface where, after the texture has been sprayed on, a metal trowel is used to flatten some areas. The heaviest texture is a heavily stippled or troweled appearance similar to rough finished

plaster. A texture is preferred whenever there is a **raking light** on the wall surface so that surface discrepancies are not quite so visible.

Gypsum board may also be installed on a curved wall by qualified dry-wall installers. Only **simple curves** may be used. **Compound curves** cannot be fabricated.

Pittcon's FRESCO™ neo-Georgian panels are actually debossed 3/16 inches below the surrounding surface of a 5/8-inch thick gypsum board to simulate paneling. This product comes in two parts, a lower portion (32 inches × 48 inches) for a wainscot effect; or, by using the upper portion (64 inches × 48 inches) as well, a fully paneled wall can be achieved. The flat borders surrounding the "raised panel" areas provide space for attachment with drywall screws. All sheets have recessed edges for receiving tape and joint compound for finishing. FRESCO is very effective for a painted paneled appearance especially where fire codes prohibit the use of solid wood. FRESCO is shown in Figure 6–2.

When water may be present, such as in bathrooms and kitchens, most building codes require the use of a water-resistant gypsum board. When ceramic tile is used, special tile backers that are water resistant are used. If a pliant wallcovering is to be used, all plaster board must be sealed or sized, as the paper of the gypsum board and the backing of the wallcovering would become bonded together and the wallcovering would be impossible to remove. This is where the Portersept Surface Sealer may be used.

Another type of plaster board has fabric or vinyl plastic in a variety of simulated finishes, including wood grains and other textures. It can be applied directly by adhesive to the studs or as a finish layer over a pre-existing wall. The edges may be square or beveled. Wood or metal trim must be applied at both floor and ceiling to create a finished edge.

WALLPAPER/WALLCOVERING

The Chinese mounted painted rice paper on their walls as early as 200 B.C. Although mention of painted papers has been historically documented as early as 1507 in France, the oldest fragment of European wallpaper, from the year 1509, was found in Christ's College, Cambridge. This paper has a rather large-scale pattern adapted from contemporary damask. Seventeenth-century papers, whether painted or block printed, did not have a continuous pattern repeat and were printed on sheets rather than on a roll, as is the modern practice. The repetitive matching of today's papers is credited to Jean Papillon of France in the later 17th century. In the 18th century, England and France produced handprinted papers that were both expensive and heavily taxed.

Leather was one of the original materials to be used as a covering for walls. The earliest decorated and painted leathers were introduced to Europe in the 11th century by Arabs from Morocco and were popular in 17th-century Holland.

Flocked papers were used as early as 1620 in France. The design was printed with some kind of glue and then heavily sprinkled with finely chopped bits of silk and wool, creating a good imitation of damask or velvet. Flocked papers have been popular in recent decades but are now falling from favor.

Scenic papers were used in the 18th century, many of them handpainted Chinese papers. Wallpapers used in the United States were imported during the second quarter of the 18th century. Domestic manufacturing did not really start until around 1800 and even then the quality was not equal to the fine imported papers.

After the Industrial Revolution, wallpaper became available to people of more moderate means and the use of wallpaper became more widespread. In the late 19th and early 20th centuries, William Morris provided the stimulating interest in wallpapers and their designs. In the first half of the 20th century, papers imitating textures and having the appearance of wood, marble, tiles, relief plasterwork, paneling, and moire silk were in demand.

In the late 1930s and 1940s, wallpaper was in style, only to be replaced by painted walls in the 1960s, 1970s, and 1990s.

Today, designers are more discriminating with the use of wallpapers or, as they will be referred to from now on, "wallcoverings." This change of name results from the fact that although paper was the original material for wallcoverings, today these wallcoverings may be all paper, paper backed by cotton fabric, vinyl face with paper or cotton backing, or fabric with a paper backing. Foils or mylars have either paper or a nonwoven backing to ensure a smooth reflective surface.

The face of the paper wallcoverings is usually treated with a protective vinyl finish and provides a washable surface. "Washable" means wiping the surface with a sponge and mild soap and water. Solid vinyl wallcoverings backed by woven cotton are more durable and are scrubbable, meaning they can be cleaned with a soft brush and mild detergent.

Vinyl wallcovering is strippable, meaning that it peels off easily in one intact piece, without steaming or scraping, should it be necessary to remove for renovation or other purposes. When a wallcovering is peelable, the face paper peels off, but the paper backing remains adhered to the wall. This backing can be removed or a new wallcovering can be applied over it.

Patterns

There are many collections available that have been researched by the manufacturer. By using these collections, the designer will be able to create the desired atmosphere.

Many of the Early American designs were inspired by the valuable brocades and tapestries that adorned the homes of the wealthy. Katzenbach & Warren has done extensive research into New England homesteads and their early papers. Since many were created before the machine age, they were often painted entirely by hand or stenciled or printed by means of a wood block. The designs include small all-over floral patterns, floral vine patterns, and flowing arabesques. Stencils with pineapples, the symbol of hospitality, and small stylized designs were also used.

For historic wallpaper, several companies have arrangements with museums to produce their designs. Bradbury & Bradbury Art Wallpapers have meticulously researched historical collections from the last quarter of the 19th century through Art Deco (see Color Plate Figure 5). Brunschwig & Fils has arrangements with the Society of New England Antiquities, the Musé des Arts Décoratifs in Paris, the Benaki Museum in Athens, Historic Charleston, the Winterthur Museum, and a number of other American museums. Katzenbach & Warren has developed a collection from the Athenaeum of Philadelphia. This library and museum has a collection of original wallcovering documents and fabrics, from which this series was developed. Scalamandré produces wallpaper for the Preservation Society at Newport, the Smithsonian Institute, and Historic Charleston, among others. Schumacher's licensers include Colonial Williamsburg, Historic Natchez, The National Trust for Historic Preservation, and the Victorian Society. Richard E. Thibaut issues the Historic Homes of America collection based on samples from actual homes; these papers are less expensive than the hand-screen prints mentioned above.

Albert van Luit and Co., in its Winterthur Museum Collection, has meandering **chinoiserie,** and the beautiful adaptation of an eight-panel scenic is the perfect background for English style furniture. The scenic murals are hung above the chair rail. Murals are large scale, nonrepeat, handscreened patterns done on a series of panels. They may be scenic, floral, architectural, or graphic in nature. Murals are sold in sets varying from two to six or more panels per set. Each panel is normally 28 inches in width and is printed on strips 10 to 12 feet in length. The height of the designs varies greatly, but most fall somewhere between 4 and 8 feet. Some graphics go from ceiling to floor.

For a French ambience, wallcoverings with delicate scrolls or lacy patterns are suitable for a formal background, while **toile-de-Jouy** and checks are appropriate for the French Country look. Wallcoverings for a formal English feeling range from symmetrical damasks to copies of English chintzes and embroideries.

Geometrics include both subtle and bold stripes and checks, as well as polka dots and circles. The colors used will dictate where these geometrics can be used.

Trompe l'oeil patterns are three-dimensional designs on paper. Examples of realistic designs are a cupboard with an open door displaying some books, a view from a window, or a niche with a shell top containing a piece of sculpture. These trompe l'oeil patterns are sold in a set.

Pattern repeats are often mentioned in wallcovering books:

> The pattern repeat is the distance between one point to the next repeated same point. This may vary from no repeat or match (as in a texture) to repeats as large as 48 inches. Therefore, for an exceptionally large repeat, additional paper should be ordered.
>
> When a patterned wallcovering is hung, the left side of a strip will match or continue the design with the right side of the previous strip. If this match is directly across on a horizontal line, then it would be called a straight match. If the second strip has to be lowered in order to continue the design, this is called a drop match. A drop match does not necessarily mean that more wallcovering must be ordered, but must be taken into consideration when cutting the strips.[1]

Types

Textures include embossed papers, which hide any substrate unevenness, solid color fabrics, and grasscloths. Embossed papers have a texture rolled into them during the manufacturing process. Care should be taken not to flatten the texture of embossed papers when hanging them.

Anaglypta® is an embossed product made from paper that has been imported from England since the turn of the century. Designed to be painted, this wallcovering provides the textured appearance of sculptured plaster, hammered copper, or even hand-tooled Moroccan leather. These highly textured wallcoverings are applied to the wall like any other product. Once painted, the surface becomes hard and durable. The advantage of these wallcoverings is that not only are they used on newly constructed walls in residential and commercial interiors, but they may also be applied after minimal surface preparation. In older dwellings and Victorian restoration projects, they provide the added advantage of actually stabilizing walls while covering moderate cracks and blemishes. Friezes, with ornate embossed designs, are part of the heavier Lincrusta® line, the original extra-deep product. Low-relief and vinyl versions are also available (Figure 5–7).

Fabrics should be tightly woven, although burlap is frequently used as a texture. The walls are pasted with a nonstaining paste and the fabric, with the selvage removed, is brushed onto the paste. Custom Laminations, Inc., paperbacks fabrics for wallcoverings.

Grasscloth is made of loosely woven vegetable

Figure 5–7
The texture of Anaglypta is shown in this photograph. The dado is Anaglypta Dado RD 668, and the border is Anaglypta Border RD 691. (Photograph courtesy of Crown Corporation, NA.)

fibers backed with paper. These fibers may be knotted at the ends and are a decorative feature of the texture. Because these are vegetable fibers, width and color will vary, thus providing a highly textured surface. Because of the natural materials, it is impossible to obtain a straight-across match, so the seams will be obvious. Woven silk is frequently included in grasscloth collections, and this finer texture gives a more refined atmosphere to a room.

Flocked papers, as has been mentioned before, are one of the oldest papers on record. They are currently manufactured by more modern methods but still resemble pile fabrics. One problem with flocked papers is that through abrasion, or constant contact with the face of the paper, the flocking may be removed and a worn area will appear. A seam roller should never be used to press down seams, as this also flattens the flocking.

Foils and mylars provide a mirrored effect with a pattern printed on the reflective surface. It is because of this high shine that the use of a lining paper is suggested to provide a smoother substrate. Foils conduct electricity if allowed to come in contact with exposed wires. In moist areas, some of the older foils had a tendency to show rust spots. This is why most "metallic" wallcoverings are presently made of mylar. To achieve the best effect from foils, there should be an abundance of light in the room in order to reflect off the foil surface.

Kraft papers are usually hand-printed on good quality kraft paper that is similar to the type used for wrapping packages. Unless specially treated, these kraft papers absorb grease and oil stains, so care should be taken in placement of these types of wallcoverings.

For a cork-faced paper, razor-thin slices of cork are applied by hand to tinted or lacquered ground papers. The base color shows through the natural texture of the cork and may blend or contrast with the cork itself. The sliced cork may also be cut into definite shapes for a repetitive pattern or it may be printed with a design on top of the cork. Cork also comes in 12-inch square tiles varying in thickness from 1/8 to 5/8 of an inch. These solid cork tiles are of varying texture and provide good heat and sound insulation.

Leather is cut into designs or blocks much like Spanish tiles because the limited size of the hide prohibits large pieces from being used. The color of the surface varies within one hide and from one hide to another; therefore, a shaded effect is to be expected.

Coordinated or companion fabrics are used to cre-
ate an unbroken appearance where wallcovering and draperies adjoin. When using coordinated paper and fabric, the wallcovering should be hung first and then the draperies can be adjusted to line up with the pattern repeat of the wallcovering. The tendency is to call these companion fabrics "matching fabrics," but this is incorrect. It is extremely important to realize that paper or vinyl will absorb dyes in a different manner than will a fabric, and many problems will be resolved by the strict avoidance of the word "matching."

Lining paper is an inexpensive blank paper recommended for use under foils and other fine quality papers. It absorbs excess moisture and makes a smoother finished wall surface. A heavier canvas liner is available for "bad walls."

Printing of Wallcoverings

Roller printing is used for the less expensive wallcoverings. The inks are transferred from a metal roller with raised design blocks to a large printing roller and then to the paper as it is fed through the press.

There are several means by which a wallcovering can be hand-printed. First of all, it may be silk screened. A separate screen must be made up for each color used and the screens must be meticulously positioned so that the patterns match at the edges. In silk screening, the wallcovering must be allowed to dry between application of the different colors (Figure 5–8).

Block printing produces a similar effect to silk screening, only instead of the paint being squeezed through the open pores of the silk screen, the paint or color is rolled on a block where the negative, or unwanted, areas have been cut away. Block printing also requires positive positioning when printing. This method is the same as the potato blocks often made in grade schools.

Because silk-screening and block printing are hand processes, a machine-like quality is not possible or perhaps even desirable. The pattern does not always meet at the seams as positively as does the roller-printed one. Matching should be exact in the 3- to 5-foot area from the floor, where it is most noticeable.

Adhesives

There are several materials available to attach a wallcovering to the wall. The old standby is the wheat-base paste and this is used for many wallcoverings.

Figure 5–8
Small orders of custom screening are still done by hand as shown above. Large orders are now done with rotary screen printing machines.

However, certain wallcoverings such as wetlook vinyls, handprints, naturals, and foils require a special adhesive. The manufacturer will always specify which type of adhesive is to be used. If fabric or grasscloth is to be hung, a nonstaining cellulose paste should be used. Regular vinyls are hung using a vinyl adhesive that is not the same as the special adhesive mentioned above.

Prepasted papers come with a factory-applied dehydrated cellulose or wheat paste. To activate this paste, cut strips are soaked in water for a designated number of seconds and then applied the same as regular wallpaper. The prepasted papers are usually less expensive and are mainly for use by the homeowner in a do-it-yourself project.

Most machine-printed wallcoverings are **pretrimmed** at the factory, but the majority of handprints and handmade textures are untrimmed.

Packaging

A single roll of American wallcovering used to contain 36 square feet, but only the cloth-backed vinyls now have this amount. All others are metric and use the European measurement equivalent to 28 square feet. To make allowance for waste and matching patterns, it is advisable to calculate 30 usable square feet for the cloth-backed vinyls and 24 usable square feet for the metric system. This allowance is sufficient for a room with an average number of doors and windows, but for a room with window walls, more precise calculations should be made.

All wallcovering is priced by the single roll, but it is packaged in two- or three-roll bolts. A double roll bolt is a continuous bolt containing the equivalent of two single rolls. The cost is twice the single roll price. The same applies to a triple roll bolt. By packaging wallcovering in bolts rather than in single rolls, the paperhanger has more continuous lineal yardage with which to work and, therefore, less waste. When ordering handprints from a retail store, there are a few things one must know. There is a cutting charge if the wallcovering order requires a cut bolt. As the shading and even the positioning of the pattern on the roll may vary between dye lots or runs, SUFFI-CIENT BOLTS SHOULD ALWAYS BE ORDERED when the order is placed. The particular dye lot, which is stamped on the back of the roll, may not be available if it is necessary to order more in the future. Opened or partially used bolts are not returnable, and unopened bolts may be subject to a restocking charge.

Commercial Wallcoverings

Commercial wallcoverings are the exception to the single roll containing up to 28 square feet. Commercial wallcoverings are usually 52 to 55 inches wide and are packaged in 30-yard or more bolts. These wider coverings require a highly skilled professional paperhanger and a helper. The final appearance of the walls depends on the ability of the paperhanger.

Commercial wallcoverings are classified according to federal minimum performance standards. Until 1983, the specifications for commercial wallcoverings were based on the number of ounces per square yard. Previously 100 percent cotton was used as a backing, but today a blend of polyester and cotton is used. Polyester fibers are not as bulky as cotton fibers, but they have more **tensile strength.** Tensile strength is the single most important performance feature in commercial wallcovering. Abrasion resistance is important but mainly in key areas such as outside corners.

A second major change is the inclusion of washability, scrubability, and stain-resistance requirements. These qualities increase from Type I to the most durable Type III. The three types are further classified into Class 1: not mildew resistant and Class 2: mildew resistant. Advanced technology has produced a unique backing for Type II vinyl wallcoverings called "apertured nonwoven." This backing combines the best qualities of regular woven and nonwoven backs, and provides excellent print quality and pattern definition. This backing also allows for superior hangability and ease of application.

Mildew is a fungus that flourishes in a moist, dark environment. If mildew is present or even suspected, the walls should be washed with a mixture of equal parts of household bleach and water. The correct paste or adhesive will also help prevent mildew from forming under newly hung wallcovering. If proper precautions are not taken, any mildew that forms will permanently discolor the wallcovering.

Portersept® with Intersept Wallcovering Adhesive is a premixed wallcovering adhesive providing excellent initial tack, slip, and opentime for easier positioning. It can be used with light to heavy weight wallcovering Types I, II, and III and cleans up with water. This nonflammable product contains Intersept to protect against microorganisms. (See Chapter 1, page 7.)

J. M. Lynne stocks its Bordeaux Prints fabric-backed vinyl wallcovering in two widths, 27 inches as well as 54 inches. The 54-inch width is required for corporate interiors whereas the 27-inch widths are needed for hospitality and health care installations, particularly in rest rooms where 54-inch material is awkward to work with (Figure 5–9). J. M. Lynne also carries the Byzantine series, a 54-inch vinyl wallcovering designed by the Roscoe award winner Patty Madden.

From NuMetal Surfaces comes a flexible metal

Figure 5–9
Examples of the Bordeaux prints from J. M. Lynne. (Photograph courtesy of J. M. Lynne Co. Inc.)

wallcovering for use in contract and residential interiors. The patterns are abstract and are individually fabricated. The pattern continues from one 27 3/16-inch by 10-foot high panel to the adjacent one with as many as 22 panels in one order. This product was given the 1991 Roscoe award for wallcoverings.

Forbo-Vicrtex Inc. has consistently won design awards for its vinyl collections. The 1993 best of Neo-Con/Gold award was for the Vicrtex Collection, inspired by the southwest region of the United States. These include Taos, a multicolor sandstone texture; Raku, a geological texture; Botero, a multihued, natural fresco texture recalling the sun and sandstone hues of the desert; and Prism, an etched surface of cut gem forms, handcrafted to capture and reflect light from every angle. The Adagio pattern won the 1993 ASID award. Adagio is a small-scale pattern that creates a tactile interest of light-reflecting, geometric shapes that alter and create multitonal values.

With plain textures, grasscloths, and suedes, it is advisable to reverse the direction of every other strip. This will make a better finished appearance particularly if one side of the covering happens to be shaded a little more than the other.

As mentioned before, commercial wallcovering usually comes in 52- to 54-inch wide bolts. However, MDC Wallcoverings has a wallcovering, Quantex™, that is 106 inches wide and endless in length. The total width of all the walls is the length ordered. This woven textile has the best characteristics of olefins, such as durability and cleanability, but because of its extreme width, provides seamless installations and avoids panel shading. This wallcovering is made to be railroaded; in other words, instead of hanging Quantex vertically, it is hung horizontally.

Koroseal® vinyl wallcoverings (with the exception of Tiffany Suede, Surface, and Fresco patterns) contain the Early Warning Effect formulation that, when heated to about 300°, gives off a harmless, odorless, and colorless vapor that will set off the alarm on an ionization smoke detector located in the same room. These vinyls are also UL approved to Class A federal standards and contain antimicrobial and mildew-resistant elements. Koroseal Wallcoverings also has Textiles for Walls in 54-inch widths. (Textile Wallcoverings do not include the Early Warning Effect formulation.)

Tassoglas, a globally accepted and specified wallcovering, is available in a variety of textures and patterns and is designed to be painted. Tassoglas offers tremendous design flexibility as an unfinished, paintable wallcovering. It is made of all natural, environmentally friendly woven glass textile yarns and comes 39 inches wide with pretrimmed edges. This product combines the versatility of paint with the strength and benefits of woven glass fiber yarns to provide a highly breatheable, mold and mildew resistant, durable, and long-lasting wallcovering. Beneath the surface, Tassoglas reinforces the substrate, easily bridges cracks, hides roughness or minor imperfections, and is ideal for use in both new construction and renovations. Tassoglas has also received the stringent European approval of OKO-TEX Confidence in Textiles for no harmful substances.

If wood paneling is not permitted under the existing fire or building codes, a product called Flexwood® may be specified. Flexwood is of two-ply construction, veneer and cloth backing. Flexwood is made of carefully selected wood veneers permanently laminated to a woven cloth backing. It can be applied to straight or curved walls and wrapped around columns. Flexwood is available in 50 domestic and imported woods, with the veneers so carefully matched that joints are practically invisible after installation. Every sheet is factory matched and numbered in sequence to ensure panoramic matching of the wall.

The recommended finish for Flexwood is a good alkyd varnish, which has a fast drying time and a low gloss matte finish. Flexwood has a Class 1 flame-spread rating of 15 when applied with the recommended adhesive.

A new concept in commercial wallcovering is the deeply embossed PVC or expanded vinyl wallcoverings, which are not only attractive but offer acoustic values. They are packaged in full bolts, 29 inches wide by 55 yards in length.

All textile wallcoverings have good acoustic qualities and also good energy-saving insulation qualities. Textiles may be backed by paper and the fiber content may be 100 percent jute, or a combination of synthetics and wool and jute and/or linen and cotton. These textiles usually have a flame spread rating of 25 or less.

Tretford Broadloom, a concentric ribbing in 38 colors from Eurotex is, in Europe, mainly used for floors, but in the United States it is also used on walls. Face yarns are 80 percent wool/mohair and 20 percent nylon, with a primary backing of polyvinyl chloride (PVC) and a secondary backing of jute. With a flamespread of 5, it is very suitable for contract work and absorbs sound, cushions impact, insulates to save energy, and is an excellent display surface that accepts Velcro® and push pins. Tretford can be installed on any dry, smooth surface such as concrete, dry wall, plaster, wood paneling, particleboard, etc. Installation on cinder or cement blocks or on surfaces covered with wallpaper or vinyl wallcovering is *not* recommended. Tretford is installed with an adhesive applied with a notched trowel, and maintenance involves brushing lightly in the direction of ribs and periodically vacuuming the surface.

Sisal is another wallcovering that has high sound absorption and is also static-free. Rolls are either 4 or 8 feet wide and 100 feet long. Sisal has an extremely prickly texture, as opposed to the other textiles, but this roughness can be an asset as in the following case: A school found that when students lined up outside the cafeteria, there was a tendency for the wall to get very dirty and be defaced by graffiti. Installation of sisal prevented both problems and also reduced the noise level.

One of the special surface treatments for wallcoverings is Tedlar®. This is a tough, transparent fluoride plastic sheet that is very flexible; chemically inert; and extremely resistant to stains, yellowing, corrosive chemicals, solvents, light, and oxygen. Most commercial wallcovering manufacturers have wallcovering products that are, or may be, surfaced with Tedlar. Another stain-resistant product is PreFixx™, available on Essex 54 products, which protects invisibly with no loss of texture.

Some companies offer special-order printing, with minimums of 50 rolls or more. These may be designs already in their line or custom designs. Because these are handprints, they are expensive; but they may solve a particular design problem.

In large public buildings, different colors of vinyl wallcovering are often used as a pathfinding aid to patrons.

Installation. Before hanging any wallcovering, the walls must be sized. Sizing is a liquid applied to the wall surface that serves several purposes. It seals the surface against alkali, also known as hot spots; it reduces absorption of the paste or adhesive to be used; and it provides tooth for the wallcovering. The sizing must be compatible with the paste or adhesive to be used.

Wallcoverings are installed in either of the following manners:

1. Table trimmed with a straight edge. This means cutting the selvage from both edges so that the panels can be butted. This procedure reduces the amount of surface adhesive residue and facilitates clean up.

2. Panels are overlapped on the wall and seams are made by double cutting through both sheets. Care

must be taken NOT to cut into the substrate surface. Various hooked knife-type cutting tools are available for this procedure. After the cut is made, the face strip may be removed and the adhesive cleaned off. Vicrtex® Wallcovering has the following extremely useful suggestions in its "Suggested Specification, Installation Instructions, Care and Maintenance" booklet: "Remove excess paste from a seam before making the next seam. Vertical joints should occur at least 6 inches from inside and outside corners." Vicrtex has also provided much of the information in this section.

Paste or adhesive is applied by means of a wide brush to the back of the wallcovering. Particular attention should be paid to the edges because this is where any curling will occur. The wallcovering is folded or **booked,** without creasing. This allows the moisture in the adhesive to be absorbed by the fabric substrate or backing, thus allowing for any shrinkage before being applied to the wall surface. Booking also makes an 8- or 9-foot strip easier to handle and transport from the pasting table.

The first strip is always hung parallel to the **plumb line,** which has been previously marked. A seam roller is used on most wallcoverings, except as noted before. As has been mentioned already, for some wallcoverings, the paste must be applied to the wall rather than to the backing. THE MANUFACTURER'S INSTRUCTIONS FOR INSTALLATION METHODS SHOULD ALWAYS BE FOLLOWED. Inspect each roll before cutting the first strip. If a damaged roll has been cut into, it cannot be returned.

Maintenance. All stains or damage should be corrected immediately. Paper-faced wallcoverings should be tested to ascertain if the inks are permanent before cleaning fluids are applied. Vinyls may be scrubbed with a soft brush and water if they have been designated scrubbable. Foils are washed with warm water and wiped with a soft cloth to avoid any scratching. Hard water does have a tendency to leave a film on the reflective surfaces of foil.

Grasscloths, suedes, fabrics, sisal, and carpeting may be vacuumed to remove the dust. Again, always follow the manufacturer's instructions for maintenance.

It is suggested that vinyl-covered walls be washed at least once or twice a year. Grease and oils in particular should not be allowed to accumulate.

1. For routine dirt and grime, use a mild detergent dissolved in warm water.

2. For severe dirt conditions use a concentrated solu-

tion of a mild detergent applied with a stiff brush. Remove the grimy suds by padding with a damp sponge. The wall should then be rinsed with clean water to remove detergent residue.

3. For surface stains such as lipstick, ball-point ink, heel marks, shoe polish, carbon smudges, and the like, use anhydrous isopropyl alcohol as an efficient cleaner for removal of such stains from vinyl wallcovering. Ethyl alcohol or denatured alcohols are also efficient. Do not use strong alkaline or abrasive cleaners.[2]

TAMBOURS

Tambours may be solid wood, wood veneer, metallic-face laminate, or cork, laminated to a tempered hardboard core with brown fabric backing approximately 3/16 of an inch thick overall. Slats are cut 1/2 to 1 inch o.c. with the angle of the groove varying between 28° and 90°. Depending on the face material, dimensions may be 24-inch by 96-inch slat length or 48-inch by 96-inch slat length. A 120-inch length is available from some companies. Solid hardwood slats are also available in oak and maple. Because of their flexibility tambours are used for curved walls as well as for roll-up doors in kitchen appliance garages (Figure 5–10).

Flexible mirror may be clear, bronzed, or colored. This mirror is also bonded to a cloth back in square, rectangular, or diagonal pattern cuts and gives a multifaceted or broken reflection. Both the tambour and flexible mirror may be used on straight or curved walls.

Installation. The method of installation depends on the surface to which the tambour is to be attached. A special adhesive is usually required, but the manufacturers' instructions should always be followed.

WOOD

When selecting a wood or veneer, designers should ascertain whether it comes from a renewable source. It is possible for wood to be sustainable with proper management.

Figure 5–10
The variety of materials available in tambour form are shown in one photograph. (Photograph courtesy of Flexible Materials) A white oak wood tambour was used to cover the dividers of the telephone area at the Indianapolis International Airport. (Photograph courtesy of National Products Inc.)

Wood is a good natural insulator because of the millions of tiny air cells within its cellular structure. For equal thickness, it is four times as efficient an insulator as cinder block, six times as efficient as brick, 15 times as efficient as stone, 400 times as efficient as steel, and 1,770 times as efficient as aluminum. The production of the final product is also energy efficient. One ton of wood requires 1,510 Kilowatt hours to manufacture, whereas one ton of rolled steel requires 12,000 Kilowatt hours, and one ton of aluminum requires 67,200 Kilowatt hours.

Wood for walls comes in two different forms: solid wood strips and plywood.

Solid wood may be used on the walls of residences, but it is not usually used for commercial applications, unless treated, because of the fire and building code restrictions. For residential use redwood, cedar, and knotty pine are the most commonly used woods, but walnut, pecan, and many others may also be used.

There are several grades of redwood from which to choose. The finest grade of redwood is Clear All Heart, with the graded face of each piece free of knots. Clear All Heart gives a solid red color, whereas Clear redwood is also top quality but does contain some cream-colored sapwood and may also contain small

Figure 5–11
This beach house in California has 1-inch by 6-inch tongue-and-groove Clear All Heart redwood used horizontally in the children's bathroom. Architects: Neumann and Scott Rowland, Santa Barbara, California. Photographer: Marvin Sloben. (Photograph courtesy of the California Redwood Association)

knots. This cream-colored sapwood may be attractive to some, but to others its random appearance is bothersome; therefore, the client needs to know the difference in appearance as well as cost between the Clear All Heart and Clear. B Heart is an economical all-heartwood grade containing a limited number of tight knots and other characteristics not permitted in Clear or Clear All Heart. B Grade is similar to B Heart except that it permits sapwood as well as heartwood (Figures 5–11 and 6–3).

Redwood is available in vertical grain, which has straight vertical lines, and flat grain, cut at a tangent to the annual growth rings, exposing a face surface that appears highly figured or marbled. The smooth-faced redwood is referred to as surfaced; saw-textured lumber has a rough, textured appearance.

There are two types of cedar: aromatic cedar, which is used for mothproof closets; and regular cedar, which is used for both interior and exterior walls. Another soft wood frequently used for residential interiors is knotty pine, where knots are part of the desired effect, unlike the top grade redwood.

Boards may be anywhere from 4 to 12 inches wide with tongue-and-groove for an interlocking joint, or **shiplap** for an overlapping joint. The tongue-and-groove may have the edges beveled for a V-joint or may be rounded or even elaborately molded for a more decorative effect. Shiplap boards come with their top edges beveled to form a V-joint, or with straight edges to form a narrow slot at the seams.

Square-edged boards are used in contemporary settings and may be board and batten, board on board, reverse board and batten, or contemporary vertical. Board and batten consists of wide boards spaced about one inch apart, and a narrow 1-inch × 2-inch strip of batten is nailed on top to cover the 1-inch gap. Board on board is similar to board and batten, except that both pieces of wood are the same width. Reverse board and batten has the narrow strip under the joint or gap. In contemporary vertical installations, the battens are sometimes placed on edge between the wider boards (Figure 5–12).

For acoustical control, boards are often placed on edge and spaced about 2 to 3 inches apart on an acoustical substrate.

The National Oak Flooring Manufacturer's Association (NOFMA) suggests using oak flooring on the walls and ceiling. It is now possible to obtain a Class "A" 0–25 flamespread rating (often required in commercial structures) by job-site application of an intumescent coating. The NOFMA supplies literature showing that using Albert DS Clear by American Vameg meets this standard. A beveled oak strip floor-

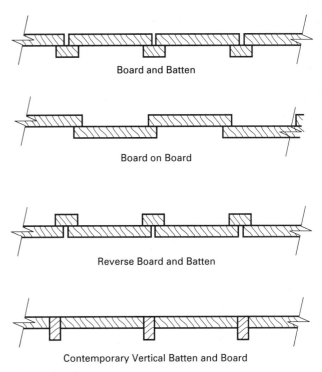

Board and Batten

Board on Board

Reverse Board and Batten

Contemporary Vertical Batten and Board

Figure 5–12
Board and battens.

ing gives a three-dimensional effect when installed on a wall.

Several companies manufacture paneling that comes prepackaged in boxes containing approximately 64 square feet. The longest pieces are 8 feet and the shortest 2 feet, with the edges beveled and tongue-and-grooved sides and ends. This type of paneling, although more expensive than regular strips, eliminates waste in a conventional 8-foot-high room.

Installation. Siding, plank, or strips may be installed horizontally, vertically, or diagonally. Each type of installation will give a completely different feeling to the room. Horizontal planking will appear to lengthen a room and draw the ceiling down, while vertical adds height to a room and is more formal. Diagonal installations appear a little more active and should be used with discretion or as a focal point of a room. Diagonal or herringbone patterns look best on walls with few doors or windows. Different application methods require different substrates.

If installed horizontally or diagonally over bare studs or gypsum board, no further preparation of the surface is needed. The strips are attached in the tongue area as with hardwood flooring, except that with wall applications, the nails penetrate each stud.

Vertical installations require the addition of nail-

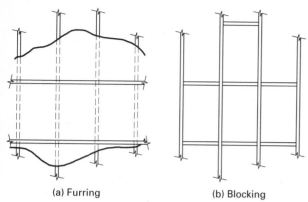

(a) Furring   (b) Blocking

Figure 5–13
Furring and blocking.

ing surfaces. The two types of nailing surfaces are blocking and furring. Blocking is filling in horizontally between the studs with a 2- to 4-inch piece of wood, in order to make a nailing surface. This blocking also acts as a fire stop. Furring is thin strips of wood nailed across the studs (Figure 5–13).

When wood is to be used on an outside wall, a vapor barrier such as a polyethylene film is required. Also, wood should be stored for several days in the area in which it is to be installed so it may reach the correct moisture content. Some manufacturers suggest several applications of a water-repellent preservative to all sides, edges, and especially the more porous ends. This is particularly important where high humidity persists.

There are several suggested finishes for wood walls: wax, which adds soft luster to the wood; or a sealer and a matte varnish, where cleaning is necessary. The paneling may also be stained, but it is important to remember that if solid wood is used, the natural beauty of the wood should be allowed to show through.

PLYWOOD PANELING

Plywood is produced from thin sheets of wood veneer, called plies, which are laminated together under heat and pressure with special adhesives. This produces a bond between plies that is as strong or stronger than the wood itself.

Plywood always has an odd number of layers that are assembled with their grains perpendicular to each other. Plywood may also have a lumber core, medium density fiberboard core, or a particle board core; however, lumber core plywood is virtually never used today in fine architectural woodworking (Figure 5–14).

The Architectural Woodwork Institute (AWI) is a not-for-profit organization representing the architectural woodwork manufacturers located in the United States and Canada. The following section would not be possible without the assistance and cooperation of AWI.

The side of the panel with the best quality veneer is designated as the face, and the back may be the same or of lesser quality, depending on its uses. The Hardwood Plywood & Veneer Association (HPVA)-sponsored plywood standard has seven plywood veneer grade classifications; however, AWI utilizes only the upper three grades, Grade AA, Grade A, and Grade B.

Grade AA. The best quality face grade for high-end use such as architectural paneling, doors and cabinets, case goods, and quality furniture.

Grade A. Where AA is not required but excellent appearance is very important, as in cabinets and furniture.

Grade B. Where the natural characteristics and appearance of the species are desirable.

A more detailed description of these three grades can be found in *Interim Voluntary Standard for Hardwood and Decorative Plywood,* available from HPVA. It is also found in the AWI Quality Standards under section 200-S-7, Veneer Face Grades.

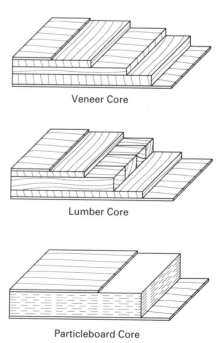

Veneer Core

Lumber Core

Particleboard Core

Figure 5–14
Types of plywood.

AWI's Architectural Woodwork Standards provide for three grades: Custom, Premium, and Economy.

Custom Grade: The grade specified for most architectural woodwork. This grade provides a well-defined degree of control over the quality of workmanship, materials, and installation of a project. The vast majority of all work produced is Custom Grade.

Premium Grade: The grade specified when the highest degree of control over the quality of the execution of the design intent, and the quality of the materials, workmanship, and installation is required. Usually reserved for special projects, or feature areas within a project.

Economy Grade: The grade that defines the minimum expectation of quality, workmanship, materials, and installation within the scope of AWI Standards.

When the AWI Quality Standards are referenced as a part of the contract documents and no grade is specified, AWI Custom Grade standards will prevail.[3]

Types of Veneer Cuts

The manner by which a log segment is cut with relation to the annual rings will determine the appearance of the veneer. When sliced, the individual pieces of veneer, referred to as "leaves," are kept in the order in which they are sliced, thus permitting a natural grain progression when assembled as veneer faces. The group of leaves from one slicing is called a **flitch** and is usually identified by a flitch number and the number of gross square feet of veneer it contains. The faces of the leaves with relation to their position in the log are identified as the "tight face" (toward the outside of the log) and the "loose face" (toward the inside or heart of the log). During slicing the leaf is stressed on the "loose" face and compressed on the "tight" face. When this stress is combined with the natural variation in light refraction caused by the pores of the wood, the result is a difference in the human perception of color and tone between "tight" and "loose" faces.

Plain or Flat Slicing is the method most often used to produce veneers for high-quality architectural woodworking. Slicing is done parallel to a line through the center of the lot. A combination of cathedral and straight grain patterns results, with a natural progression of pattern from leaf to leaf.[4]

Walnut is usually cut by this method (Figure 5–15).

Quarter Slicing simulates the quarter sawing process of solid lumber, roughly parallel to a radius line through the log segment. In many species the individual leaves are narrow as a result. A series of stripes is produced, varying in density and thickness from species to species. *Flake* is a characteristic of this slicing method in red and white oak. [See Figure 5–15.]

Rift Cut Veneers are produced most often in red and white oak, rarely in other species. Note that rift veneers and rift sawn solid lumber are produced so differently that a "match" between rift veneers and rift sawn solid lumber is highly unlikely. In both cases the cutting is done slightly off the radius, minimizing the "flake" associated with quarter slicing. [See Figure 5–15.]

Rotary—the log is center mounted on a lathe and peeled along the general path of the growth rings like unwinding a roll of paper, providing a generally bold random appearance. Rotary cut veneers may vary in width, and matching at veneer joints is extremely difficult. Almost all softwood veneers are cut this way. Except for a specific design effect, rotary veneers are the least useful in fine architectural woodwork. [See Figure 5–15.][5]

Other decorative veneer patterns may be obtained by using the crotch, burl, or stump of the tree. The crotch pattern is always reversed so that the pointed part, or V, is up. Burl comes from an area of damage of the tree, where the tree has healed itself and grown over the injury. It is a very swirly pattern. Olive burl is frequently used in contemporary furniture.

Matching Between Adjacent Veneer Leaves

It is possible to achieve certain visual effects by the manner in which the leaves are arranged. As noted, rotary cut veneers are difficult to match; therefore, most matching is done with sliced veneers. The matching of adjacent veneer leaves must be specified. Special arrangements of leaves such as "diamond" and "box" matching are available. Consult your AWI woodworker for choices. The more common types are:

Book matching is the most commonly used match in the industry. Every other piece of veneer is turned over so adjacent pieces (leaves) are opened like the pages of a book. [Figure 5–16.]

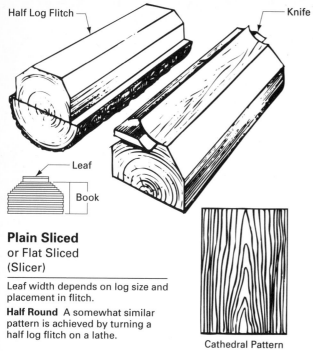

Plain Sliced
or Flat Sliced
(Slicer)

Leaf width depends on log size and placement in flitch.

Half Round A somewhat similar pattern is achieved by turning a half log flitch on a lathe.

Cathedral Pattern

(a) Plain Slicing (or Flat Slicing)

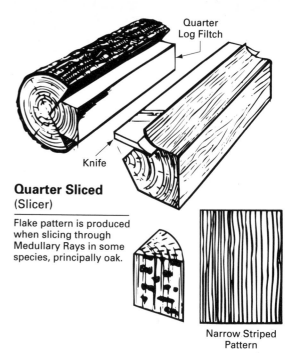

Quarter Sliced
(Slicer)

Flake pattern is produced when slicing through Medullary Rays in some species, principally oak.

Narrow Striped Pattern

(b) Quarter Slicing (or Quarter Cut)

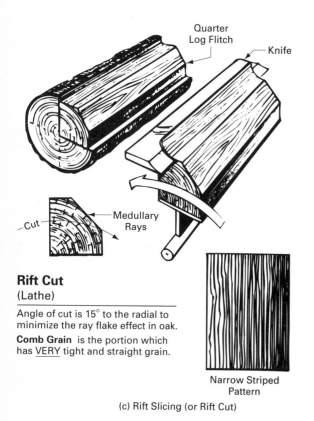

Rift Cut
(Lathe)

Angle of cut is 15° to the radial to minimize the ray flake effect in oak.

Comb Grain is the portion which has VERY tight and straight grain.

Narrow Striped Pattern

(c) Rift Slicing (or Rift Cut)

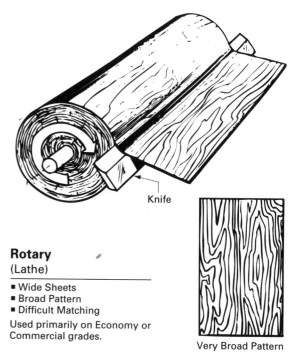

Rotary
(Lathe)

- Wide Sheets
- Broad Pattern
- Difficult Matching

Used primarily on Economy or Commercial grades.

Very Broad Pattern

(d) Rotary

Figure 5–15
Veneer types. (Reproduced by permission of the Architectural Woodwork Institute)

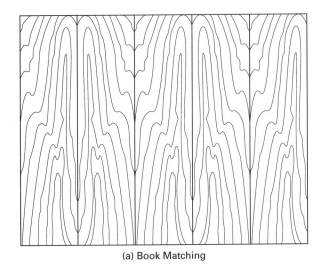

(a) Book Matching

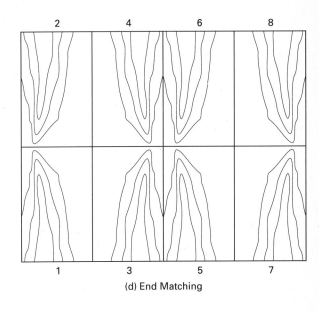

(d) End Matching

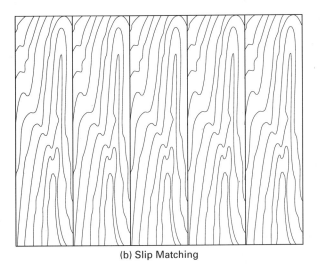

(b) Slip Matching

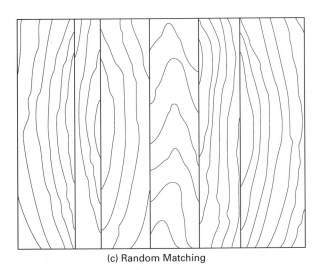

(c) Random Matching

Figure 5–16
Matching of veneers. (Reproduced by permission of the Architectural Woodwork Institute)

Visual effect—Veneer joints match creating a symmetrical pattern. Yields maximum continuity of grain. When sequenced panels are specified, prominent characteristics will ascend or descend across the match as the leaves progress from panel to panel.

NOTE: May be used with plain, quarter, or rift sliced veneers. Because the "tight" and "loose" faces alternate in adjacent leaves, they reflect light and accept stain differently, and this may yield a noticeable color variation in some species or flitches.

Slip matching is often used with quarter sliced and rift sliced veneers. Adjoining leaves are placed (slipped out) in sequence, without turning, resulting in all the same face sides being exposed (see Figure 5–16).

Visual effect—Grain figure repeats but joints do not show grain match.

NOTE: The lack of grain match at the joints can be desirable. The relatively straight grain patterns of quartered and rift veneers generally produce pleasing results and a uniformity of color because all faces have the same light refraction.

In *random matching,* veneer leaves are placed next to each other in a random order and orientation, producing a "board-by-board" effect in many species (see Figure 5–16).

Visual effect—Random matching produces a casual or rustic appearance, as though individual boards from a random pile were applied to the product. Conscious effort is made to mismatch grain at joints.

NOTE: Degrees of contrast and variation may change from panel to panel. This match is more difficult to obtain than Book or Slip Match, and must be clearly specified and detailed.

End matching is often used to extend the apparent length of available veneers for high wall panels and long conference tables. End matching occurs in two types: Architectural End Match, where leaves are individually book (or slip) matched, first end-to-end and then side-to-side, alternating end and side (see Figure 5–16). The visual effect is the best for continuous grain patterns for length as well as width.

For *Panel End Match,* leaves are book (or slip) matched on panel sub-assemblies, with sequenced sub-assemblies end matched, resulting in some modest cost savings on projects where applicable. The visual effect for most species is a pleasing, blended appearance and grain continuity.

Matching Within Individual Panel Faces

The individual leaves of veneer in a sliced flitch increase or decrease in width as the slicing progresses. Thus, if an AA number of panels are manufactured from a particular flitch, the number of veneer leaves per panel face will change as the flitch is utilized. The manner in which these leaves are "laid-up" within the panel requires specification and is classified as follows:

RUNNING MATCH—Each panel face is assembled from as many veneer leaves as necessary. This often results in a nonsymmetrical appearance, with some veneer leaves of unequal width. Often, the most economical method at the expense of aesthetics is the standard for Custom Grade and must be specified for other grades. Running matches are seldom "sequenced and numbered" for use as adjacent panels. Horizontal grain "match" or sequence cannot be expected. [Figure 5–17.]

BALANCE MATCH—Each panel face is assembled from veneer leaves of uniform width before edge trimming. Panels may contain an even or odd number of leaves, and distribution may change from panel to panel within a sequenced set. While this method is the standard for Premium Grade, it must be specified for other grades, and it is the most common assembly method at moderate cost (see Figure 5–17).

BALANCE AND CENTER MATCH—Each panel face is assembled of an even number of veneer leaves of uniform width before edge trimming. Thus, there is a veneer joint in the center of the panel, producing horizontal symmetry. A small amount of figure is lost in the process. Considered by some to be the most pleasing assembly at a modest increase of cost over Balance Match [see Figure 5–17].[6]

Methods of Matching Panels

1. *Premanufactured Sets—Full Width.* These are one step above "stock" plywood panels, usually made and warehoused in 4-foot × 8-foot or 4-foot × 10-foot sheets in sequenced sets. They may be produced from a single flitch or

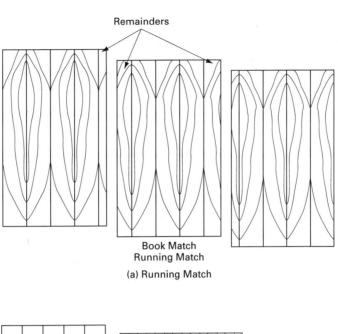

Book Match
Running Match

(a) Running Match

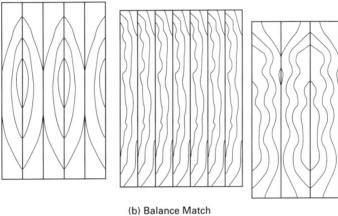

(b) Balance Match

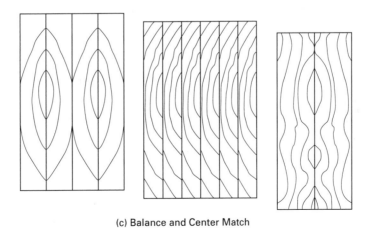

(c) Balance and Center Match

Figure 5–17
Matching within individual panel faces. (Reproduced by permission of the Architectural Woodwork Institute)

a part of a flitch, usually varying in number from 6 to 12 panels. If more than one set is required, matching between sets cannot be expected. Similarly doors or components often cannot be fabricated from the same flitch materials, resulting in noticeable mismatch. This is often the most economical type of special panel products [see Figure 5–18 a].

2. *Premanufactured Sets—Selectively Reduced in Width.* These are panels just like Premanufactured Sets—Full Width, usually made and warehoused in 4-foot × 8-foot and 4-foot × 10-foot sheets in sequenced sets. They are often selected for continuity, recut into modular widths, and numbered to achieve the appearance of greater symmetry. If more than one set is required, matching between the sets cannot be expected. Similarly, doors or components often cannot be fabricated from the same flitch materials, resulting in noticeable mismatch [Figure 5–18 b].

3. *Sequence Matched Uniform Size Set.* These sets are manufactured for a specific installation to a uniform panel width and height. If more than one flitch is required to produce the required number of panels, similar flitches will be used. This type of panel matching is best used when panel layout is uninterrupted and when the design permits the use of equal width panels. Some sequence will be lost if trimming is required to meet field conditions. Doors and components within the wall cannot usually be matched to the panels. Moderate in cost, sequenced uniform panels offer a compromise between price and aesthetics [Figure 5–18 c].

4. *Blueprint-Matched Panel and Components.* This method of panel matching achieves maximum grain continuity, since all panels, doors, and other veneered components are made to the exact sizes required and in exact veneer sequence. If possible, flitches should be selected that will yield sufficient veneer to complete a prescribed area or room; if more than one is needed, flitch transition should be accomplished at the least noticeable predetermined location. This method requires careful site coordination and relatively long lead times. Panels cannot be manufactured until site conditions can be accurately measured and detailed. This panel matching method is more expensive and expresses veneering in its most impressive manner [Figure 5–18 d].[7]

Rooms treated with paneling always produce a feeling of permanency. Architectural paneling is as different from ready-made paneling as a custom-made Rolls Royce is from an inexpensive production car. The ready-made paneling will be discussed later.

Fire Retardant Panels/Flame Spread Classification

The various codes utilize "flame spread" classifications for wood and other materials. It is the responsibility of the specifier to determine which elements, if any, of the woodworking require special treatment to meet local codes. In most codes, the panel products used to fabricate casework and furniture are not regulated. For more detailed information, please refer to the AWI publication *Fire Code Summary.* Typical model code classifications are:

Class I or A	0–25
Class II or B	26–75
Class III or C	76–200

Flame Spread Factors

A. *Core*—The fire rating of the core material determines the rating of the assembled panel. Fire retardant veneered panels must have a fire retardant core. Particleboard core is available with a Class I (Class A) rating and can be used successfully with veneer or rated high pressure decorative laminate faces. MDF (medium density fiberboard) is not currently available with a fire rating.

B. *Face*—Existing building codes, except where locally amended, provide that facing materials 1/28 of an inch or thinner are not considered in determining the flame spread rating of the panel. In localities where basic panel building codes have been amended, it is the responsibility of the specifier to determine whether the application of the facing material specified will meet the code.

Face veneers are not required to be fire retardant treated, and such treatment will adversely affect the finishing process.[8]

There are several methods of installing panels for acoustic control. The panels may be floated or raised, or batten mouldings of wood, metal, or plastic may also be used (Figure 5–19).

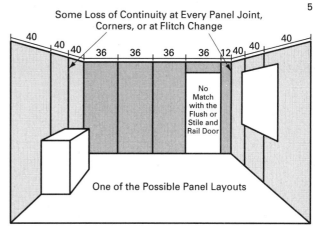

(a) Premanufactured Sets–Full Width

(b) Premanufactured Sets–Selectively Reduced in Width

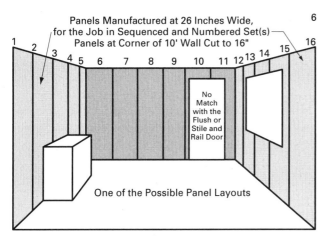

(c) Sequence Matched Uniform Size Set

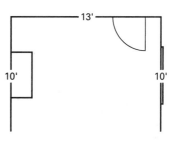

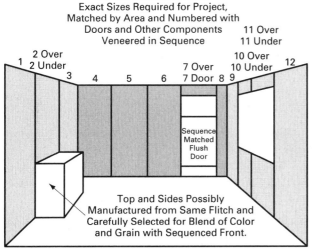

(d) Blueprint Matched Panels and Components

Figure 5–18
Matching of panels within an area. (Reproduced by permission of the Architectural Woodwork Institute)

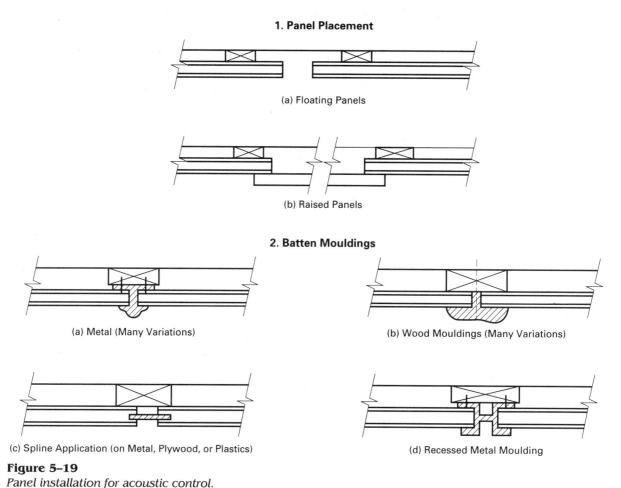

1. Panel Placement

(a) Floating Panels

(b) Raised Panels

2. Batten Mouldings

(a) Metal (Many Variations)

(b) Wood Mouldings (Many Variations)

(c) Spline Application (on Metal, Plywood, or Plastics)

(d) Recessed Metal Moulding

Figure 5–19
Panel installation for acoustic control.

Finishing. The Architectural Woodwork Institute has specific standards for factory finishing of woodwork, and its publication entitled *Architectural Woodwork Quality Standards* should be consulted.

PREFINISHED PLYWOOD

Prefinished plywood paneling varies from 1/4- to 1/2-inch thick, and standard panel size is 4 × 8 feet but is also available in 7- and 10-foot heights. The face of the plywood is grooved in random widths to simulate wood strips. This also hides the joining where each panel is butted up to the next, as outside edges are beveled at the same angle as the grooves.

The finish on this type of paneling is clear acrylic over a stained surface.

Some plywood paneling has a woodgrain reproduction on plywood or on a paper overlay applied to **lauan** plywood and then protected with an oven-baked topcoat.

Installation. As with all wood products, panel-ing should be stored in the room for 24 hours to condition for humidity and temperature. Paneling may be applied directly to the stud framing, but it is safer from a fire hazard point of view to install over gypsum board. A 1/4-inch sound-deadening board used as a backing decreases the sound transmission. Nails or adhesive may be used to install the panels. If nails are used, they may be color-coated when exposed fasteners are acceptable, or countersunk and filled with colored putty.

Maintenance. Prefinished plywood panels require frequent dusting in order to prevent a buildup of soil, which dulls the finish. Each manufacturer supplies instructions for maintenance of its particular product, and these should be followed.

HARDBOARD

Sheets or planks of hardboard are manufactured of compressed wood fibers by means of heat and pressure. Hardboard sheets or planks consist of a hardboard base that is textured during the pressing process, usually in a wood grain pattern. A dark base coat is then placed on top. This layer gives the dark color to the V-joints. On top is the light precision coat that does not cover the V-joints. This precision coat is grained and coated with a melamine topcoat that is baked on and is resistant to most household chemicals and such staining agents as cosmetics and crayons. Tape should not be applied to the panel surface because it may damage the surface.

Paneling is also available in 4 × 8-foot sheets and may utilize harmonizing mouldings between panels or may be butted. Pigmented vertical grooves simulate joints of lumber planks, and edges are also pigmented to match face grooves and to conceal butt joints. Hardboard panels are not to be used below grade, over masonry walls, in bathrooms, or in any area of high humidity.

When hardboard is covered with a photo-reproduction of wood, it does not have the depth or richness of real wood and is probably best used for inexpensive installations where price and durability are more important than the appearance of real wood. Because this paneling is not wood-veneered but rather a reproduction, the same manufacturing methods may be used for solid colors or patterns. Fast food restaurants and many businesses requiring the same features of durability and easy cleaning use Marlite plank. The plank may be used vertically, horizontally, and diagonally, provided furring strips have been installed over any sound, solid substrate.

Some hardboard is available in a stamped grille-type pattern or with holes (commonly known as Peg-Board®). The grille types are framed with wood and used for dividers. The perforated board is useful when hanging or storing items. Special hooks and supports are available for this purpose and are easily installed and removed for adjustment.

Installation. Thicknesses of hardboard vary from 1/8 and 3/16 of an inch to 1/4 of an inch. The 1/8-inch and 3/16-inch thicknesses must be installed over a solid backing, such as gypsum board. Panels are glued or nailed to the substrate.

Maintenance. To remove surface accumulation such as dust and grease, a lint-free soft cloth dampened with furniture polish containing no waxes or silicones may be used. More stubborn accumulations may require wiping with a soft cloth dampened in a solution of lukewarm water and a mild detergent. The hardboard must be wiped dry with a clean dry cloth immediately following this procedure. (An inconspicuous area or scrap paneling should be used for experimental cleaning.)

DECORATIVE LAMINATE

Decorative laminates are made from layers of kraft paper that have been impregnated with phenolic resins, giving flexibility to the final product. The pattern layer is placed on top and covered by a translucent overlay of melamine, a plastic that provides durability. When all these layers are bonded with heat, 300°, and pressure, 1,000 psi, the top translucent layer becomes transparent and forms the wearlayer. The pattern layer may be a solid color, or a photo of wood, fabric, or an artist- or computer-drawn image.

The vertical surface may be .050 of an inch general purpose or .030 of an inch vertical surface. The .030 inch type is not recommended on surfaces exceeding 24 inches in width. Decorative laminate for walls is quite often installed on the job site.

Balancing or backing laminates are used to give structural balance and **dimensional stability.** They are placed on the reverse side of the substrate to inhibit moisture absorption through the back surface.

Custom laminates are now available from Wilsonart®. They may be seamless inlay, where a piece of Wilsonart patterned decorative paper is cut out like a stencil and then backed by another Wilsonart decorative paper, which when bonded under heat and pressure, results in a two-color seamless inlay. The screen-print process is used when more than two colors are required. A multicolor, detailed image is screened onto a sheet of decorative paper, which is then made into a seamless, single sheet laminate (Figure 5–20).

Wilsonart Decorative Metal line now consists of 26 decorative metals. New options include mirror-quality aluminum panels, with three solids in chrome, gold, and bronze, and seven etched patterns in chrome (Figure 5–21). In response to the increasing popularity and demand for a matte finish, three cross-brushed patterns were added to the existing line of anodized aluminum metals along with a new brushed stainless steel look.

Where antistatic properties are required, a standard grade laminate is available. Several manufacturers of decorative laminate produce a laminate that does not have the usual dark edge associated with a square edge installation such as SOLICOR® and COLORCORE®.

Many manufacturers of **HPDL** produce a fire-resistant type that, when applied with approved adhesives to a fire-resistant core, results in wall paneling with Class 1 or "A" flamespread rating.

Wilsonart has twelve different finish options available, with varying degrees of light reflectance, to suit any project.

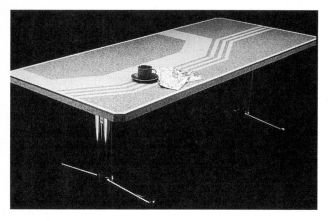

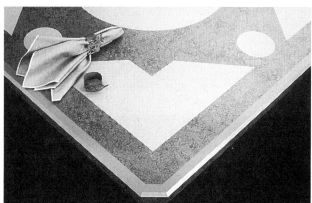

Figure 5–20
Using a special "seamless inlay" process, Wilsonart Custom Laminates allow the designer to specify a combination of two laminate patterns, or a pattern and a solid color, which are fused together into a single sheet of laminate and easily applied to counter tops, cabinetry, or other fixtures, shown here on table surfaces. Since laminate is made up of layers of paper, shapes that are cut out of the "top sheet" are seen as whatever color or pattern the "bottom sheet" happens to be specified in. The result is a custom-designed, unified sheet of laminate without the usual seams where delamination or dirt collection may occur. (Photographs courtesy of Wilsonart®)

Installation. When decorative laminates are to be used on the wall, 3/4-inch hardwood-faced plywood or particleboard should be used as a core. The use of an expansion type joint or reveal is suggested (Figure 5–22). To permit free panel movement and to avoid visible fastenings, AWI recommends that panels be hung on the walls, utilizing metal panel clips or interlocking wood wall cleats.

Maintenance. Wilsonart recommends that decorative laminates be cleaned with warm water and mild soaps such as those used for hands or dishes. If spots remain, use an all-purpose cleaner or bathroom cleaner, such as Formula 409®, Glass Plus®, or Mr. Clean®.

For very stubborn stains, make a paste with baking soda and water, applying it to the stain with a soft bristle brush. The last resort is undiluted household bleach such as Clorox®, followed by a clean water rinse. Use of abrasive cleansers or "special" cleansers should be avoided because they may contain abrasives, acids, or alkalines.

Metallic laminates other than solid polished brass may be cleaned as above. However, always wipe the surface of metallics completely dry with a clean soft cloth after washing. Stubborn smudges may be reuse in high-abuse public areas such as hospitals and food-processing and preparation areas. It is also available with writing board surfaces that double as projection screens. Widths are from 2 to 4 feet, and lengths are from 6 to 12 feet. Weight varies from 1.60 to 2.75 pounds per square foot. This material is also used for toilet partitions in public rest rooms.

Maintenance. Maintenance is the same as that for ceramic tile.

GLASS

Glass, one of our most useful products, is also one of the oldest (first used about 4000 B.C.). In ancient times, formed pieces of colored glass were considered as valuable as precious stones. In the past, glass was used mainly for windows, permitting light and sun to enter the interior of a home or building. Currently, as a result of modern construction methods, glass is used for interior walls or partitions. Of course, one disadvantage of glass is that it is breakable, but there are products specially made to reduce this problem.

There are three methods of manufacturing glass. The first is for sheet or window glass, where the molten glass is drawn out and both sides are subjected to open flame. This type, which is not treated after manufacture, can show distortions and waviness. Plate glass has both surfaces ground and polished, rendering its surfaces virtually plane and parallel. Float glass is a more recently developed and less expensive process of manufacturing; molten glass is floated over molten metal and is used interchangeably with plate glass.

Insulating glass consists of two or three sheets of glass separated by either a dehydrated air space or an inert gas-filled space, together with a **desiccant.** This insulating glass limits heat transference and, in some areas of the country, may be required by the building codes in all new construction for energy conservation purposes. It also helps to eliminate the problem of condensation caused by a wide difference in outside and inside temperatures.

There are various types of safety glass. The one with which we are most familiar is **tempered,** the kind used in entry doors or shower doors, where a heavy blow breaks the glass into small grains rather than sharp, jagged slivers. Another, which has a wire mesh incorporated into its construction, can break under a blow but does not shatter.

Laminated glass can control sound, glare, heat,

Figure 5–21
Bands of Wilsonart Decorative Metal help turn this 1950s-retro bar into a custom-tailored fixture for current times. Metallic accents, inlaid into the green Wilsonart Laminate background, help reflect light and move the eye down the bar's sweeping shape. The frosted plastic window, backlit from within, makes the unit even more noticeable. (Photograph courtesy of Wilsonart®)

moved with a dry cloth and a thin, clean oil. For solid polished brass surfaces, use only glass cleaners free of petroleum products. The surface may be touched up with Fill 'n Glaze™ and a good grade of automobile wax. Follow the manufacturer's instructions carefully when applying.

PORCELAIN ENAMEL

Porcelain enamel is baked-on 28-gauge steel, laminated to 3/16 to 21/32 of an inch gypsum board or hardboard. It comes in many colors and finishes for

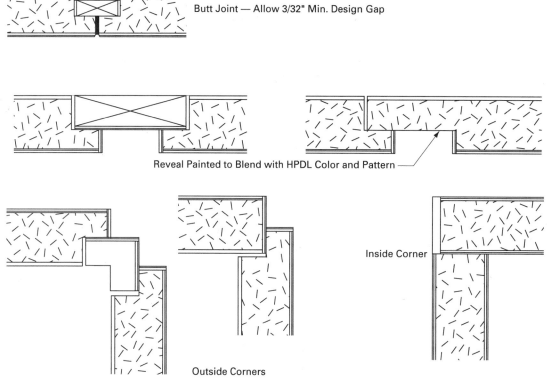

Butt Joint — Allow 3/32" Min. Design Gap

Reveal Painted to Blend with HPDL Color and Pattern

Inside Corner

Outside Corners

Figure 5–22
Reveals. (Reproduced by permission of the Architectural Woodwork Institute)

and light transmission. It offers security and safety through high resistance to breakage and penetration. In interior areas where glass is desired, laminated acoustical glass is effective in reducing sound transmission. Where exterior sounds (traffic, airplanes, etc.) are present and distracting, laminated acoustical glass may be used. This glass may be clear or colored. Another form of glass used for energy conservation is a laminated glass with a vinyl interlayer that, depending on the color of the interlayer, may absorb or transmit light in varying degrees. The tinted glass may have a bronze, gray, green, blue, silver, or gold appearance, and these tints cut down on glare in a manner similar to sunglasses or the tinted glass in an automobile. Where 24-hour protection is required, such as in jewelry stores, banks, and detention areas, a security glass with a high-tensile polyvinyl butryal inner layer is highly effective. There are even bullet-resistant glasses on the market.

For those involved in historical restorations, there is Restoration Glass™ from Bendheim. This glass is handmade using the original cylinder method, yet the glass easily meets today's tougher building codes. It is available in two levels of distortion—"full," for thicker and more distorting effects; and "light," for thinner and less distorting effects.

N. E. G. Company has NeoClad, a product manufactured by the crystallization of specially formulated sheet glass. In the process, it gains remarkable strength, a soft color, and a smooth high-gloss surface. The edges can be shaped with various types of bevels on the front or back. This product is for both interior and exterior use and is extremely resistant to environmental pollution and graffiti (Figure 5–23).

The 3M Company has a Priva-See film that, at the flip of a switch, changes interior and exterior windows from clear to translucent. This option provides open vistas and a sense of spaciousness that can be converted for privacy and security.

Transwall has glass movable walls that are modular and may be combined with acoustical panels and/or a variety of other components (Figure 5–24).

Figure 5–23
NeoClad wall cladding is extremely resistant to stains, graffiti, and environmental pollution. The polished quality of NeoClad can be seen by the reflections on the right-hand wall. Birmingham Financial Center, Birmingham, Alabama. Architects: Moody & Associates. (Photograph courtesy of N. E. G. America)

MIRROR

The mirrors used two thousand years ago by the Egyptians, Romans, and Greeks were highly polished thin sheets of bronze. Today, many of these metal mirrors may be seen in museums. The method of backing glass with a metallic film was known to the Romans, but it was not until 1507 that the first glass mirrors were made in Italy. Plate glass was invented in France in 1691, enabling larger pieces of glass to be manufactured. The shape of mirrors used in various periods of design should be studied by interior designers, but mirrors are no longer just accessories hung on the wall for utilitarian or decorative purposes. Walls are often completely covered with these highly reflective surfaces (see Figure 5–11).

Quality mirrors are made of float glass and are silvered on the back to obtain the highly reflective quality. Also used under certain circumstances are the two-way mirrors, where from one side, the viewer can see out, but from the other side it appears to be an ordinary mirror. These two-way mirrors have many uses, such as in apartment doors, child observation

Figure 5–24
*Transwall Corporate Designer Series creates an office with ceiling
height movable walls. Designer: Kelsh Wilson Design, Inc.,
Philadelphia, Pennsylvania. Photographer: Tom Crane Photography
Inc., Bryn Mawr, Pennsylvania. (Photograph courtesy of Transwall
Corporation)*

areas, department stores, banks, and prison security
areas.

Mirrors used on wall installations may be clear
and brightly reflective or grayed or bronze hued. The
latter are not as bright, but do not noticeably distort
color values. The surface may also be antiqued, producing a smoky, shadowy effect. Mirrored walls always enlarge a room and may be used to correct a size
deficiency or to duplicate a prized possession, such as

a candelabra or chandelier. Mirrored walls may also
display all sides of a piece of sculpture or double the
light available in a room.

Mirrors are available for wall installations in
many sizes, ranging from large sheets to small mosaic
mirrors on sheets similar to mosaic tile. Sometimes, a
perfect reflection is not necessary and the mirrors may
be in squares, **convex** or **concave,** acid etched, engraved, or beveled.

Mirror Terminology

The following terminology was provided by the National Association of Mirror Manufacturers:

Acid Etch: A process of producing a specific design or lettering on glass, prior to silvering but cutting into the glass with a combination of acids. This process may involve either a frosted surface treatment or a deep etch. This process can also be done on regular glass.

Antique Mirror: A decorative mirror in which the silver has been treated to create a smoky or shadowy effect. The antique look is often heightened by applying a veining on the silvered side in any one or more of a variety of colors and designs.

Backing Paint: The final protective coating applied on the back of the mirror, over copper, to protect the silver from deterioration.

Concave Mirror: Surface is slightly curved inward and tends to magnify reflected items or images.

Convex Mirror: Surface is slightly curved outward to increase the area that is reflected. Generally used for safety or security surveillance purposes.

Edge Work: Among numerous terms and expressions defining types of edge finishing, the five in most common usage are listed here.

> *Clean-Cut Edge:* Natural edge produced when glass is cut. It should not be left exposed in installation.
>
> *Ground Edge:* Grinding removes the raw cut of glass, leaving a smooth satin finish.
>
> *Seamed Edge:* Sharp edges are removed by an abrasive belt.
>
> *Polished Edge:* Polishing removes the raw cut of glass to give a smooth-surfaced edge. A polished edge is available in two basic contours.
>
> *Beveled Edge:* A tapered polished edge, varying from 1/4 of an inch to a maximum of 1 1/4 inches thick, produced by machine in a rectangular or circular shape. Other shapes or ovals may be beveled by hand, but the result is inferior to machine bevel. Standard width of bevel is generally 1/2 of an inch (Figure 5–25).

Electro-Copper-Plating: Process of copper-plating by electrolytic deposition of copper on the back of the silver film, to protect the silver and to assure good adherence of the backing paint.

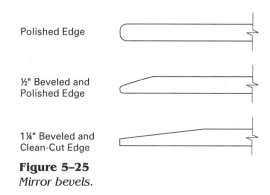

Polished Edge

½" Beveled and Polished Edge

1¼" Beveled and Clean-Cut Edge

Figure 5–25
Mirror bevels.

Engraving: The cutting of a design on the back or face of a mirror, usually accomplished by hand on an engraving lathe.

Finger Pull: An elongated slot cut into the glass by a wheel, so that a mirrored door or panel, for instance, may be moved to one side.

First-Surface Mirror: A mirror produced by deposition of reflective metal on front surface of glass, usually under vacuum. Its principal use is as an automobile rear-view mirror or transparent mirror.

Framed Mirror: Mirror placed in a frame that is generally made of wood, metal, or composition material and equipped for hanging.

Hole: Piercing of a mirror, usually 1/2 inch in diameter and generally accomplished by a drill. Often employed in connection with installations involving rosettes.

Mitre Cutting: The cutting of straight lines by use of a wheel on the back or face of a mirror for design purposes. Available in both satin and polished finishes.

Rosette: Hardware used for affixing a mirror to a wall. A decorative rose-shaped button used in several places on the face of a mirror.

Sand Blasting: Engraving or cutting designs on glass by a stream of sand, usually projected by air.

Shadowbox Mirror: Mirror bordered or framed at an angle on some or all sides by other mirrors, creating multiple reflections of an image.

Stock-Sheet Mirrors: Mirrors of varying sizes over 10 square feet, and up to 75 square feet, from which all types of custom mirrors are cut. Normally packed 800 to 1,000 square feet to a case.

Transparent Mirror: A first surface mirror with a thin film of reflective coating. To ensure most efficient use, the light intensity on the viewer's side of the mirror must be significantly less than on the subject side. Under such a condition, the viewer can see through the mirror as through a transparent glass, while the subject looks into a mirror.

Installation. Both mastic and mechanical devices such as clips or rosettes should be used in order to install a mirror properly. Clips are usually of polished chrome and are placed around the outside edges. Rosettes are clear plastic type fasteners and require a hole to be drilled several inches in from the edge, in order to accept the fastening screws and rosettes. Because of the fragile quality of mirror, use should be limited to areas where the likelihood of breakage is minimal.

Installation of Ceramic, Metal, and Mirror Tile. Because of the force of gravity, mortar cement cannot be troweled directly onto the wall without sagging. To prevent this sagging, a metal lath, similar to the one used for a plaster wall, is attached to the solid backing and then troweled with mortar. The metal lath acts as a stabilizing force. The backing may be wood, plaster, masonry, or gypsum board. This is equivalent to the thick-set method of floor installation. For wall use over gypsum board, plaster, or other smooth surfaces, an organic adhesive may be used. This adhesive should be water resistant for bath and shower areas.

The *Handbook of Ceramic Tile Installation,* available from the Tile Council of America Inc. and also found in *Sweet's Catalogs,* is the nationally accepted guideline for tile installation, even for materials other than ceramic tile.

CERAMIC TILE

Ceramic tile is frequently used on walls when an easily cleaned, waterproof, and durable surface is desired. One use of ceramic tile is as a **backsplash** in the kitchen, as a continuation of the couter. When it is used for this purpose, the grout may be sealed by use of a commercial sealer or by using a lemon oil furniture polish. Ceramic tile is also used for the surrounds of showers and bathtubs, and for bathroom walls in general (Color Plate Figure 3). These three uses are probably the most common ones, but ceramic tile may also be used on the walls in foyers and hallways, either plain, patterned, or in logos, and as a heat-resistant material around fireplaces and stoves. Ceramic tile for counter tops will be discussed later in Chapter 9.

If the walls are completely covered with ceramic tile, there will be no need for trim pieces. However, in bathrooms or kitchens, or any place where tiling will not be continued from wall to wall or from ceiling to floor, trim pieces must be added to cover the unglazed and uncolored side of the tile. These trim pieces are different in appearance, depending on the type of installation, thick or thin set. For specific installation methods, refer to Table 5–2.

A bullnose for thick-set installations has an overhanging curve piece, whereas a bullnose for thin-set is the same thickness as the surrounding tiles, but has a curved finished edge. For bath and shower installations, angle trims for the top and inside edges are used, and for walls meeting the floor, a cove is used (see Figure 3–12).

This interesting note comes from the Tile Council of America:

> Use of wall-washer and cove type lighting, where the lights are located either at the wall/ceiling interface, or mounted directly on the wall, are popular techniques of producing dramatic room lighting effects. When proper backing surfaces, installation materials and methods, and location of light fixtures are not carefully coordinated, these lighting techniques may produce shadows and undesirable effects with ceramic tiles. Similar shadows are created from side lighting interior walls and floors when light shines at that angle through windows and doors.

GLASS TILE

Edward Lowe, the inventor, is now producing through Edward Lowe Glass Designs, Inc. (ELGDI), a unique hand-cast glass tile for interior and exterior use in any type of residential or commercial architecture. ELGDI tiles are actually three pieces of glass laminated together to produce a tile with a high degree of depth and richness of color. The result is a tile unique to any other, with the color in the tile instead of just on the surface. ELGDI can customize both colors and patterns to fit any design need.

ELGDI tiles are installed using the same methods as ceramic tile. Because the tiles are impervious to water, acids, and other chemicals, the tiles have no area to harbor the growth of microorganisms—an excellent feature when considering tile installment in kitchens, bathrooms, and aqueous surfaces such as pools, spas, and fountains. Furthermore, ELGDI tiles can be easily cleaned with biocidal solution. ELGDI won a 1994 ASID product award.

TABLE 5–2
Wall Tiling Installation Guide

Simplest methods are indicated; those for heavier services are acceptable. Some very large or heavy tile may require special setting methods. Consult ceramic tile manufacturer.

SERVICE REQUIREMENTS	WALL TYPE (numbers refer to Handbook Method numbers)					
	Masonry or Concrete	*Page*	*Wood Studs*	*Page*	*Metal Studs*	*Page*
Commercial Construction—Dry or limited water exposure: dairies, breweries, kitchens.	W202 W221[a] W223	20 21 21	W223 W231 W243 W244	21 22 23 23	W223 W241 W242 W243, W244	21 22 22 23
Commercial Construction—Wet: gang showers, tubs, showers, laundries.	W202 W211 W221[a]	20 20 21	W231 W244 B411 B414	22 23 24 25	W241 W244 B411 B414, B415	22 23 24 25
Residential & Light Construction—Dry or limited water exposure: kitchens and toilet rooms, commercial dry area interiors and decoration.	W221[a] W223	21 21	W222[a] W223 W243 W244	21 21 23 23	W222[a] W242 W243 W244	21 22 23 23
Residential & Light Construction—Wet: tub enclosures and showers.	W202 W211 W223	20 20 21	W222[a] W223 W244 B412, B413 B415, B416	21 21 23 24 25	W222[a] W241 W244 B412, B413 B415, B416	21 22 23 24 25
Exterior	W201 W202	20 20	W231	22	W241	22

[a]Use these details where there may be dimensional instability, possible cracks developing in or foreign coating (paint, etc.) on structural wall which includes cleavage membrane (15 lb. felt or polyethylene) between wall surface and tile installation.

Source: 1994 Handbook for Ceramic Tile Installation. Copyright © Tile Council of America, Inc. Reprinted with permission.

METAL

In the latter part of the 19th century, during the Victorian era, stamped tin panels were used on ceilings and dadoes of rooms. The dadoes even had a molded chair rail incorporated into them. Today Pinecrest manufactures 26-gauge tin in 24- by 96-inch panels stamped with dies dating back to the Civil War. These panels are virtually indestructible and come with a silver tin finish. They may be painted with an oil-base paint, if desired. Matching cornices are also available.

ACOUSTICAL PANELS

Several manufacturers produce a mineral fiberboard or fiberglass panel that, when covered with fabric, absorbs sound and also provides an attractive and individually designed environment. Because of the textured, porous surface and the absorbent substrate, sound is absorbed rather than bounced back into the room. These panels may also be used as tack boards for lightweight pictures and graphics. In open-plan office areas, different colors can be used to direct the flow of traffic through an open office and to differentiate between work areas. In addition to the acoustical qualities of these panels, there are two other beneficial features. One is that the panels are fire retardant and the other is that, when installed on perimeter walls, there is an insulating factor that varies with the type of board used.

The panels may take the form of appliques in sizes of 2 × 4 feet, 2 × 6 feet, or they may cover the wall completely in panel sizes of 24 or 30 inches × 9 feet.

Vinyl or fabric faced acoustic panels may be designed for various types of installation. For use on an existing wall, only one side needs to be covered. For open-plan landscapes, both surfaces are covered to absorb sound from both sides. Some panels are covered on the two side edges for butted installation while another portable type is wrapped on all surfaces and edges. Sculptwall, with its rounded contour, provides an acoustical and aesthetic solution for sound absorbency. The surface area of the arc is 24 inches wide, which covers 18 inches of wall surface. The internal construction is either 1- or 2-inch molded fiberglass core, which is adhered with the fabric or wall-covering of your choice.

A 1993 Interior Design Product Award was given to Armstrong World Industries for its Soundsoak Woodwinds Wall Rail System. The pre-engineered chair rail molding system is specifically crafted for use with acoustical wall panel systems. The judges said the chair rail system offers availability in standard components and looks custom-designed when assembled.

Installation. As there are numerous types of acoustic panels, no one installation method covers all panels. Depending on the type of panel, panels may be attached to the wall by means of an adhesive and/or may have moulding concealing the seams. Manufacturers' recommended installation methods should be followed.

Maintenance. Surface dirt is removed by vacuuming or light brushing. Spots can be treated with dry-cleaning fluid or with carpet shampoo.

CORK

Cork tiles are available in 12 × 36 inches in 1/2-, 3/4-, 1-, and 1 1/2-inch thicknesses and may be used in residential, commercial, educational, and institutional buildings. Because of its porous nature, cork can breathe and, therefore, can be used on basement walls or on the inside surface of exterior support walls without the risk of moisture difficulties. Because of the millions of dead-air spaces in the cork particles themselves, cork also has good insulating properties.

Installation. Panels are applied by using a 1/8 × 1/8 of an inch notched trowel and the recommended adhesive.

Maintenance. Vacuuming periodically with the brush attachment is recommended. A light, dust-free sealing coat of silicone aerosol spray will give dust protection; a heavier spray protects against dust and gives the surface a glossier finish, providing more light reflection. However, a heavy spray tends to close the pores of the cork, thus decreasing its sound deadening and insulating qualities. An alternative to the silicone spray is a 50–50 blend of clear shellac and alcohol.

OTHER MATERIALS

Surface Design and Technology Inc. has metal graphics that are materials for elevator door and cab facings, wall and ceiling panels, door claddings, column covers, etc.

VITRICOR® is a high molecular acrylic from Nevamar and is very suitable for vertical surfaces that require a reflective gloss appearance with deep, rich, saturated color much like that of hand-lacquered finishes.

BIBLIOGRAPHY

Ackerman, Phyllis. *Wallpaper, Its History, Design and Use.* New York: Frederick A. Stokes Company, 1923.

Architectural Woodwork Institute. *Architectural Woodwork Quality Standards*, 6th ed. Version 1.1. Centreville, VA: Architectural Woodwork Institute, 1994.

Entwisle, E. A. *The Book of Wallpaper, A History and an Appreciation.* Trowbridge, England: Redwood Press Ltd., 1970.

Kicklighter, Clois E. *Modern Masonry.* South Holland, IL: Goodheart-Wilcox Co., 1980.

Landsmann, Leanne. *Painting and Wallpapering.* New York: Grosset & Dunlap, 1975.

Pittsburgh Corning Corporation. *PC Glass Block® Products Specification Guidelines.* Pittsburgh, PA: Author, 1994.

Plumridge, Andrew and Wim Meulenkamp. *Brick-

work, Architecture and Design. New York: Harry N. Abrams, Inc., 1993.

Schumacher. *A Guide to Wallcoverings.* New York: Schumacher.

Time-Life Books. *Paint and Wallpaper.* New York: Time-Life Books, 1981.

Time-Life Books. *Walls and Ceilings.* Alexandria, VA: Time-Life Books, 1980.

Wilson, Ralph Plastics Co. *The ABC's of Easy Care for Wilsonart® Brand Decorative Laminate.* Temple, TX: Author, 1985.

ENDNOTES

[1]Schumacher, *A Guide to Wallcoverings* (New York: Author, n.d.).

[2]Vicrtex Wallcoverings, "Suggested Specification, Installation Instructions, Care and Maintenance" (New Jersey: Author, n.d.).

[3]*Architectural Woodwork Quality Standards,* 6th Edition, Version 1.1 1994, by Architectural Woodwork Institute (Centreville, VA 22020), page 6. All quotes from *Architectural Woodwork Quality Standards* reproduced with permission.

[4]Ibid., page 59.

[5]Ibid., pages 59–60. (Emphasis added)

[6]Ibid., pages 60–62.

[7]Ibid., pages 63–66.

[8]Ibid., page 62.

GLOSSARY

Ashlar. Precut stone (see Figure 5–2).

Backsplash. The vertical wall area between the kitchen counter and the upper cabinets.

Beads. Rounded formed pieces of metal used in finishing the edges of gypsum board.

Booked. Folding back of pasted wallcovering so that pasted sides are touching.

Book match. Every other leaf is turned over, so the right side of a leaf abuts a right side, and a left side abuts a left side.

Casing. Exposed trim or moulding (see Figure 6–1).

Chinoiserie. (French) Refers to Chinese designs or manner.

Cobble. Similar in appearance to fieldstone.

Compound curves. Curving in two different directions at the same time.

Compressive strength. Amount of stress and pressure a material can withstand.

Concave. Hollow or inward curving shape.

Convex. Arched or outward curving shape.

Cramps. U-shaped metal fastenings.

Desiccant. Substance capable of removing moisture from the air.

Dimensional stability. Ability to retain shape regardless of temperature and humidity.

Drywall. Any interior covering that does not require the use of plaster or mortar.

Evacuated. Air is removed.

Feathering. Tapering off to nothing.

Fieldstone. Rounded stone.

Flake. A pattern produced when slicing through the medullary rays in some species, principally oak.

Flitch. Portion of a log from which veneer is cut.

Header. End of an exposed brick (see Figure 5–4).

Header course. Headers used every sixth course (see Figure 5–4).

Head. Horizontal cross member supported by the jambs.

HPDL. High pressure decorative laminate.

Jamb. Vertical member at the sides of a door.

Laminated glass. Breaks without shattering. Glass remains in place.

Lauan mahogany. A wood from the Philippines that although not a true mahogany, does resemble mahogany in grain.

Mortar stain. Stain caused by excess mortar on face of brick or stone.

Nonferrous. Containing no iron.

Plumb line. True vertical line.

Pretrimmed. Selvages or edges have been removed.

Raking light. Light shining obliquely down the length of the wall.

Rubble. Uncut stone (see Figure 5–2).

Scratch coat. In three-coat plastering, it is the first coat.

Shiplap. An overlapping wood joint.

Simple curve. Curving in one direction only.

Stile. Outside vertical member of paneling (see Figure 7–5).

Stretcher. Long side of an exposed brick (see Figure 5–4).

Struck. Mortar joint where excess mortar is removed by a trowel.

Suction. Absorption of water by the gypsum board from the wet plaster.

Tambours. Thin strips of wood or other materials attached to a flexible backing for use on curved surfaces. Similar in appearance to a roll-top desk.

Tensile strength. Resistance of a material to tearing apart when under tension.

Tempered glass. Glass toughened by heating and rapid cooling.

Toile-de-Jouy. Similar to the printed cottons made by Oberkampf in France during the 18th and 19th centuries.

Trompe l'oeil. French for "fooling the eye." Also used on painted surfaces such as walls or furniture.

_____ *Chapter 6*

Ceilings

Early Greeks and Romans used lime stucco for ceilings, on which low, medium, and high **reliefs** were carried out. The Italians in the 15th century worked with plaster, and Henry VIII's Hampton Court has very highly decorative plasterwork ceilings. In the Tudor and Jacobean periods, the plasterwork for ceilings had a geometric basis in medium and high relief. This was followed by the classicism of Christopher Wren and Inigo Jones, an admirer of Palladio. In the later 18th century, the Adam brothers designed and used cast plaster ornaments with **arabesques, paterae,** and urns (Figure 6–1).

Stamped tin ceilings used in the 19th and 20th centuries disappeared from use in the 1930s but are now staging a comeback. In private residences, tin ceilings were occasionally used in halls and bathrooms. In commercial buildings, metal ceilings were used in order to comply with the early fire codes.

Today, the ceiling should not be considered as just the flat surface over our heads that is painted white. The ceiling is an integral part of a room, affecting space, light, heat, and sound, and consideration should be given to making it fit the environment. There are many ways of achieving this integration, such as beams for a country or Old World appearance, a stamped metal ceiling for a Victorian ambience, a wood ceiling for contemporary warmth, or acoustical for today's noisier environments. Ceiling treatments are limited only by the imagination.

PLASTER

There are times when the ceiling should be the unobtrusive surface in a room. When this is required, plastering is the answer. The surface may be smooth or highly textured or somewhere in between. A smooth surface will reflect more light than a heavily textured one of the same color.

The plaster for a ceiling is applied in the same manner as for walls, although it will require scaffolding so that the surface will be within working reach. It will take a longer period of time to plaster a ceiling when compared with a similar wall area, because of the overhead reach.

The ornately carved ceilings of the past are obtained today by using one of three means:

1. Precast plaster, either in pieces or tiles
2. Molded polyurethane foam
3. Wood mouldings, mainly used as **crown mouldings**

The moulded urethane foam mouldings will be discussed in detail in the next chapter, under the heading "Mouldings."

Figure 6–1
*The Matthew Keenan Building, a historical landmark building in
Milwaukee, Wisconsin, used the Coffered Egg & Dart for the
ceiling. Architect: Jordon Miller. Photographer: Eric Oxendorf.
(Photograph courtesy of Above View Mfg. by Tiles Inc.)*

GYPSUM BOARD

The main difficulty with the installation of gypsum board for ceilings is the weight. However, 1/2-inch ceiling panels are specially designed to resist sagging and are equal to 5/8-inch wallboard, installed perpendicular to framing. Gypsum board does require more labor and, again, scaffolding. It may be applied to a flat or curved surface. The seams and screw holes are filled in the same manner as for gypsum board walls. The surface may be perfectly smooth, lightly or heavily textured, with the smooth surface not only reflecting the most light, but also showing any unevenness of the ceiling joists.

By using FRESCO ceiling sheets from Pittcon Industries, a paneled ceiling can be achieved. The 48-inch × 48-inch × 5/8-inch gypsum board raised panel sheets consist of nine 12-inch square panels separated by 4-inch borders and surrounded by a 2-inch border. When joined to an adjacent sheet, these combined borders continue the same 4-inch spacing throughout the installed surface (Figure 6–2).

Figure 6–2
FRESCO™, a raised panel drywall, is designed to replace wood panels, seen here on a ceiling. (Photograph courtesy of Pittcon Industries, Inc.)

BEAMS

This is probably the oldest of ceiling treatments. Originally, the ceiling beams of the lower floor were the floor joists of the room above. The old New England houses had hand-hewn timbers that ran the length of the room; the larger-sized **summer beam** ran across the width. The area between the beams was covered by the floor boards of the room above, or in the case of a sloped ceiling, the wood covering the outside of the roof timbers. Later these floorboards were covered with plaster and the timbers were left to darken naturally. The plaster in between the timbers had a rough or troweled surface. Today, instead of plaster, sometimes a plank ceiling is used in combination with beams.

Today, beamed ceilings are used for a country setting with an Old World or contemporary feeling. The original beams were made of one piece of wood 12 inches or more square, but today, beams of this size are very difficult to obtain.

Very large beams can now be fabricated by gluing strands of veneer together. The technology, pioneered by Trus Joist MacMillan, uses a patented microwave process to bond the strands together, producing a beam that is actually straighter and stronger than a piece of solid sawn lumber. The company is capable of manufacturing a beam that is 66 feet × 11 inches × 19 inches.

There are several methods of imitating the solid heavy look of hand-hewn beams. A box beam may be built as part of the floor joists or as a surface addition. In order to make a box beam appear similar to a hand-hewn beam, the surface must be treated to avoid the perfectly smooth surface of modern lumber.

In contemporary homes, **laminated beams** are used. These consist of several pieces of lumber (depending on the width required) glued together on the wider flat surfaces. Because of the type of construction, laminated beams are very strong. Laminated beams are commonly referred to as "lam" beams.

WOOD

A natural outgrowth of the beamed ceiling is using wood planks or strips to cover the ceiling joists. With the many types of wood available on the market today, wood ceilings are used in many homes, particularly contemporary ones (Figure 6–3).

Almost all types of strip flooring and solid wood for walls may be used on the ceiling. Because of the dark-

Figure 6–3
This beach house in California has 1-inch × 6-inch tongue-and-groove Clear All Heart redwood used horizontally on the walls and ceilings. Floors are of rough-textured Chinese green slate. Architects: Neumann and Scott Rowland, Santa Barbara, California. Photographer: Marvin Sloben. (Photograph courtesy of the California Redwood Association)

ness of wood, it is more suitable for a cathedral or shed ceiling as the darker color appears to lower the ceiling.

Armstrong VX wood ceilings have 24-inch lay-in panels that can be installed in a standard T-bar grid for accessibility and cost-efficient retrofit.

ACOUSTICAL CEILINGS

Residential

As a result of the ceiling being the largest unobstructed area in a room, sound is bounced off the surface without very much absorption. Just as light is reflected from a smooth, high-gloss surface, so sound is reflected or bounced off the ceiling. This is the reason for the textured tiles on the market today, for both residential and commercial interiors. Uncontrolled reverberations transform sound into noise, muffling music and disrupting effective communication.

Acoustical ceilings, however, do not prevent the transmission of sound from one floor to another. The only answer to sound transmission is mass—the actual resistance of the material to vibrations caused by sound waves.

Sound absorption qualities may be obtained by using different materials and different methods. The most well-known is the acoustical **tile** (a 12-inch square) or **panel** (larger than 1 square foot) composed of mineral fiber board. Other materials such as fiberglass, metal, plastic-clad fiber, and fabric may also be used. Sound absorption properties are produced by mechanical dies perforating the mineral fiber board after curing. Metal may also be perforated to improve its acoustical qualities if backed with an absorptive medium.

The Noise Reduction Coefficient (**NRC**) is a measure of sound absorbed by a material, and the NRC of different types of panels may be compared. The higher the number, the more sound reduction is indicated. When making a comparison, be sure tests are made at the same **Hertz** (Hz) range.

The Sound Transmission Class (**STC**) is a single number rating that is used to characterize the sound-insulating value of a partition (wall or ceiling). A partition prevents sound from being transmitted from one area to another; the STC rating denotes approximately how much the sound will be reduced when traveling through the partition. The higher the rating, the less sound will be transmitted through the wall or floor/ceiling.

The Ceiling Attenuation Class (**CAC**) refers to the sound attenuation ability of ceiling systems. CAC rates how much sound will be reduced when it is transmitted through the ceiling of one room into an adjacent room through a shared **plenum.** A higher rating indicates that the material will allow less sound transmission.

Another heading often found in acoustical mineral fiberboard charts is Light Reflectance (**LR**), which indicates the percentage of light reflected from a ceiling product's surface. This LR varies according to the amount of texture on the surface and the value of the color. Some ceiling panels have a mineral fiber substrate with a needle-punched fabric surface.

A 1993 Interior Design Product Award went to Armstrong World Industries for its Cirrus Themes. This product brings whimsy to ceiling design, creating a surrounding that encourages fun, comfort, and a sense of well-being. It can be used in health and daycare facilities, with designs that include Primaries, Letters and Numbers, Trains, Critters, Animal Paw Prints, Stars, or Leaves (Figure 6–4).

The Cirrus Borders™ help to break up a large ceiling expanse with a choice of classical, transitional, or contemporary panel detailing. Panel designs combine to create borders, continuous patterns, or island focal areas on the ceiling (see Figure 6–4).

Installation. In private residences, two or three methods of installation are used. If the tiles are to be

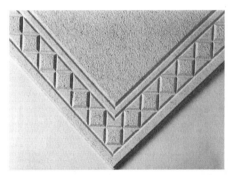

Figure 6–4
"Trains" from the Armstrong Cirrus Themes series is especially suitable for daycare centers and pediatric hospitals. Also part of the Cirrus series are the borders as shown in the second picture. (Photographs courtesy of Armstrong World Industries, Inc.)

used over an existing ceiling, they may be cemented to that ceiling provided the surface is solid and level. Tiles have interlocking edges that provide a solid joining method as well as an almost seamless installation. If the existing ceiling is not solid or level, furring strips are nailed up so that the edges of the tile may be glued and stapled to a solid surface.

The third type of installation is the suspended ceiling, which consists of a metal spline suspended by wires from the ceiling or joists. The tiles are laid in the spline so that the edges of the panels are supported by the edge of the T-shaped spline. The splines may be left exposed or they may be covered by the tile. There are several advantages to using a suspended ceiling:

1. Damaged panels are easily replaced.
2. The height of the ceiling may be varied according to the size of the room or other requirements.

With an exposed spline, it is easy to replace a single panel; the damaged panel is merely lifted out. However, if the spline is covered, the damaged panel or panels are removed and when replacing the last panel, the tongue is removed.

Maintenance. Celotex suggests that a soft gum eraser be used to remove small spots, dirt marks, and streaks. For larger areas, or larger smudges, a chemically treated sponge, rubber pad, or wallpaper cleaner is used. The sponge rubber pad or wallpaper cleaner must be in fresh condition. Nicks and scratches may be touched up with colored chalks. Dust is removed by brushing lightly with a soft brush, clean rag, or by vacuuming with the soft brush attachment.

Do not moisten tile excessively. Never soak tile with water. Wash by light application of sponge dampened with a mild liquid detergent solution: about 1/2 cup in 1 gallon of water. After saturating the sponge, squeeze it nearly dry, and then lightly rub the surface to be cleaned. Use long, sweeping, gentle strokes. Clean in the same direction as the texture if tile is ribbed or embossed.

When painting, avoid clogging or bridging surface openings. Use a paint of high hiding power since it is desirable to keep the number of coats to a minimum on acoustical tile. Paint greatly affects the NRC of the acoustical material.

Hiding character of paint is a particularly important consideration when a single coat is expected to cover stains or change the color of the tile. Some paint manufacturers provide specific formulations that have high hiding power and low combustibility and are not likely to bridge opening in the tile. Wherever possible, apply paint of this type. In all cases, apply paint as thinly as necessary.

Commercial

Acoustical ceiling products have become a mainstay of commercial installations. Because of the flexibility of the movable office partitions, audio privacy is very necessary. In this day of electronic word processors and data processing equipment, the noise of an office has been somewhat reduced from the noisy typewriters of the past, but telephones and voices can still cause distracting sounds. Productivity is increased in a quieter environment, but a noiseless environment is easily disrupted.

The advantages of a residential suspended acoustical ceiling also apply to commercial installations, but the major reason for using a suspended ceiling in commercial work is the easy access to wiring, telephone lines, plumbing, and heating ducts.

The traditional approach to lighting is **luminaires** recessed at specific intervals into the acoustical ceiling. The fixtures are often covered by lenses or louvers to diffuse the light.

Today, not only lighting but also heating and cooling are incorporated into the installation. This is done in several ways. The heating and cooling duct may be spaced between the modules in one long continuous line or individual vents may be used. One interesting innovation is that in which the whole area between the suspended ceiling and the joists is used as a plenum area with the conditioned air entering the room below through orifices in the individual tiles.

One word of warning: If you are replacing a ceiling that may contain asbestos, OSHA has some very stringent regulations and safety precautions that must be strictly adhered to.

METAL

Metal ceilings were originally introduced in the 1860s as a replacement for the ornamental plasterwork that decorated the walls and ceilings of the most fashionable rooms of the day. Once in place, it was discovered that these ceilings had other benefits. Unlike plaster, the metal could withstand rough use and could also be more easily maintained than plaster, which would flake, crack, and peel. Many of today's metal ceilings are actually steel, which can be prepainted, or plated with copper, brass, or chrome.

Shanker uses a 665-ton press built in 1928 (completely rebuilt to modern manufacturing standards in

1986) to stamp its 2-foot × 4-foot panels, which can be painted or left steel gray, protected by a coat of clear polyurethane. Copper and brass plating are also available as are color coatings baked onto the metal.

Stamped metal ceilings now come in 1-foot squares or come 1 foot × 2 feet, 2 feet × 4 feet, or 2 feet × 8 feet and are installed by tacking the units to furring strips nailed 12 inches apart. These stamped metal ceilings are very suitable for Victorian restoration work.

A contemporary metal ceiling is made up of 3-inch to 7-inch wide strips of painted or polished aluminum, which clip to special carriers. The polished metals also include bronze and brass finishes and can provide an almost mirrored effect. These ceilings may be used in renovations over existing sound ceilings or for new construction.

The metal strips may be installed as separate strips with the area between the strips left open to the plenum, or the open space may be covered with an acoustical pad. They may also be covered with a joining strip on the face to form a flush surface, or on the back for a board-on-batten effect.

Steel or aluminum panels, perforated or unperforated, are available in 12-inch squares or as large as 24 × 48-inch panels. Armstrong produces the Cassettes metal ceilings, 24-inch square aluminum panels perforated or nonperforated, installed with stainless steel spring clips and hidden edge details that allow all panels to move laterally for 100 percent downward panel access. These are perfect for tight plenum conditions found in corridors, computer rooms, and many rehab ceiling applications.

OTHER CEILING MATERIALS

A vinyl-coated, embossed aluminum, bonded to the mineral fiber substrate, results in an easily maintained, corrosion-resistant, durable product. Grease vapor concentrations may be wiped clean with a sponge or a mild detergent solution, thus providing a suitable ceiling for commercial kitchens, laboratories, and hospitals.

Mirrors are not recommended for ceilings; instead, A-Look Mirror Quality Decorative Metals from Wilsonart® may be used. (A-Look Mirror Quality Decorative Metals are supplied by Mitsubishi KASEI America Inc.) Colors available are chrome, bronze, and gold. There are also seven etched designs (Figure 6–5).

Another product, the Classique™ lay-in panels

from Chicago Metallic, can also provide a reflective finish. These panels are all metal so there are no fibers to create dust or dirt. Typical applications for metal panels are in high traffic areas such as restaurants, retail outlets or lobbies, and in "clean room" areas such as hospitals, high-tech computer rooms, audiovisual facilities, and laboratories. The noncombustible metal surface is easily cleaned with mild soap or window cleaner.

Now being manufactured in this country are Barrisol® Stretch Ceilings. The mirror-like finish of Barrisol will visually enlarge areas with a variety of colors and textures. The stretch material can be used for flat, inclined, or vaulted ceilings. Barrisol is impermeable to moisture and is rated Class I within the requirements of the ASTM E84 Flame Spread Test. When a blunt instrument makes a deep depression in this material, it will return to its original shape when slight heat is applied, and it is so strong it will support a person's weight. Additionally, this product can be installed over an existing ceiling, thereby lowering labor costs and eliminating disposal problems.

The use of an acoustical mineral fiberboard will also increase fire resistance. Custom-designed fiberglass core panels are used to upgrade existing ceilings as well as for new custom-designed ceiling construction. This same material may be used for baffles constructed of 1-, 1 1/2-, or 2-inch thick panels. They are hung from the ceiling by means of wire attached to eyelets installed in the top edge.

Baffles hung perpendicular to a ceiling are an established and highly effective way to create additional sound-absorbing surfaces, especially in interiors lacking sufficient surfaces for wall-mounted panels. Baffles are not only functional, but decorative too, and can be used for signage or to denote areas or departments within a larger space. As with other Panel Solutions products, baffles may be covered with the fabric or wallcovering of your choice.

With the increasing awareness of making buildings earthquake proof, the Seismic Panel from Simplex Ceiling Products fulfills that requirement. Seismic is an aluminum ceiling with a completely concealed suspension system that will resist failure as a result of multidirectional movement during an earthquake. The panels will not disengage from the suspension regardless of what motion the earth's surface may make during an earthquake.

Not all acoustical ceilings are flat. Many are **coffered** in 2- to 4-foot square modules. These panels may or may not include luminaires. A cell system from Hunter Douglas dramatizes design while masking plenum clutter.

Figure 6–5
A-Look from Wilsonart was used for the ceiling of the Chicago O'Hare Airport over the moving sidewalk, creating interesting reflections. (Photograph courtesy of Ralph Wilson Plastics)

Compässo™ is a suspension trim from USG Interiors. The Compässo Design Kit includes a special template of the standard curves available to a 1/4 and 1/8 of an inch scale—it even includes a supply of graph paper. You can sketch your design using ideas such as those listed.

Place dramatic accents with soffits a few inches below the ceiling.

Suspend floating island far below the ceiling plane.

Build powerful peninsulas extending prominently from the wall.

Separate or emphasize areas; create distinct spaces within spaces.

Bring special lighting or acoustical privacy closer.

USG then provides, at no charge, an AutoCAD® drawing for your approval, complete with parts identification. The grid can also be used without the panels for an open-cell effect.

CERAMIC TILE

For a ceiling that is easy to wipe clean, or in very moist areas such as bathrooms and showers, ceramic tile may be installed.

BIBLIOGRAPHY

Rothery, Guy Cadogan. *Ceilings and Their Decoration.* London, England: T. Werner Laurie, 1978.

Time-Life Books. *Walls and Ceilings.* Alexandria, VA: Time-Life Books, 1980.

GLOSSARY

Arabesque. Elaborate scroll designs either carved or in low relief.

CAC. Ceiling Attenuation Class. The CAC rates how much sound will be reduced when it is transmitted through the ceiling of one room into an adjacent room through a shared plenum.

Coffered. Recessed panels in the ceiling. May or may not be decorated.

Crown moulding. The uppermost moulding next to the ceiling.

Hertz. Unit of frequency measurement. One unit per second. Abbreviation: Hz.

Laminated beam. Several pieces of lumber glued to form a structural timber.

LR. Light Reflectance. The amount of light reflected from the surface.

Luminaires. Lighting fixture, with all components needed to be connected to the electric power supply.

NRC. Noise Reduction Coefficient. The average percentage of sound reduction at various Hz levels.

Panel. A ceiling unit larger than one square foot.

Patera. A round or oval raised surface design.

Plenum. The space between the suspended ceiling and the floor above.

Reliefs. A design that is raised above the surrounding area.

STC. Sound Transmission Class. A number denoting the sound-insulating value of a material.

Summer beam. A main supporting beam in old colonial homes, in the middle of the room, resting on the fireplace at one end and a post at the other.

Tile. Ceiling tile (12-inch square).

___ *Chapter 7*

Other Components

MOULDINGS

To an interior designer, trim and mouldings are what icing is to a cake; they cover, enhance, and decorate a plain surface. Basically, heavily carved or ornate trim is used in a traditional setting, whereas the simpler trim is used where a contemporary feeling is desired.

Materials for trim and mouldings should be constructed from easily shaped stock. When wood is desired, both pine and oak are used, providing details that are easily discernible and smooth. Trim should always be **mitered** at the corners; that is, the joint should be cut at a 45° angle.

Other materials include solid surface materials, such as Corian®, or Gibraltar® used for counters. These are also fairly easy to shape, depending on the thickness, and are used most often in commercial and medical installations.

Bases are universally used to finish the area where the wall and floor meet. There are several reasons for the use of a base or skirting: It covers any discrepancy or expansion space between the wall and the floor; it forms a protection for the wall from cleaning equipment; and it may also be a decorative feature. The word *base* is used to describe all types of materials, including those mentioned earlier as well as vinyl or rubber.

Baseboard is the term used for wood bases only.

When a plain baseboard is used, the wood should be smoothly sanded on the face and particularly on the top edge to facilitate cleaning. The exposed edge should be slightly beveled to prevent breaking or chipping. The more traditional baseboard usually has a shaped top edge with a flat lower part. This may be achieved with one piece of wood 3 1/2 to 7 inches wide or may consist of separate parts, with a base moulding on top of a square-edged piece of lumber. A base shoe may be added to either type. Traditional one-piece baseboards are available as stock mouldings from the better woodworking manufacturers (Figure 7–1).

For residential use, windows come prefabricated with the **brickmold** or exterior trim attached. The interior casing (the exposed trim) may be flat or molded and is applied after the window and walls have been installed and the windows **caulked,** an extremely necessary step in these days of energy conservation. The interior casing usually matches the baseboard design, although the size may vary (see Figure 7–1).

Doors, particularly for residential use, often come **prehung,** and after installation of the door frame, the space between the jamb and the wall is covered by a casing. This casing matches the profile of the one used around the windows, with the width of the casing determined by the size, scale, and style of the room.

Crown and **bed mouldings** are used to soften the sharp line where ceiling and walls meet. Cove mould-

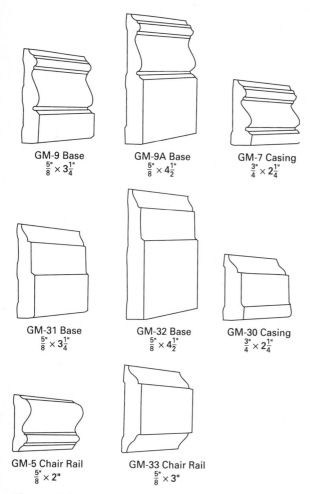

Figure 7–1
Wood bases, chair rails, and casings. (Courtesy of Granite Mill)

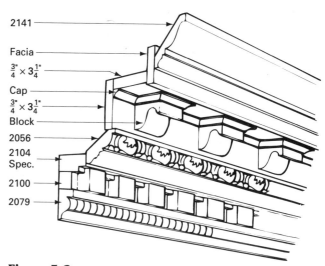

Figure 7–2
Ten piece wooden ceiling cornice. (Drawing courtesy of Driwood Period Moulding)

ings also serve the same purpose, the difference being that crown mouldings are more intricately shaped and cove mouldings have a simple curved face. Cove mouldings may be painted the same color as the ceiling, thus giving a lowered appearance to the ceiling. Cornice mouldings may be very ornate and made up of as many as ten separate pieces of wood (Figure 7–2).

Chair rails are used in traditional homes to protect the surface of the wall from damage caused by the backs of chairs. These rails may be simple strips of wood with rounded edges or may have shaped top and bottom edges, depending upon the style of the room (see Figure 7–1). The installed height should be between 30 and 36 inches. When trim is to be painted, it should be made of a hard, close-grained wood. If it is to be left natural, it should be finished in the same manner and be of the same material as the rest of the woodwork.

When plywood panels are used on the walls, the edges are sometimes covered with a square-edge batten. In more traditional surroundings, a molded batten is used.

Picture mouldings, as the name implies, were used to create a continuous projecting support around the walls of a room for picture hooks. The picture moulding has a curved top to receive the picture hook. Of course, when pictures are hung by this method the wires will show, but this method is used in older homes, museums, and art galleries where frequent rearranging is required. No damage is done to the walls, as with the more modern method of hanging paintings by means of concealed wires. The picture moulding is placed just below or several inches below the ceiling. Wherever the placement, the ceiling color is usually continued down to the top of the moulding.

An infinite variety of patterns may be used for mouldings. They may be stock shapes and sizes, custom ordered, or shaped to the designer's specifications by the use of custom-formed shaper blades. This latter method is the most expensive but does achieve a unique moulding.

Wood mouldings may also be covered with metal in many finishes, including bright chrome, brass, copper, or simulated metal finishes for use as picture frame moulding, interior trim, and displays.

All the mouldings discussed thus far have been constructed of wood. When a heavily carved cornice moulding is required, the material may be a **polymer.** NMC Focal Point makes a polymer moulding by direct impression from the original wood, metal, or plaster article. This direct process gives the reproduction all the personality, texture, and spirit of the original, but with several advantages. The mouldings are much less expensive than the hand-carved originals. They are lighter weight and therefore easier to handle; they may be nailed, drilled, or screwed; and they are receptive to sanding. Another feature is that, in many cases, the original moulding consisted of several pieces, but modern technology has produced these multiple mouldings in a one-piece strip, thus saving on installation costs. For contract installations where fire-rated materials must be used, Specicast™ meets the ASTM E-84, Class A specifications.

NMC Focal Point is the licensee for architectural details for the Victorian Society in America, Colonial Williamsburg Foundation, National Trust for Historic Preservation, and the Historic Natchez Foundation. Nor is the contemporary market being ignored; NMC Focal Point has Santa Fe and Taos step mouldings.

Polymer mouldings are factory-primed in white;

however, if a stained effect is desired, the mouldings may be primed beige and stained with Mohawk non-penetrating stain. Careful brush strokes will simulate grain and, when skillfully applied, the effect is very convincing.

In Chapter 6, ceiling medallions were mentioned as a form of ceiling decoration. Originally, when these medallions were used as **backplates** for chandeliers, they were made of plaster, but again the polymer reproductions are lightweight and easy to ship. The medallions are primed white at the factory, ready to paint. The use of a medallion is not limited to chandeliers, but is also used as a backplate for ceiling fans (Figure 7–3).

Other materials used in ornate ceiling cornices are gypsum with a polymer agent that is reinforced with glass fibers for added strength. A wood fiber combination may also be used.

Some products used internationally are light weight

Figure 7–3
On the left, the D'Evereux Rim from NMC Focal Point. On the right, the Woodlawn Stair Brackets from the Classic Collection of NMC Focal Point. (Photographs courtesy of NMC Focal Point)

QUARRYCAST® or glass-reinforced gypsum and ce-
ment-cast architectural products, including all types of
mouldings as mentioned above. Also available are
round or tapered column covers, with capitals and bases.

Other reproductions from the past include the
dome and the niche cap. When first designed, they
were made of plaster or wood, which was then hand
carved. These domes and niche caps can provide a
touch of authenticity needed in renovations; in fact,
many of NMC Focal Point's designs have been used in
restoration of national historical landmarks. Niche
caps have a shell design and form the top of a curved
recess that usually displays sculpture, vases, flowers,
or any other prized possession.

Stair brackets are another form of architectural detail and are placed on the finished stringer for a decorative effect (see Figure 7–3).

DOORS

Doors for residential use are commonly constructed of
wood, although metal may also be used. In commercial applications, however, doors are more likely to be
made of metal or laminate because of fire codes and
ease of maintenance.

Wood Doors

Flush doors are perfectly flat and smooth with no decoration whatsoever (Figure 7–4). There are several
methods of construction. A hollow core is used for
some interior residential flush doors. The core of the
door is made up of 2- to 3-inch wide solid wood for
the **rails** and 1 to 2 inches of solid wood for the **stiles,**
with an additional 20-inch-long strip of wood called a
lock block in the approximate hardware location. The
area between the solid wood is filled with a honeycomb or ladder core. In less expensive doors, this is
covered by the finish veneer. More expensive doors
have one or two layers of veneer before the finish veneer is applied. Thus, a flush door may be of 3-, 5-, or
7-ply construction.

The better flush door is constructed with a lumber
core, also known as staved wood, where wood blocks
are used in place of the honeycomb or ladder core of
the hollow-core door. The staved or lumber core may
or may not have the blocks bonded together. With
staved-core doors, the inside rails and stiles are narrower because this type of construction is more rigid
(see Figure 7–4).

Another method of construction utilizes a particleboard or flakeboard core with a crossband veneer

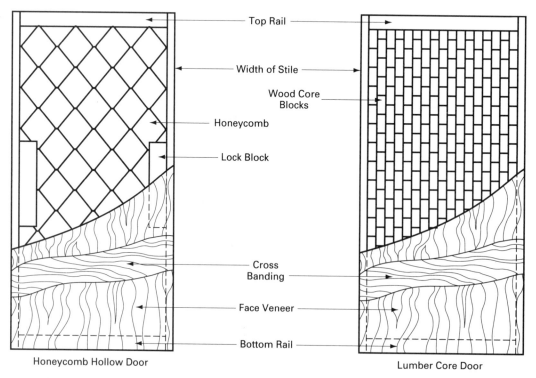

Top Rail

Width of Stile

Wood Core
Blocks

Honeycomb

Lock Block

Cross
Banding

Face Veneer

Bottom Rail

Honeycomb Hollow Door

Lumber Core Door

Figure 7–4
Door construction.

to which the face veneer is attached. A particleboard door core is warp resistant, solid, with no knots or voids, and it has good insulation values and sound resistance, thereby limiting heat loss and transfer of sound waves.

Flush doors for commercial installations may have a high-pressure decorative laminate (HPDL) as the face veneer or, for low maintenance, a photogravure or vinyl covering similar to the paneling discussed in Chapter 5.

Commercial installations do not always require a moulding; they are merely set into the wall. In other words, the wall meets the door jamb.

There are three methods of achieving the paneled look in doors. One uses a solid ornate **ogee** sticking; in other words, the stiles and rails are shaped so that the moulding and stile or rails are all one piece of wood. The second method is the same as above only using a simpler **ovolo** sticking. The third method uses a **dadoed** stile and rail, and the joining of panel and stile is covered by a separate applied moulding. If the panel is large, it will be made of plywood and a moulding used; if under 10 inches in width, it may be of solid wood. Paneled doors reflect different periods, as do paneled walls. When period paneling is used, the doors should be of similar design (Figure 7–5).

Dutch doors for residential use consist of an upper and a lower part. Special hardware joins the two parts to form a regular door or, with the hardware undone, the top part may be opened to ventilate or give light to a room, with the lower part remaining closed. Dutch doors are sometimes used commercially as a service opening. In this case, a shelf is attached to the top of the bottom half (Figure 7–6).

Louvers are used in doors where ventilation is needed, such as in cleaning or storage closets or to aid in air circulation. Louvers are made of horizontal slats contained within stile-and-rail frames. Louvers may be set into wood or metal doors, with the louver either at the top and/or bottom, or the center may be all louvered. Some louvers are vision-proof, some adjustable, and others may be lightproof or weatherproof (see Figure 7–6).

One of the most common residential uses for a louvered door is in a bifold door for a closet. For a narrow opening, a bifold door consists of two panels, with larger openings requiring a double set, opening from the middle. The center panel of each pair is hung from the track, and the outer panels pivot at the jamb (see Figure 7–6).

A pocket door, or recessed sliding door, requires a special frame and track that is incorporated into the inside of the wall. The finished door is hung from the track before the casing is attached. The bottom of the door is held in place by guides that permit the door to slide sideways while preventing back and forth movement (see Figure 7–6).

Folding or accordion doors are used where space needs to be temporarily divided. These folding doors operate and stack compactly within their openings. The panels may be wood-veneered lumber core, or particleboard core with a wood-grained vinyl coating. Each panel is 3 5/8 inches or under in width, and the folding doors are available in heights up to 16 feet 1

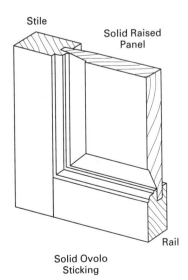

Solid Ovolo
Sticking

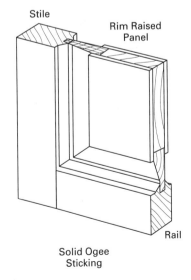

Solid Ogee
Sticking

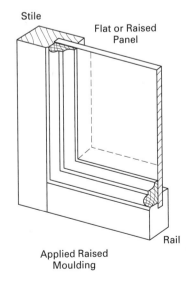

Applied Raised
Moulding

Figure 7–5
Paneled doors.

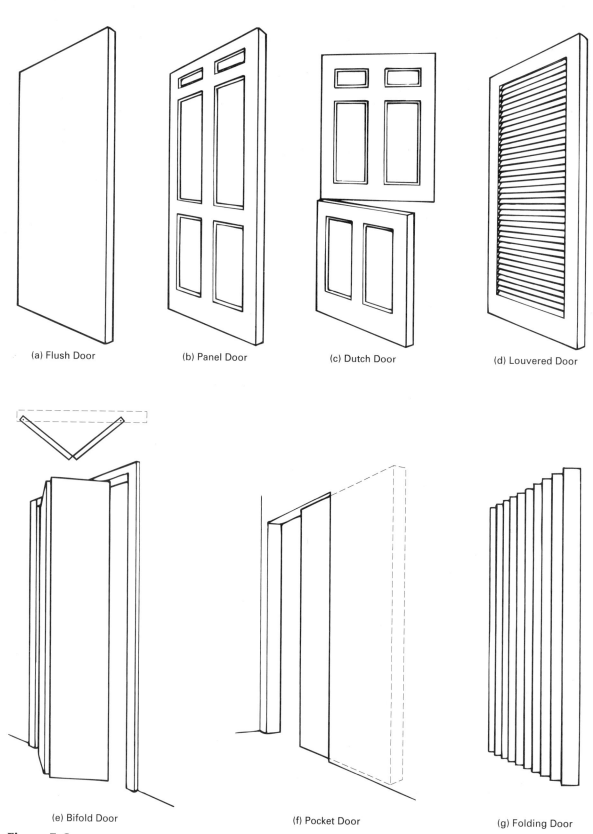

(a) Flush Door (b) Panel Door (c) Dutch Door (d) Louvered Door

(e) Bifold Door (f) Pocket Door (g) Folding Door

Figure 7–6
Types of doors.

inch. Folding doors operate by means of a track at the top to which the panels are attached by wheels. The handle and locking mechanism is installed on the panel closest to the opening edge (see Figure 7–6).

For an Oriental ambience, fixed or sliding Shoji panels are available; these are wood framed with syn-skin inserts, which have an Oriental rice paper look. Pinecrest has a wide variety of Shoji panels, standard or custom, both fixed and sliding (Figure 7–7).

Glass Doors

Sash doors are similar in construction and appearance to panel doors, except that one or more panels are replaced with glass. French doors are often used in residences to open out onto a balcony or patio. They have wood frames and may consist of one sheet of plate glass or may have multiple **lights** in each door. French

doors are most often installed in pairs and usually open out.

When French doors or other styles of doors are installed in pairs, one is used as the primary door. The second one is stationary with a flush bolt or special lock holding it tight at top and bottom. To cover the joining crack between the pair of doors and to make them more weathertight, an **astragal** is attached to the interior edge of the stationary door. If required, both doors may be used to enlarge the opening.

Instead of using large sliding glass doors, the trend seems to be to use patio doors, either singly or in pairs. These are similar in appearance to the double French doors, except that they open into the house instead of out. If double doors are used, the astragal is on the exterior edge of the secondary door.

Glass doors for residential use may have a wood or metal frame and may pivot on hinges or have one

Figure 7–7
*Pinecrest Shoji panels were used at Mitsui & Co. (USA) Inc., in
Houston, Texas, by Architectural Woodwork Corp., Houston, Texas.
(Photograph courtesy of Pinecrest)*

sliding panel with the second panel stationary. Whenever full-length glass is used, by law it must be tempered or laminated.

Commercial glass doors must also be made of tempered or laminated glass and are subject to local building codes. The door may be all glass, framed with metal at the top and/or bottom, or framed on all four sides. Because of the nature of an all-glass door, the most visible design feature is the hardware.

Specialty Doors

When X-ray machines are used, special doors must be specified. These flush panel doors have two layers of plywood with lead between; then a face veneer of wood, hardboard, or laminate is applied.

Firedoors have an incombustible material core with fire-retardant rails and stiles covered by a wood veneer or high-pressure decorative laminate. These doors are rated according to the time they take to burn. Depending on materials and construction, this time will vary between 20 minutes and 1 1/2 hours. Local building codes should be consulted before specifying.

Metal Doors

Most metal doors are made of steel, although some are available in aluminum. In the past, metal doors had a commercial or institutional connotation, but today many interior and exterior residential doors and many bifold doors are made of metal. Exterior metal doors were shunned in the past because wood exterior solid core doors had better insulating qualities. The use of polystyrene and polyurethane as a core has now provided a residential metal exterior door with similar insulating qualities, plus it is not as susceptible to temperature changes and warping as is the wood door. Metal doors are available coated with a rust-resistant primer for finishing on site, or they may be prefinished with a heavy baked-on coating.

Exterior Doors

For exterior use, a wood door must be of solid construction. Hand-carved doors are available for exterior use, but manufacturer's specifications must be studied carefully, because a door that appears to be hand carved may actually be molded to imitate hand carving at less expense, but with less aesthetic appeal.

Specifications for Doors. Most doors are

available prehung, that is, assembled complete with frames, trim, and sometimes hardware. The bored hole is ready for installation of the lock. This bored hole must have a **backset** that corresponds to the selected hardware. Most prehung doors come predrilled with a 2 3/8-inch hole; however, most designer type hardware looks better with a 2 3/4-inch backset or even more. The 2 3/8-inch backset, with knob type hardware, can sometimes result in scraped knuckles.

For prehung doors, door hand is determined by noting hinge location when the door opens away from the viewer (i. e., if the hinge jamb is on his/her right, it is a right-hand door). In the case of a pair of doors, hand is determined from the active leaf in the same way. If prehung doors are specified, door handing should be included (see Figure 7–12).

The following additional information should be provided when specifying doors:

Manufacturer.

Size—including width, height, and thickness.

Face description—species of wood, type of veneer, rotary or sliced. If not veneer, then laminate, photogravure, vinyl coating, or metal.

Construction—crossbanding thickness, edge strips, top and bottom rails, stiles, and core construction.

Finishing—prefinished or unfinished.

Special detailing—includes specifying backset for hardware and any mouldings. Special service such as glazing, firedoors.

Warranty—differs whether for interior or exterior use.

Door Hardware

Some of the following material is excerpted, by permission, from the Tech Talk bulletin, "Butts and Hinges," published by the Door and Hardware Institute's (DHI) bulletin. This material is very technical and has been simplified for ease of understanding.

Hinges

The two parts of a hinge consist of metal plates known as **leaves** and are joined by a pin that passes through the **knuckle** joints. **Counter-sunk** holes are predrilled in the leaves. **Template hardware** has the holes drilled so accurately as to conform to standard drawings, thus assuring a perfect fit. Template **butt hinges** have the holes drilled in a crescent shape (Figure 7–8).

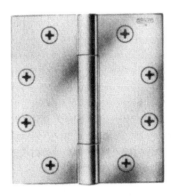
Full Mortise

Half Mortise

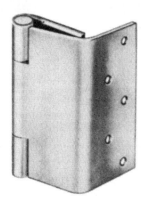
Half Mortise Swing Clear

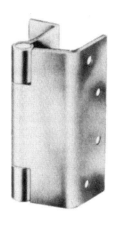
Full Mortise Swing Clear

Full Surface

Half Surface

Full Surface Swing Clear

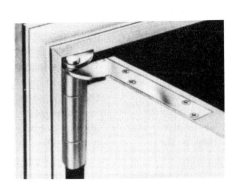
Pivot Reinforced

Half Surface Swing Clear

Figure 7–8
Types of hinges.

Hardware in general is not thought of unless it does not work properly, and the door unit will not function properly if the proper hinging device is not specified.

There are hinges that will meet all types of application. The standards developed by the Builders Hardware Manufacturers Association (BHMA) and promulgated through the American National Standards Institute (ANSI) are extremely helpful in making the correct selection of the proper hinge. These standards include ANSI/BHMA A156.1, A156.7, and A156.17.

The following eight points are intended to assist in proper hinge selection.

1. Determine the Type of Hinge. Before the type of hinge can be selected, there are several pieces of information that are needed, because certain types of hinges can be used with only certain types of construction. A door may be made of wood (WD) or hollow metal (HM), and the frame may be wood, hollow metal, or channel iron frame (CIF).

The four classifications of hinges are

Full Mortise. Both leaves are **mortised,** one leaf to the door and one leaf to the frame (WD or HM with WF or HMF).

Half Mortise. One leaf is mortised to the door and the other is surface applied to the frame (HM with CIF).

Full Surface. Both leaves are applied to the surface, one to the door and the other to the frame (metal core door [MCD] or HM with CIF).

Half Surface. One leaf is mortised to the frame and the other is surface applied to the face of the door (WD with WF or MCD with HMF).

There is one easy way to remember what the hinge is called. The full mortise and the full surface really are no problem. However, the half mortise and the half surface sometimes are difficult to keep straight.

You need only remember that the name of the hinge refers to what is done to the door. A half mortise hinge is mortised to the door and surface applied to the frame. A half surface hinge is surface applied to the door and mortised to the frame.

There are several features available for the full mortise hinge that must be indicated before going further.

Swaging is a slight offset to the hinge leaf at the barrel (or pin area). This offset permits the leaves to come closer together when the door is in the closed position. If the hinge were to be left in the natural state after the knuckle was rolled, the hinge would be referred to as **flatback.** A flatback hinge has a gap between the leaves of approximately 5/32 of an inch. This would allow heat and air conditioning to escape, not to mention the unsightly gap between the door and the frame.

The standard swaging on standard weight and heavy weight Full Mortise hinges provides 1/16 of an inch clearance between the leaves when the leaves are in the closed position.

The four types mentioned above are named after the manner in which they are attached on the door. There are several special use hinges that should also be mentioned here.

One is the *Swing Clear* type. This is used mostly in hospitals and institutional buildings when the passage area must be the full width of the opening. One such use would be an 8-foot-wide corridor that required the full opening for the passage of two beds or carts. With the use of Swing Clear hinges this passage can be accomplished.

The hinges are designed to swing the door completely clear of the opening when the door is opened 95°. The standard way to accomplish this degree of opening is to build a pocket in the wall to accept the door. This allows the door to be concealed in the wall and not obstruct the flow of traffic.

Concealed hinges are used on doors when the design precludes the use of visible hinges. With concealed hinges, one side is mounted on the inside of the frame and the second side is mortised into the door. These hinges are available in 90° to 100° openings or 176° (Figure 7–9).

Concealed hinges for cabinets are different in construction. They are not visible from the outside of the cabinet but are surface mounted on the inside of the cabinet door (see Figure 7–9).

Spring hinges may be single acting or double acting and are used when automatic closing is required. In some cases the spring hinge is used as a substitute for door closers. This is a less costly product than the standard door closer, but it does not have the control or back check features that a door closer will offer. The tension is adjustable.

2. Select the Proper Weight and Bearing Structure. Two factors determine the weight and structure of the hinge: weight of door and frequency of use. Because of the large variety of door sizes and weights, hinges are placed into three groups:

Figure 7–9
Concealed hinges. (Courtesy Grass America and Soss)

Heavy weight—Ball bearing

Standard weight—Ball bearing

Standard weight—Plain bearing

Bearings may be ball, oil impregnated, or antifriction. Ball bearing hinges are packed with grease to assure a quiet, long-life hinge. These types of bearings should always be specified for doors equipped with door closers.

3. *Determine the Size of the Hinge.* In order to determine the proper size of the hinge, several pieces of information are necessary:

Door height

Door width

Door thickness

Door weight

Trim dimension required

One hinge for every 30 inches of door height or fraction thereof is the general rule of thumb to determine the number of hinges per door leaf.

Doors up to 60 inches in height—2 hinges

Doors over 60 inches but not over 90 inches in height—3 hinges

Doors over 90 inches but not over 120 inches in height—4 hinges

4. *Determine Type of Material.* There are three base materials from which hinges are manufactured: steel, stainless steel, and brass. Each base material has different qualities.

Steel—has great strength but is a corrosive material. If the atmosphere in which steel is used is not stable, it will begin to rust. The best application for steel is in a controlled environment, such as inside a building where the temperature and humidity are controlled.

Stainless Steel—also has great strength. It is rust resistant and has decorative value in that it can be polished to a satin or bright finish. Other considerations may be geographical, such as on the seacoast or in industrial areas where acids or atmospheric conditions exist.

Brass—is noncorrosive, rust resistant, and very decorative; however, it has less strength than the steel or stainless steel material. Brass is often used where appearance is of great concern. It may be polished and plated in many various finishes.

Both steel and stainless steel hinges may be used on listed or labeled door openings. Brass material may not be used on fire-rated or labeled openings because of its low melting point.

5. *Determine the Type of Finish.* All steel and brass material hinges can be plated to match the available finishes that are listed in ANSI/BHMA A156.18 Materials and Finishes. Reading this standard will be extremely helpful during the specification process.

6. *Determine Handing.* This was discussed under the Door section, page 132.

7. *Determine Pin and Tip Style.* The pins may be **loose, nonrising** loose, nonremovable loose, or **fast.**

A loose pin hinge enables a door to be removed easily from the frame by merely pulling out the pin. A loose pin type of hinge is used for hanging less expensive residential doors. One problem with a loose pin is that the pin has a tendency to rise with use. If the pin of the loose pin hinge is visible, even a locked door can be removed from its frame by simply removing the pin. A nonrising loose pin has the same advantage as the loose pin but without the rising problem.

The nonremovable pin has a small set screw in the body of the barrel. This set screw is tightened down against the pin. In most cases the pin has a groove in the position where the set screw makes contact, allowing the set screw to seat. The set screw is positioned so it cannot be reached unless the door is opened. If pin removal is necessary, the set screw merely is removed and the pin tapped from the bottom in the usual manner.

Fast-riveted pins are pins that are **spun** on both ends, making the pin permanent.

Another security feature in hinges is the security safety stud, which places a stud in one leaf and a locking hole in the other leaf. When the door is closed the stud is anchored into the opposite leaf. Even if the hinge pin is removed, the door is secure because the leaves are locked together.

An important point must be made here. All of these features are intended as deterrents only. If someone wants to gain entry through a door badly enough, eventually the intruder will get through!

The tips of the pins may be flat button or decorative. Flat button tips are normally furnished unless something else is specified. Decorative type tips also are available from most manufacturers, such as Acorn, Ball, Steeple, and Urn. These are used in highly

decorative areas of offices and in more expensive residences. Steeple tips are used on colonial hinges.

8. *Electric Hinges.* Over the past fifteen years, hinge manufacturers have made some changes that have revolutionized the hardware industry. With the introduction of electric hinges, we now have the ability to monitor the position of the door, transfer power, and incorporate both functions into the same hinge. With this technology, it is now possible to electrify other hardware items such as locks and exit devices.

Electric hinges can be modified to be either exposed on the surface of the hinge or concealed in the hinge. When concealed, the modifications are not visible and normally go undetected by personnel using the openings.

Electrically modified hinges are for low voltage power transfer only (50 volts or under). Normally modifications are made to full mortise hinges. However, monitoring can be supplied on a half surface hinge when the need arises.

Most manufacturers will require the use of a mortar box or jamb box in order to protect the wire terminations on the inside of the frame. If this box is not used, the grout that may be poured into the frame will destroy the wiring and usually will void the warranty on the product.

Locks

The needs of the client and the expected usage of a lock will determine which lock will be selected. For residential uses, security is probably the foremost criterion, whereas for a commercial installation, heavy usage will necessitate not only a secure lock, but also one built to withstand constant use.

There are three weights or grades of locks. The most expensive is heavy duty; then comes standard duty. The least expensive is the light duty or builders grade. The first two types are made of solid metal with a polished, brushed, or antique finish; the light duty grade has a painted or plated finish that may be removed with wear.

The **Door & Hardware Institute** describes the four types of locks and bolts as follows:

BORED TYPE—These types of locks are installed in a door having two round holes at right angles to one another, one through the face of the door to hold the lock body and the other in the edge of the door to receive the latch mechanism. When the two are joined together in the door they comprise a complete latching or locking mechanism [Figure 7–10].

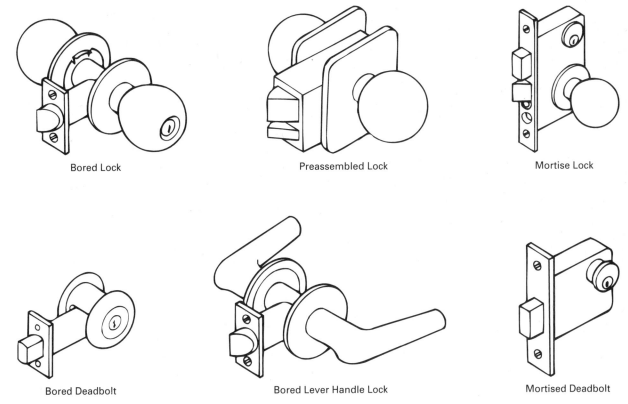

Figure 7–10
Types of locks.

Bored type locks have the keyway (cylinder) and/or locking device, such as push or turn buttons, in the knobs. They are made in three weights: heavy, standard, and light duty.

PREASSEMBLED TYPE—The preassembled lock is installed in a rectangular notch cut into the door edge. This lock is one that has all the parts assembled as a unit at the factory; when installed, little or no disassembly is required.

The assembly must be tight on the door, without excessive play. Knobs should be held securely in place without screws, and a locked knob should not be removable. **Roses** should be threaded or secured firmly to the body mechanism. The trim has an important effect in this type of lock because working parts fit directly into the trim. Regular backset for a bored lock is 2 3/4 inches but may vary from 2 3/8 to 42 inches.

Preassembled type locks have the keyway (cylinder) in the knobs. Locking devices may be in the knob or in the inner case. Regular backset is 2 3/4 inches. The lock is available only in heavy duty weight [see Figure 7–10].

MORTISE LOCK—A mortise lock is installed in a prepared recess (mortise) in a door. The working mechanism is contained in a rectangular-shaped case with appropriate holes into which the required components, cylinder, knob, and turn-piece spindles are inserted to complete the working assembly. Regular backset is 2 3/4 inches. These locks are available in heavy duty and standard duty weights. **Armored** fronts are also available.

In order to provide a complete working unit, mortise locks, except for those with **deadlock** function only, must be installed with knobs, levers, and/or other items of trim as described in the section on door knobs and handles. Regular backset is 2 3/4 inches. These locks are available only in heavy duty weight.

The lock achieves its function by means of various types of bolts. The bolt is a bar of metal that projects out of the lock into a strike prepared to receive it.

LATCH BOLTS—The function of a latch bolt is to hold the door in a closed position. A latch bolt is spring actuated and is used in all swinging door locks except those providing **deadbolt** function only. It has a beveled face and may be operated by a knob, handle, or turn.

AUXILIARY DEAD LATCH—An auxiliary dead latch is a security feature and should be required on all locks used for security purposes unless a deadbolt function is specified. This feature deadlocks the latch bolt automatically and makes it virtually impossible to depress the latch bolt when the door is closed.

DEADBOLT—A deadbolt is a bolt having no spring action and is activated by a key or thumb turn. It must be manually operated. Deadbolts provide security. When hardened steel inserts are used, the security is greater. The minimum **throw** should be 1/2 inch, but today most throws are 1 inch.

LOCK STRIKES—A **lock strike** is a metal plate mortised into the door jamb to receive and to hold the projected latch bolt and, when specified, the deadbolt also, thus securing the door. It is sometimes called a keeper. The proper length lip should be specified so that the latch bolt will not hit the door jamb before the strike.

A wrought box should be installed in back of the strike in the jamb. This box will protect the bolt holes from the intrusion of plaster or other foreign material, which would prevent the bolt from projecting properly into the strike.[1]

Electric Strike. This is an electromechanical device that replaces an ordinary strike and makes possible remote electric locking and unlocking. When a control mechanism actuates the electric strike, this allows the door to be opened without a key and relocked when closed. It is used in secured apartment buildings.

Rim Locks. Rim locks were first used at the beginning of the 18th century and are attached to the inside of the door stile. They are used today in restoration work or in new homes of medieval English, Salt Box, Cape Cod, or colonial styles. Because they are exposed to view, the case and other parts are finished brass.

The simplest type of door hardware is the passage set in which both knobs are always free and there is no locking mechanism. An example would be the door between a living or dining room and a hallway. A **springlatch** holds this type of door closed.

Bathroom doors require a privacy lock. This type

locks from the inside in several ways. Some have a push button located on the interior rose, some have a turn or push button in the interior knob, and still others have a turnpiece that activates a bolt. In the case of an emergency entrance, all privacy locks have some means of opening from the outside, either with an emergency release key or by using a screwdriver.

When the type of use has been decided upon, the style of handle, rose, and finish is selected. There are many shapes of knobs from ball to round with a semi-flat face to round with a concave face that may even be decorated. Knobs may be made of metal, glass, porcelain, or wood (Figure 7–11). Grip handle entrance locks combine the convenience of button-in-the-knob locking with traditional grip handle elegance. Grip handles should be of cast brass or cast bronze. Interior colonial doors may have a thumb latch installed on the stile surface.

Natural finishes take the color of the base metal in the product and may be either high or low luster. Applied finishes result from the addition by plating of a second metal, a synthetic enamel, or other material.

Polished brass and bronze finishes are produced by buffing or polishing the metal to a high gloss before applying a synthetic coating. Satin brass and natural bronze finishes are obtained by dry buffing or scouring, and the resulting finish is then coated. The most popular of the plated finishes are the chromiums, both polished and satin.

Locks, which include all operating mechanisms, come with numerous finishes, including brass, bronze, chrome, and stainless steel in bright polish, satin, antique, or oil rubbed.

Lever handles must be specified for all public and commercial doors, as per ADA. When blind persons have access to areas that might be dangerous, such as a doorway leading to stairs, the knob must be knurled or ridged to provide a tactile warning. Schlage has an access bow key with an easily identifiable 1 1/4-inch top.

Roses are used to cover the bored hole in the door and may be round or square and may also be decorated. Some locks, particularly the mortise type, have **escutcheon** plates instead of roses. These are usually rectangular in shape.

Security, function, and handing are all factors to be considered with regard to mortise locks.

In the architectural hardware industry the position of the hinges on a door—in terms of right or left as viewed from the outside of the building, room or space to which the doorway leads—determines the hand.

The outside is the side from which security is

(a)

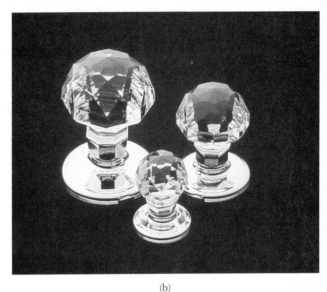

(b)

(c)

(d)

Figure 7–11
The wide variety of door hardware is shown. (a) Decorated porcelain knobs are shown in three sizes, for doors, bifold doors, and cabinet knobs. (b) Twenty-four percent lead crystal door knobs in the same three sizes. (Photographs courtesy of Gainsborough Hardware Industries Inc.) (c) Knobs and levers may be traditional or contemporary with a variety of finishes. (Photograph courtesy of Baldwin Hardware Co.) (d) An exterior grip handle thumb latch suitable for use in a colonial home. (Photograph courtesy of Schlage Lock Company)

necessary. In a series of connecting doors (as in a hotel suite) the outside will be the side of each successive door as one comes to it proceeding from the entrance. For two rooms of equal importance with a passage between, the outside is the passage side.

Strictly speaking, the door itself is only right or left hand; the locks and the latches may be reverse bevel. However, it is necessary to include the term reverse and to specify in accordance with the con-

ventions shown here. This will prevent any confusion as to which side is the outside—especially important when different finishes are desired on opposite sides of the door.

Hardware in general may be:

1. *Universal.* Used in any position. (Example: surface bolt)
2. *Reversible.* Hand can be changed by revolving

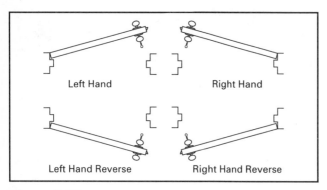

Figure 7–12
Door handing.

from left to right, or by turning upside down or by reversing some part of the mechanism. (Example: many types of locks and latches)

3. *Handed.* (Not reversible) Used only on doors of the hand for which designed. (Example: most **rabbeted** front door locks and latches)

Although the hardware item specified may be reversible, or even universal, it is good practice to identify the hand completely, in accordance with the conventions stated here.[2]

While some locks are reversible and may be used on a right- or left-hand door, others must be ordered as right- or left-handed (Figure 7–12).

Security has become an important feature of lockset selection. Schlage H-Series Interconnected locks are recommended by the experts. From the outside a key must be used. The lock features simultaneous retraction of both the latch and the deadbolt from the inside, by turning the knob or lever, providing panic-proof exiting. It is recommended by police and fire departments to provide compliance with many life safety and security codes.

Another security type lock is InnerKey Digital Deadbolt from InteLock® (Figure 7–13). Simply turn the knob right or left (as you would a combination lock) to enter the three- or four-digit secret access code. The numbers appear one by one in the bright, easy-to-read LED display. Once the correct sequence has been entered, the 1-inch thick deadbolt can be released simply by turning its outside ring. Without the right code, the ring spins freely, resisting attempts to wrench or pry it open. If an intruder doesn't enter the correct code within 30 seconds of trying to unlock the door, a tamper alarm will sound. Easily activated by a switch, a temporary code allows guests and tradespeople to enter without revealing the master code.

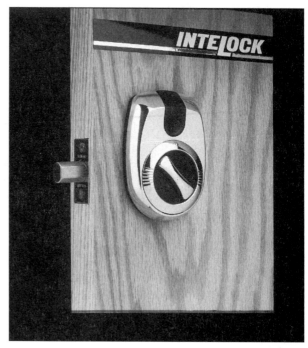

Figure 7–13
On the left is the InnerKey Digital Deadbolt from the outside, the key side. On the right is the interior side. (Photographs courtesy of InteLock Technologies)

This code can be changed in seconds. InnerKey comes preprogrammed and includes batteries that will last up to 3 years, and InnerKey warns you 3 months in advance of the batteries' becoming low.

A door should be controlled at the desired limit of its opening cycle in order to prevent damage to an adjacent wall, column, equipment, the door or to its hardware. This control is achieved by stops and holders, which may be located at the floor, wall or overhead.

Floor stops are available in varied heights, sizes, shapes, and functions. They may have a mechanism such as a hook or friction device to hold the door open at the option of the user. Height of door from floor, shape of stops, and location in relation to traffic are important considerations.

Wall stops or bumpers have the advantage of being located where they do not conflict with floor coverings or cleaning equipment and do not constitute a traffic hazard.

There are two commonly used types of floor holders; the spring-loaded "step-on" type and the lever or "flip-down" type. Neither type acts as a stop.[3]

Door controls used in commercial installations may be overhead closers, either surface-mounted or concealed, and floor-type closers. These devices are a combination of a spring and an oil-cushioned piston that dampens the closing action inside a cylinder. Surface-mounted closers are more accessible for maintenance, but concealed closers are more aesthetically pleasing. Overhead installations are preferred because dirt and scrub water may harm the operation of a floor-type closer (Figure 7–14). A 3-second delay is required to provide safe passage for a handicapped person.

In public buildings, all doors must open out for fire safety. A push plate is attached to the door, or a fire exit bar or panic bar is used. Slight pressure of the bar releases the rod and latch. For handicapped use, this bar should be able to be operated with a maximum of 8 pounds of pressure.

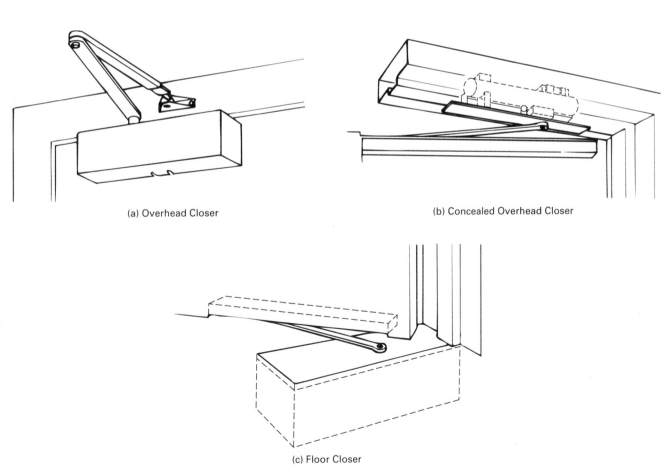

(a) Overhead Closer

(b) Concealed Overhead Closer

(c) Floor Closer

Figure 7–14
Door controls.

Door opening may also be accomplished by the use of an electronic eye; when the beam is broken, the door opens. For areas requiring special security, doors can be opened by a specially coded plastic card similar to a credit card, or a numbered combination may be punched in. The combination may be changed easily, thus eliminating the need to reissue keys.

These security systems are being used more and more in restrooms of office buildings and other special areas where access is restricted to certain personnel.

To eliminate having to carry several keys for residential use, all the locksets for exterior doors may be keyed the same. This may be done when the locks are ordered, or a locksmith can make the changes later but at a greater expense.

When specifying locksets, the following information must be provided: manufacturer's name and style number; finish; style of knob and rose; backset, wood or metal door; thickness of door; and door handing.

Installation should be performed by a professional locksmith or carpenter to ensure correct fit, with no door rattles or other fitting problems.

HOSPITAL HARDWARE

Hardware for hospitals and health-related institutions includes items that might not be found in any other type of building. Because it may be used by aged, infirm, sick, or handicapped persons, the hardware must meet all the ADA requirements of safety, security, and protection, and yet be operable with a minimum amount of effort.

Modifications of hinges may include hospital tips for added safety, special length and shape of leaves to swing doors clear of an opening, and hinges of special sizes and gauges to carry the weight of lead-lined doors.

Hospital pulls are designed to be mounted with the open end down allowing the door to be operated by the wrist, arm, or forearm when the hands are occupied.[4]

BIBLIOGRAPHY

Buchard, H. Matt, Jr., AHC. "Butts and Hinges." *Tech Talk.* McLean, VA: Door and Hardware Institute, 1990.

Ortho Books. *Finish Carpentry Techniques.* San Francisco: Chevron Chemical Company, 1983.

National Particleboard Association. *Builder Bulletin, Particleboard Shelf Systems.* Gaithersburg, MD: National Particleboard Association, 1988.

Time-Life Books. *Doors and Windows, Home Repairs & Improvement.* Alexandria, VA: Time-Life Books, 1978.

ENDNOTES

[1]*Basic Architectural Hardware.* McLean, VA: Door and Hardware Institute, 1985, pages 5, 8–10.
[2]Ibid., page 25. (Emphasis added)
[3]Ibid., page 23.
[4]Ibid.

GLOSSARY

Armored. Two plates are used to cover the lock mechanism in order to prevent tampering.

Astragal. Vertical strip of wood with weather-stripping.

Backplate. An applied decorative moulding used on ceilings above a chandelier or ceiling fan.

Backset. The horizontal distance from the center of the face-bored hole to the edge of the door.

Bed moulding. Cornice moulding.

Brickmold. Exterior wood moulding to cover gap between door or window frame.

Butt hinges. Two metal plates joined with a pin, one being fastened to the door jamb or frame and the other to the door (see Figure 7–8).

Caulk. Filling a joint with resilient mastic. Also spelled calk.

Chair rail. Strip of wood or moulding that is placed on the wall at the same height as the back of a chair to protect the wall from damage (see Figure 7–1).

Counter-sunk. Hole prepared with a bevel to enable the tapered head of a screw to be inserted flush with the surface.

Dado. A groove cut in wood to receive and position another member.

Deadbolt or deadlock. Hardened steel bolt with a square head operated by a key or turn piece (see Figure 7–10).

Door and Hardware Institute (DHI). Represents the industry.

Escutcheon. Plate that surrounds the keyhole and/or handle.

Fast pin. Pin is permanently in place. Nonremovable.

Flatback. Hinge with a gap between the leaves of approximately 5/32 of an inch.

Knuckle. Cylindrical area of hinge enclosing the pin.

Leaves. Flat plates of a pair of hinges (see Figure 7–10).

Lights. Small panes of glass, usually rectangular in shape.

Lock strike. A plate fastened to the door frame into which the bolts project.

Loose. Able to be removed.

Mitered. Two cuts at a 45° angle to form a right angle. See Figure 8–2.

Mortised. Set in to the surface.

Mullions. Center vertical member of paneling.

Nonrising. Pins that do not ride up with use.

Ogee. A double curved shape resembling an S-shape.

Ovolo. A convex moulding, usually a quarter of a circle.

Polymer. A high-molecular weight compound from which mouldings are made.

Prehung. Frame and door are packaged as one unit.

Rabbeted. A longitudinal slot in a piece of wood.

Rails. Cross members of paneling, whether on walls or doors.

Rose. The plate, usually round, that covers the bored hole on the face of the door.

Springlatch. Latch with a spring rather than a locking action.

Spun. Moving the metal by means of a spinning action and applied pressure that changes the shape of the metal.

Sticking. The shaping of moulding.

Stiles. Vertical members of paneling, whether on walls or doors.

Swaging. A slight offset to the hinge at the barrel.

Template hardware. Hardware that exactly matches a master template drawing, as to spacing of all holes and dimensions (see Figure 7–8, full mortise hinge).

Throw. The distance a bolt penetrates when fully extended.

Figure 5
Dining room with Bradbury & Bradbury Neo-Grec roomset, Terra cotta colorway. (Photograph courtesy of Bradbury & Bradbury)

Figure 6
A commercial style range with stainless steel hood is flanked by Wood-Mode's Cherry cabinets with the Colony door style featuring a square recessed panel. Its classic, clean lines adapt to a variety of design motifs – from colonial cottage to contemporary postmodern. The Chef's Accessory System, an innovative modular system mounted on both sides of the range, puts practically everything you might need during meal preparation at your fingertips. The refrigerator on the back wall features appliance panels that are designed to precisely match the door and drawers of the cabinetry. (Photograph courtesy of Wood-Mode)

Figure 7

This light and airy kitchen, which features Wood-Mode's Newport alpine white, includes cabinets for various types of storage: open shelving and mullion glass door cabinets for display pieces; wall cabinets for grocery items and dinnerware; drawers for cookware and small appliances; and even an easy access tambour cabinet for whatever you choose to put in it. (Photograph courtesy of Wood-Mode)

Figure 8

The interest in this conventionally sized room by Bernson, ASID, is achieved through the use of angles, curves, and different elevations. The softness and radii of the plumbing pieces counter the look and feel conveyed by the stone. The sharply angled planters and steps are softened by foliage and suede-like wallcovering. Kohler fixtures include Pillow Talk™ pedestal lavatory, toilet with seat, and bidet with cover in Black Black™; Watersilk™ whirlpool with pillows in Black Black; and Taboret™ lavatory faucet. (Photograph courtesy of Kohler)

_____ Chapter 8

Cabinet Construction

To properly select or design well-made cabinet work, it is necessary to become familiar with furniture construction. By studying the casework joints, specifiers will be able to compare and contrast similar items and make an informed decision on which piece of furniture, or which group of cabinets, is the most value for the money.

When designing casework and specifying materials, several parts need definition. AWI has the following "Identification of Parts":

A. Exposed Parts—Surfaces visible when:
   1. Drawer fronts and doors are closed.
   2. Cabinets and shelving are open-type or behind clear glass doors.
   3. Bottoms of cabinets are seen 42" (1067 mm) or more above finish floor.
   4. Tops of cabinets are seen below 78" (1981 mm) above finish floor, or are visible from an upper floor or staircase after installation.

B. Semi-Exposed Parts—Surfaces visible when:
   1. Drawers/doors are in the open position.
   2. Bottoms of cabinets are between 30" (762 mm) and up to 42" (1067 mm) above finish floor.

C. Concealed Surfaces—Surfaces are concealed when:
   1. Surfaces are not visible after installation.
   2. Bottoms of cabinets are less than 30" (762 mm) above finish floor.
   3. Tops of cabinets are over 78" (1981 mm) above

finish floor and are not visible from an upper level.
   4. Stretchers, blocking, and/or components are concealed by drawers.[1]

Note: A toe space is required for such items as kitchen cabinets and dressers, to provide a recessed space for toes under the doors or drawers. This toe strip is usually 3 inches high and 3 inches deep. These measurements vary slightly with the European kitchen cabinets having a height of 5 7/8 inches.

The three grades mentioned in the wood paneling section of Chapter 5 still apply to cabinetry (Figure 8–1).

JOINERY OF CASE BODY MEMBERS

The type of joinery used for case construction varies according to the grade. For Tops, Exposed Ends, and Bottoms the only acceptable joint for Custom is Spline or Biscuit, glued under pressure (approximately 3 per foot of joint). For Premium a Stop Dado, glued under pressure, and either nailed, stapled or screwed (fasteners will not be visible on exposed parts) or doweled, glued under

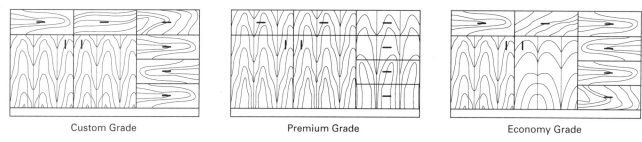

Custom Grade   Premium Grade   Economy Grade

Figure 8–1
Illustration of grades in cabinetry. (Reprinted with permission from Architectural Woodwork Institute)

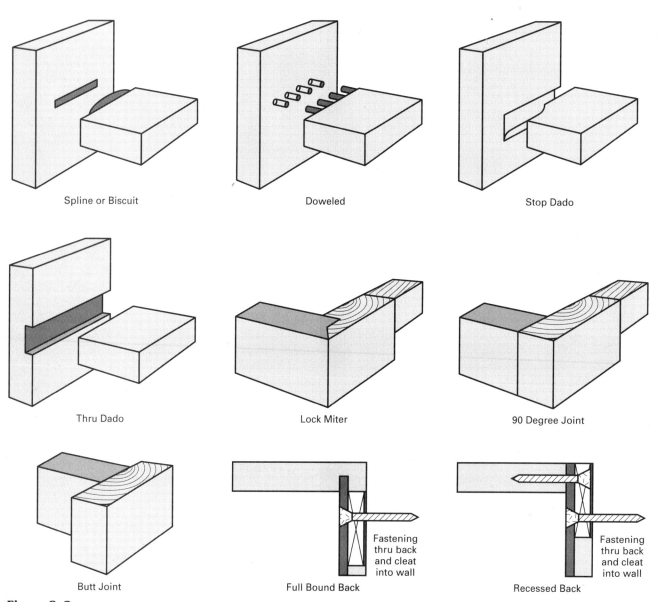

Spline or Biscuit   Doweled   Stop Dado

Thru Dado   Lock Miter   90 Degree Joint

Butt Joint   Full Bound Back   Recessed Back

Fastening thru back and cleat into wall

Fastening thru back and cleat into wall

Figure 8–2
Joinery of face frames to cabinet body members. (Reprinted with permission from Architectural Woodwork Institute)

pressure (approximately 4 dowels per foot) and for Economy Thru Dado, glued under pressure.

For the exposed end corner details and face frame attachment, Custom requires butt joint, glued and finish nailed; for Premium, mitered joint: Lock miter or spline or biscuit, glued under pressure (no visible fasteners) or non-mitered joints, i.e., 90 degree applications: glued under pressure (no visible fasteners and Economy butt joints, finish nailed are acceptable [Figure 8–2].[2]

EDGE TREATMENTS

Edge banding is required when materials other than solid wood are used. This edge treatment is used for case body members and shelves but varies according to the grade and finish of the work. When a transparent finish is used for premium grade, the visible edge should be banded with the same species as the face and pressure glued. In custom grade the banding should be a compatible species, pressure glued, and for economy grade the compatible species may be nailed. When an opaque finish is used, premium grade requires close-grain material, pressure glued, custom grade uses close-grain material glued and nailed, and economy grade edge is filled and sanded (Figure 8–3).

DRAWERS/DOORS

Drawer or door fronts may be of one of the three following design categories, and construction will vary with the grade. Custom Grade will use glue and finish nail, Premium Grade pressure will be glued (no nails or other visible fasteners), and Economy Grade may be nailed.

1. Conventional Flush Construction—with face frame
   Conventional Flush Construction—without face frame
2. Overlay—flush
   Overlay—reveal
3. Exposed face frame—lipped

Figure 8–3
Edge treatments. (Reprinted with permission from Architectural Woodwork Institute)

Conventional Flush Construction. With this style of construction, door and drawer faces are **flush** with the face of the cabinet. This style is highly functional and allows the use of different thicknesses of door and drawer fronts. Conventional as well as concealed hinges are available for a variety of door thicknesses (see Chapter 7 and Figure 8–4[e]).

This is the most expensive of the five styles because increased care is necessary in the fitting and aligning of the doors and drawers, as well as the cost of providing the face frame. This style does not lend itself to the economical use of decorative laminate covering.

Conventional Flush Construction—Without Face Frame. The design features of this casework style are the same as conventional flush with face frame except that the face frame has been eliminated resulting in a cost savings. This style does not lend itself to the economical use of decorative laminate covering. (See Figure 8–4[d].)

Flush Overlay Construction. This kind offers a very clean, contemporary look since only the doors and drawer fronts are visible in elevation. When specified, grain matching between doors and drawer fronts can be achieved by having all pieces cut from the same panel. This style is increasingly popular and lends itself well to the use of decorative laminate for exposed surfaces. Conventional as well as concealed hinges are available for a variety of door thicknesses (see Chapter 7 and Figure 8–4[a]).

Reveal Overlay Construction. In this style, the separation between doors and drawer fronts is accented by the **reveal**. The style is equally suited to either wood or decorative laminate construction. Although the detail shown here incorporates a reveal at all horizontal and vertical joints, this can be varied by the designer. It should be noted that a reveal over 1/2 inch would require the addition of a face frame, and therefore, an increase in cost. The addition of a face frame would also change the hinge requirement. With or without a face frame, this style allows the use of conventional or concealed hinges (see Figure 7–8 for types of hinges and also Figure 8–4[b] and [c]).

Exposed Face Frame—Lipped. The lipped design is the type used in traditional furniture. The door or drawer fronts are similar to reveal overlay construction except that the fronts have an overlapping edge that partially covers the frame. It is an economical style since the fitting tolerances of the doors and drawers are less critical. (See Figure 8–4[f].)

When an exposed face frame with a flush drawer front is designed, a **stop** must be incorporated to prevent too much inward travel. As has been mentioned before, flush doors and drawers are the most expensive form of design because of the tolerances and hand-fitting of such extras as drawer stops (Figure 8–4).

When doors or drawers are covered with a high-pressure laminate, a **balancing** laminate must be used on the reverse side of the substrate.

JOINTS

The type of joint for drawer construction also varies according to the grade.

Premium Grade, Multiple Dovetail, or French Dovetail. Doweled

Custom Grade, Lock Shoulder
Economy Grade, Square shoulder[3] (see Figure 8–5)

A **dado** is a cross-grain machining feature with a square or rectangular section, and a **groove** is machined along the grain of the wood with a similar section. All drawer bottoms should have a minimum thickness of 1/4 of an inch and should be captured into grooves on drawer sides, fronts, and backs. This construction creates a bottom panel that is permanently locked into position.

Wood may also be joined together with a **butt joint** by merely placing the two pieces of wood at right angles to each other. For a traditional type of paneling, **stile** and rail construction is used. This consists of a panel that may be flat, raised, or have a beveled edge. The vertical side strips are called stiles, and the horizontal strips at the top and bottom are called rails.

The rails, stiles, and **mullions** may themselves be

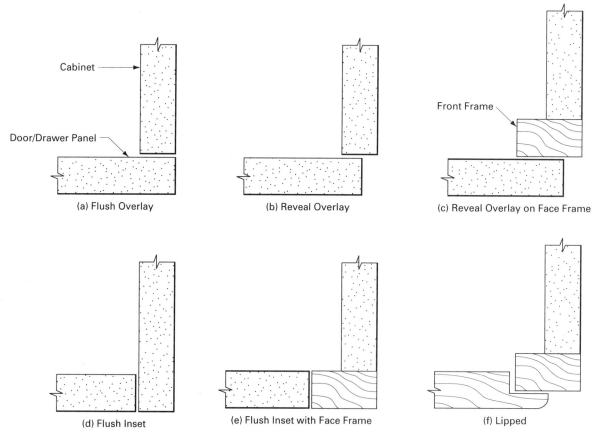

Figure 8–4
Plan view of door/drawer construction.

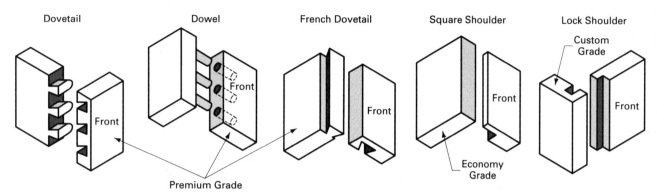

Figure 8–5
Drawer joinery. (Reprinted with permission from Architectural Woodwork Institute)

shaped into an **ovolo** or **ogee** moulding, or, to give a more intricate design, a separate moulding may be added. For raised panels under 10 inches in width, solid lumber may be used in custom grade, but for premium grade or wider panels, plywood is used with an attached edge of solid lumber, which is then beveled (see Figure 7–5).

Panels are assembled by means of mortise and tenon, or dowel joints. At the joining of the panel and the stiles and rails, a small space is left to allow for the natural expansion and contraction of the panel. This type of construction may sometimes be known as floating panel construction, and is advisable where there are great variations in humidity. Panels that are glued have no allowance for this expansion and contraction and may split if movement is excessive.

Since the detail and design options in this type of paneling are virtually unlimited, the AWI suggests that certain minimum information should be provided to properly estimate and detail this type of paneling:

Panel layout

Grain patterns and relationships

Stile and rail construction

Moulding details

Panel construction

Joinery techniques

DRAWER GUIDES

Drawer guides are an important feature of well-made casework. They may be constructed of wood or metal. If wood is selected, it should have both male and fe-

male parts made of wood. Wood drawer guides are found mainly in wood furniture and are usually centered under the drawer, but they may also be attached to the side of the case, with the drawer sides being dadoed to accommodate the wood guide. The reverse procedure may also be used, with the guide attached to the drawer side and the frame dadoes receiving the guide. Paste wax should be applied to the wood guides to facilitate movement.

The type of metal drawer slide selected depends on several factors: travel, width of drawer, action, and load factors.

Travel is the maximum extension compared to the closed length. Typically, most slides are either 3/4 or full travel. Special extension lengths are available with modified travel. Generally, the longer the travel, the less load a slide can carry and vice versa.

A "3/4 Travel" slide has extension of approximately 75% of its length.
A "Full Travel" slide has extension approximately equal to its length.
An "Over-Travel" slide has travel greater than its length.

Drawer width affects the rigidity of the installation. In wide drawers, the slides will rack from side to side. Excessive racking can degrade performance and shorten life expectancy.

The type of mechanism used to carry the load determines many of the quality aspects of a slide, such as performance, motion, noise, and the "fit and feel." Slides may use rollers, ball bearings, friction fits, or any combination in achieving movement. Generally, better action requires more rollers or ball bearings in supporting and distributing large loads.

Knape & Vogt (KV) designates drawer slides in "Pounds Class" categories. KV uses **dynamic** loading to determine load ratings. **Static** and dynamic loads affect slide performance differently. Static load capacity is significantly higher than dynamic load capacity. A fixed static weight will gain momentum and other dynamic forces when set in motion. A load in motion induces more stress and fatigue.

The "Pound Class" categories are used within the slide industry as general guidelines for drawer slide selection. These categories are general in nature, and *not* the same as actual load ratings. Specific load ratings vary by slide length and the application.[4]

Types of mounting include Side Mount, which requires adequate side clearance and drawer side height; Bottom Mount, which has limited selection, primarily for pull-out shelf applications; and Top Mount, which also has limited selection, primarily for under-counter drawers.

Other features may include "stay closed" slides that have a built-in feature to prevent unintentional opening. Self-closing drawers will close without assistance from 4" to 6" of extension. A positive stop with trip latch removal means a trip latch must be activated to affect drawer removal. (This feature prevents drawers from accidentally being pulled completely out of position.) With lift-out removal a drawer may be lifted from the cabinet when fully extended.

CABINET HARDWARE

The type of hardware selected will depend upon the design category. With an exposed face frame and a flush door, heavy-duty **exposed hinges** may be used or they may be concealed. **Concealed hinges** are recessed into the door, attached to the side of the frame, and hidden from view when the cabinet door is closed (see Figure 7–10). A half-mortise or half-surface hinge with a decorative end to the pin may be used where a semiconcealed hinge is desired. Lipped doors are hung by means of a semiconcealed hinge. Flush overlay and reveal overlay doors may be hung by using semiconcealed or concealed hinges. **Pivot hinges** are often used for fitting doors to cabinets without frames. Pivot hinges are particularly useful on plywood and particleboard doors. Only the pivot shows from the front when the door is closed (see Figure 7–9

for a pivot hinge). A piano hinge or continuous hinge is used on drop-leaf desks and on the doors of some fine furniture. Because they are installed the whole length of the edge, they support the weight of the door in an efficient manner (Figure 8–6).

Cabinet doors and drawers may be designed without pull hardware by having a finger pull either as part of the door or drawer construction, or by the addition of a piece of shaped wood, plastic, or metal to the front of the door. It is necessary to design these finger pulls in such a manner that the doors or drawers open easily without breaking fingernails.

Cabinet pull hardware may be knobs, rounded or square, or handles ranging from simple metal strips to ornately designed ones. The material from which this hardware is constructed may be wood, porcelain, plastic, or metal. It is necessary to select hardware that is compatible with the design of the cabinets or furniture. For traditional or period cabinets, authentic hardware should be chosen.

In order to hold cabinet doors shut, some form of catch is needed. There are five different types: **friction**, roller, magnetic, **bullet,** and touch catch. A friction catch, when engaged, is held in place by friction. The roller catch has a roller under tension, that engages a recess in the **strike plate.** The magnet is the holding mechanism of a magnetic catch and, in a bullet catch, a spring-actuated ball engages a depression in the plate. A touch catch releases automatically when the door is pushed. Many of these catches have elongated screw slots that enable the tension of the catch to be adjusted (Figure 8–7). Some hinges are springloaded, eliminating the need for a catch.

SHELVES

For shelves, or when the case body is exposed, the following construction methods are used: *Through dado* is the conventional joint used for assembly of case body members, and the dado is usually concealed by a case face frame. *Blind dado* has an applied edge "stopping" or concealing the dado groove and is used when case body edge is exposed. *Stop dado* is applicable when veneer edging or solid lumber is exposed (see Figure 8–5).

The span and thickness of shelves varies according to the purpose of the shelves. The AWI has the following specifications for shelves:

[For closet and utility shelving] ends and back cleats to receive clothes rods or hooks shall be 3/4 by 3 1/2 inches. Ends and back cleats which do not receive clothes rods or hooks shall be 3/4 by 1 1/2

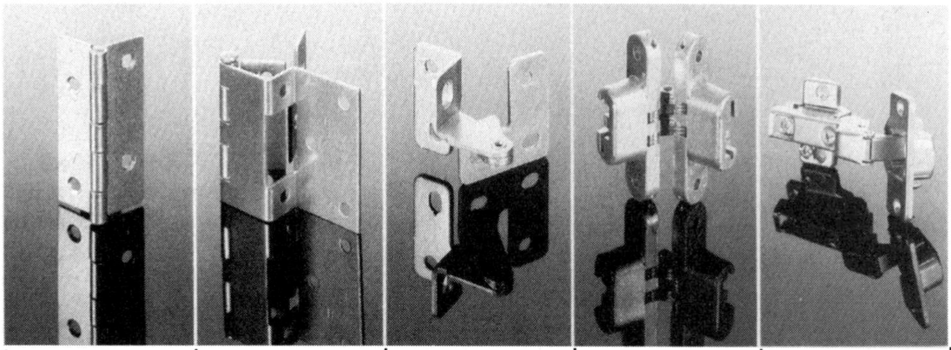

Applications	Conventional Flush Front with Face Frame	Conventional Flush Front Reveal Overlay Flush Overlay	Reveal Overlay Flush Overlay	Conventional Flush with Face Frame	Reveal Overlay Flush Overlay Conventional Flush without Face Frame
Strength	High	Very High	Moderate	Low	Moderate
Concealed when closed	No	No	Semi	Yes	Yes
Requires Mortising	Yes	Occasionally	Usually	Yes	Yes
Cost of Hinge	Low	Moderate	Low	High	High
Ease of Installation (cost)	Moderate	Easy	Moderate	Difficult	Very Easy
Can be easily adjusted after installation	No	No	No	No	Yes
Remarks	door requires hardwood edge			door requires hardwood edge	1. Specify degree of opening 2. No catch required

Figure 8–6

Architectural casework hardware. (Reprinted with permission from Architectural Woodwork Institute)

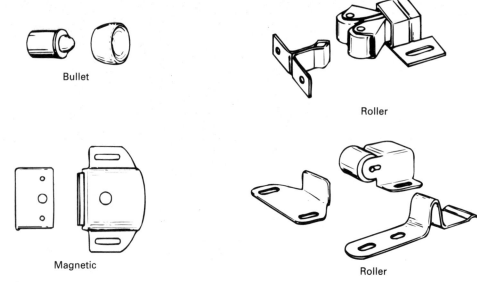

Figure 8-7
Cabinet catches.

TABLE 8-1
Maximum Shelf Spans in Inches for Uniform Loading

	END SUPPORTED MAXIMUM SPAN						MULTIPLE SUPPORTS MAXIMUM SPAN					
	INDUSTRIAL PARTICLEBOARD 1-M-2			MDF			INDUSTRIAL PARTICLEBOARD 1-M-2			MDF		
LOAD*	1/2	5/8	3/4	1/2	5/8	3/4	1/2	5/8	3/4	1/2	5/8	3/4
Inches												
50.0	15	19	23	15	19	23	21	26	31	20	25	30
45.0	16	20	24	16	19	23	22	27	32	21	26	32
40.0	17	21	25	16	20	24	22	28	34	22	27	33
35.0	17	22	26	17	21	25	23	29	35	23	28	34
30.0	18	23	27	18	22	27	25	31	37	24	30	36
25.0	19	24	29	19	23	28	26	33	39	25	32	38
20.0	21	26	31	20	25	30	28	35	42	27	34	40
17.5	22	27	32	21	26	31	29	36	43	28	35	42
15.0	23	28	34	22	27	33	31	38	45	30	37	44
12.5	24	30	35	23	29	34	32	40	48	31	39	46
10.0	26	32	38	25	31	37	34	43	50	33	41	49
7.5	28	34	40	27	33	39	37	46	54	36	45	53
5.0	31	38	44	30	37	43	41	51	60	40	49	58

*Load in pounds per square foot.

Courtesy of National Particleboard Association.

inches. Shelf thickness shall be a minimum of 3/4 of an inch if not specified, or shall be as specified by the design professional in relation to anticipated load.[5]

To increase a shelf's visible thickness, use a dropped edge or applied moulding.

The following information is used with permission of the National Particleboard Association (NPA): Particleboard and **Medium Density Fiberboard (MDF)** are often specified for shelves, and designers should be aware of fairly specific applications. Kitchen cabinets, for example, normally will be designed for a uniform load of 15 pounds per square foot (psf), closets 25 psf, and books 40 psf. (See Table 8–1 for maximum shelf spans in inches for uniform loading.) This table has been abbreviated to only include information needed by designers. The use of underlayment and overhanging shelves has been omitted. The Builders Bulletin, Particleboard Shelf Systems, may be obtained from the NPA.

Proper use of the table is explained below.

1. *Design.* The critical factor in shelf design is the span between supports and the load you expect to put on the shelf. Installation of extra support between the end supports will allow use of the Multiple Support values.

2. *Load Factor.* This table is based on pounds per square foot (psf) loading. Known weight that is not in the form of uniform loading psf will have to be converted before the table may be used. To determine the uniform load in psf, convert the inches of the shelf to square feet by dividing by 144 inches (one square foot); divide the expected load by the answer and you will get the uniform load. For example, a shelf is 9 inches x 36 inches or 324 square inches. To convert to square feet, divide by 144 inches and you get 2.25 square feet. If you have a 50-pound load, divide it by the square footage (2.25) and your uniform load is 22.2 psf.

3. *Continuous Support.* The most efficient use of load-bearing capacity involves using end supports with continuous support all along the rear edge of the shelf fastened at 6-inch intervals. For shelves up to 12 inches wide you may double the span listed under the "End Supported" heading when the same load is applied. For continuously supported shelves over 12 inches but less than 24 inches wide, first triple the load you are designing the shelf to hold. Then, find

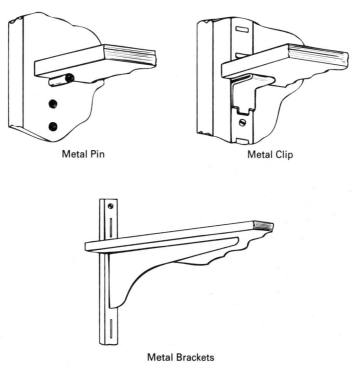

Metal Pin

Metal Clip

Metal Brackets

Figure 8–8
Shelf supports.

the span listed under the "End Supported" heading for that treble loading. Next, double that span for the original load. This analysis does not apply to shelves wider than 24 inches or longer than 6 feet.

When shelves are to be permanently installed, some form of dado may be used for positioning. The type used depends upon the frame construction. Another permanent installation uses a wood quarter round at the desired height.

If, however, the shelves are to be adjustable, there are several methods of support. The type used in fine china cabinets is a metal shelf pin. A number of blind holes, usually in groups of three, are drilled 5/8 of an inch apart in two rows on each interior face of the sides. The metal shelf pins are then inserted at the desired shelf level.

Metal shelf standards have slots every inch, with two standards on each side running from top to bottom of the shelf unit. Four adjustable metal clips are inserted at the same level into these slots. The metal strips may be applied to the inside surface of the shelf unit or they may be dadoed into the interior face.

When metal brackets are used, the shelf standards are attached to the back wall surface instead of to the sides (Figure 8–8).

BIBLIOGRAPHY

Architectural Woodwork Institute. *Architectural Woodwork Quality Standard*, 6th Edition, Version 1.1. Centreville, VA: Architectural Woodwork Institute, 1994.

ENDNOTES

[1]Architectural Woodwork Institute. *Architectural Woodwork Quality Standard*, 6th Edition, Version 1.1. (Centreville, VA: Architectural Woodwork Institute) 1994, page 88. All quotes from *Architectural Woodwork Quality Standard* reproduced with permission.

[2]Adapted from ibid., page 102.

[3]Adapted from ibid., page 110.

[4]Knape & Vogt. *Drawer Slides & Specialty Hardware,* 1994, pages 4–5.

[5]Architectural Woodwork Institute, page 153.

GLOSSARY

Apron. A flat piece of wood attached vertically along the underside of the front edge of a horizontal surface; may be for support, as in book shelves, or decorative.

Balancing sheet. In decorative laminate doors, the lighter weight laminate on the interior face.

Bullet catch. A spring-actuated ball engaging a depression in the plate (see Figure 8–7).

Butt joint. Two pieces of wood attached at right angles (see Figure 8–2).

Concealed hinge. All parts are concealed when door is closed (see Figure 6–10).

Dado. A cross-grained rectangular or square section.

Dowel joint. A joint, usually right angle, using dowels for positioning and strength (see Figure 8–2).

Dynamic load. A moving load, as opposed to static.

Exposed hinge. All parts are visible when door is closed (see Figure 7–9).

Flush. Door and frame are level and frame is completely visible when door/drawer is closed (see Figure 8–4).

Friction catch. When engaged, catch is held in place by friction.

Groove. A square or rectangular section cut with the grain.

Lipped door. A door with an overlapping edge. Partially covers the frame (see Figure 8–4).

MDF. Medium Density Fiberboard.

Mullion. Vertical member between panels.

Ogee. A double curved shape resembling an S-shape.

Overlay door. The door is on the outside of the frame and when closed, the door hides the frame from view (see Figure 8–4).

Ovolo. A convex moulding, usually a quarter of a circle.

Pivot hinge. Hinge leaves are mortised into edge of door panel and set in frame at jamb and top of door. Some pivot hinges pivot on a single point (see Figure 7–8).

Reveal. The small area of the frame that is visible when door/drawer is closed (see Figure 8–4).

Static load. A resting load without any motion. Static load capacity is significantly higher than dynamic load capacity.

Stiles. Vertical pieces on paneling (see Figure 7–5).

Stop. A metal, plastic, or wood block placed so as to position the flush drawer front to be level with the face frame.

Strike plate. Metal plate attached to the frame, designed to hold roller catch under tension.

_____ *Chapter 9*

Kitchens

The kitchen has undergone many changes over the years. In the Victorian era, the cast iron cookstove was the main source of cooking and heating and, although an improvement over the open fire of colonial days, it still required much time and labor to keep it operating. The coal or wood had to be carried into the house and the stove itself required blacking to maintain its shiny appearance. In winter, the heat radiating from the cookstove heated the kitchen and made it a gathering place for the family. But, in summer, in order to use the top for cooking and the oven for baking, the fire had to be lit, causing the kitchen to feel like a furnace.

These traditional wood/coal-burning cookstoves are still available, with some models using gas or electricity but still retaining the look of the traditional cookstove.

In the kitchens of the past, besides the cookstove, the only other pieces of furniture were tables and chairs and a sink. All food preparation was done on the table or on the draining board next to the sink. There were no counters as we know them today and no upper storage cabinets. All food was stored in the pantry or in a cold cellar. Today, the kitchen has once again become a gathering place for the family. Much family life is centered around the kitchen, not only for food preparation, but also for entertaining and socializing. In line with this, Joe Ruggiero, past Publishing Director of _Home Magazine,_ said, "The kitchen will

have more upholstery as well as new types of furniture such as armoires, entertainment centers, and custom dish-racks, instead of traditional cabinetry." He mentions the parade of gadgets such as wood-burning pizza ovens and built-in woks, to ice cream makers and sorbet freezers. "Many kitchens will be outfitted with canning centers, special preparation areas and doors opening up to herb and vegetable gardens. The trend will be to more wood in the kitchen," said Ruggiero, who now serves as a consultant and spokesman for the new Kohler Coordinates program.

Regardless of the type of kitchen desired, there are some basic requirements for all kitchens. The appliances and work areas most used in a kitchen are the refrigerator for food storage, the stove for cooking, and the sink for washing. The **work triangle** connects these three areas, and the total distance should not be over 22 feet and may be less than that in some smaller kitchens. The distance between the refrigerator and the sink should be 4 to 7 feet, with 4 to 6 feet between sink and stove, and 4 to 9 feet between stove and refrigerator. Besides an efficient work triangle, adequate lighting and adequate storage are important.

The type of kitchen desired depends upon availability of space, life style, and ages and number of family members. Expense and space are the limiting factors in kitchen design. The best utilization of space will create a functional and enjoyable working area.

Kitchens are becoming larger and now account

for almost 10 percent of the total square footage of a single-family home. They also feature more cabinetry and counter space, with barrier-free products increasing in importance.

Life style involves several factors. One is the manner of entertaining. Formal dinners require a separate formal dining room, while informal entertaining may take place just outside the work triangle, with guest and host/hostess communicating while meals are being prepared (see Color Plate Figure 7). If entertaining is done outside the home of a working host and/or hostess, then the kitchen may be minimal in size.

A small kitchen will appear larger with an open plan, that is, without a wall dividing it from the adjacent room. It will also appear larger with a vaulted ceiling.

A young couple with a beginning family might require a family room within sight of the parents. Teenagers like to be near food preparation areas for easy access to the refrigerator and snacks. All these factors need to be taken into consideration when planning a kitchen.

Some cooks prefer to work from a pantry and therefore do not need a lot of upper cabinets, while others prefer to have a bake center and work from both the upper and lower cabinets.

Ellen Cheever, CKD, ASID, gives the following work simplification techniques for planning a kitchen:

1. Build the cabinets to fit the cook.
2. Build the shelves to fit the supplies.
3. Build the kitchen to fit the family.

FLOOR PLANS

There are infinite variations on basic floor plans, and this is where the customizing comes in (Figure 9–1).

> Islands, which may function as eat-in bars, room dividers, and/or work areas are probably the most sought-after design elements in today's kitchens, because they are attractive and make efficient use of space. Varying island shape can result in interesting angles and efficiencies.[1]

(See Figures 9–3, 9–4, and Color Plate Figure 6.)

The simplest of all kitchen floor plans is the one-wall, otherwise known as **pullman**, **strip**, or **studio**. Here, all appliances and counter space are contained on one wall and, when required, folding doors or screens are used to hide the kitchen completely from

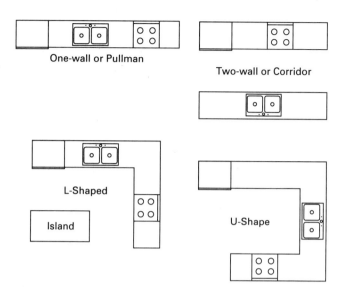

Figure 9–1
Kitchen floor plans.

view. This is a minimal kitchen not designed for elaborate or family meals.

The **corridor** or two-wall plan utilizes two parallel walls and doubles the available space over the one-wall plan. The major problem with this design is through traffic. If possible, for safety's sake, one end should be closed off to avoid this traffic. The width of the corridor kitchen should be between 5 and 8 feet. A narrower width prevents two facing doors from being opened at the same time. For energy conservation, refrigerator and stove should not face each other directly (see Figure 9–1).

In an L-shaped kitchen, work areas are arranged on two adjacent walls rather than on two opposite walls; the advantages being there is no through traffic and all counter space is contiguous. The L-shaped kitchen may also include an island or a peninsula. This island may simply be an extra work surface, contain the sink or stove, and/or may also include an informal eating area. If the island has a raised side facing an eating or seating area, the higher side will hide the clutter in the kitchen.

The U-shaped kitchen is probably the most efficient design. It has three walls of counter space, with no through traffic. Depending on the location of the window, there are at least two walls or more of upper cabinets. The work triangle is the easiest to arrange with the sink usually at the top of the U, the refrigerator on one side, and the range on the other. The refrigerator is always placed at the end of the U to avoid breaking up the counter area and also to be more easily accessible to the eating area. The stove, range, or cooktop is on the opposite side but more centered in the U (see Figure 9–1). Islands also work in a U-shaped kitchen provided there is more than 4-foot-wide passageways.

When planning any kitchen, thought should be given to the activities of each area. The sink area serves a dual purpose. First, it is used for food preparation such as washing and cleaning fruits and vegetables. Second, after the meal it is used for cleanup. In the age of the electric dishwasher, the sink area is generally used only for preliminary cleaning; but in the event of a large number of dishes, sufficient space should be provided next to the sink for a helper to dry the dishes.

Certain areas of the kitchen require a minimum amount of adjacent counter space. The sink needs 24 to 36 inches on the dishwasher side, and 18 to 36 on the other side. For cooktops, allow 18 to 24 inches either side, and regardless of the type of design, there must be at least 16 inches of counter on the handle side of the refrigerator, which should be at the end of one side of the counter near the entrance to the kitchen. Do not place the refrigerator in such a manner that the counter is broken up into small areas.

The refrigerator should be plugged into its own individual 115-volt electrical outlet on a circuit separate from those used for heating and cooking appliances. Place the refrigerator in an area that will not have direct sunlight or direct heat from the home heating system. Do not place it next to the range or dishwasher.

The cooking area is considered to be the cooktop area. Many wall ovens are now located in separate areas from the cooktop.

Kitchen Appliances

Only those appliances that are necessary to a kitchen floor plan will be discussed—in other words, what we consider major appliances. Mixers and toasters are outside the scope of this book.

Major appliance manufacturers must comply with a law enacted by Congress in 1975 (PL. 94–163). This law provides that energy costs for appliances must be calculated as so much per **kilowatt-hour** (kwh). This information must be supplied on a tag attached to the front of the appliance. Consumers can then calculate their yearly energy cost by finding out their local kwh rate. It is important to bear in mind that the higher the local rate the more important energy conservation features become. It is by using these figures that comparison shopping can be done.

Colored as well as white appliances are available. Currently, the most popular color other than white is almond, which blends very well with wood cabinets. If planning a change in the decor of the kitchen in the near future, white is always a safe choice. All-black appliances are very popular in contemporary kitchens, with black glass fronts on microwaves and ovens (see Figure 9–4). White appliances may have some chrome accents or be totally white (see Figure 9–4 and Color Plate Figure 9).

The style of appliances selected may affect the style of cabinetry. Black appliances look better with white or light-colored wood cabinets, while free standing Old World stoves may look better with French country cabinetry.

Porcelain enamel is most frequently used on surface tops and oven doors because it resists heat, acid, stains, scratches, yellowing, and fading. Baked enamel or electrostatically applied polyester is less durable than porcelain enamel because it is less resistant to stains and scratches; however, it resists chipping better than porcelain enamel.

Stainless steel is resistant to corrosion, dents, and stains and is easy to clean. However, it may turn dark if it is overheated. Chrome-plated finishes are durable and will not dent easily. Excess heat may cause chrome to discolor over a period of time.[2]

Refrigerators

The most costly kitchen appliance to purchase and to operate is the refrigerator. In fact, the Department of Energy did mandate that 1993 models operate 30 percent more efficiently than 1990 models, and this efficiency will probably increase. Different methods of refrigeration are being studied but increased cost, as always, will be a factor.

For our purposes, the word *refrigerator* will be used instead of refrigerator/freezer combination since we assume that all refrigerators have some form of freezer section. The freezer section is commonly on top (which is the most energy efficient), but some refrigerators have the freezer section below the regular food storage area. Side-by-side refrigerators have separate vertical doors for the freezer and refrigerator sections and because of the narrower doors, they require less aisle space for opening (see Figures 9–3, 9–4, and Color Plate Figure 6). Other exterior features include panel adapter kits that are used on the face of the refrigerator to match other appliances; the latest are stainless fronts for appliances. Doors that can be reversed are an important feature for those who move frequently.

For larger families, an ice-water dispenser with cubed and/or crushed ice that is accessible without opening the door may conserve energy and justify the additional expense. In its new refrigerators, GE has replaced the stirrup type of water and ice activator with a LightTouch® dispenser that delivers crushed ice, cubes, and chilled water. The Profile series from GE has several new features including a Quick Space® shelf, where the front part of the shelf simply slides back for storage of tall containers and clear-fronted meat and vegetable storage that, along with the glass shelves, prevents items from migrating to the back and being forgotten. Door bins with metal hooks make them fully adjustable to fit the family's needs.

One manufacturer even has a third door for access only to the ice cube compartment. Another has a storage unit in the door that can be opened for access to snack items without opening the full-length doors.

The most common features found in refrigerators include meat keepers, vegetable storage, unwrapped food sections, adjustable shelves, and humidity-controlled vegetable storage areas. Other interior features might include egg storage, handy cheese and spread storage, and glass shelves that prevent spilled liquids from dripping onto other shelves, although these solid glass shelves may prevent full air circulation. The shelves on the doors of both refrigerator and freezer may be fixed or adjustable. The latest feature is a door deep enough to hold gallon containers. Others have features such as frozen juice can dispensers, ice makers, and an ice cream maker within the freezer compartment.

Some companies have see-through storage bins. Frigidaire has lighted storage drawers with clear fronts. Frigidaire also features components that can be stacked or placed side-by-side or in a cubical arrangement of four units. They include wine coolers with optically-coated, double-pane thermal glass doors to protect the wine from harsh lighting. There are separate units for white and red wines, plus the conventional refrigerator and freezer components (Figure 9–2).

Some manufacturers specialize in energy conservation and efficiency has greatly improved over the past 15 years. A self-defrosting refrigerator consumes more energy than a manual defrost, but it is much more convenient.

Whirlpool Corporation won $30 million in the industry's winner-take-all Super Efficient Refrigerator Program (SERP) competition. The first model, a 22 cubic foot side-by-side refrigerator, exceeds 1993 fed-

Figure 9–2
The Frigidaire® wine cooler has two separate compartments and temperature zones, ensuring that both red and white wines are stored at their best temperatures. The cooler can store up to 70 bottles. Optically coated, double-pane thermal glass doors protect the wine from harsh lighting. Size 24 inches deep, 24 inches wide, and 71 inches high. (Photograph courtesy of Frigidaire Company)

eral standards by 29.7 percent. In addition, SERP models have CFC-free (Chloro Fluro Carbon) refrigeration systems and are therefore environmentally friendly. SERP refrigerators are being marketed by Whirlpool Corporation under the Whirlpool and KitchenAid brand names, and under the Kenmore brand by Sears, Roebuck and Co.

Frigidaire refrigerators feature an exclusive Frigi-Foam® insulation with reduced ozone-depleting CFCs. This company also has a new design feature in the gently rounded edges on the side of the UltraStyle™ refrigerator.

Refrigerators are sold by their storage capacity; in other words, by cubic feet of space. It is interesting to note that while families and kitchens generally are getting smaller, the size of the refrigerator is staying around 16 to 17 cubic feet. This may be a result of working parents with less time to shop, or more frequent entertaining. The most efficient refrigerator energy-wise is in the 15- to 20-cubic-foot range.

The average size for refrigerator/freezer combinations is 66 1/2 inches high, 35 3/4 inches wide (that is, it fits into a 36-inch space), and 30 1/2 inches deep. This depth measurement means that the door of the refrigerator extends beyond the counter by several inches. In order to design the refrigerator to be an integral part of the cabinetry, many manufacturers have recessed the coils or placed them above the refrigerator, which makes the refrigerator flush with the edge of the counter; however, this type is usually considerably higher in price. The door can be covered to match the cabinets and even have custom handles. Because there is no bottom vent, the toe-kick panel can extend from the cabinet across the base of the refrigerator. For new construction, allow 37 inches even if the planned unit is narrower, and make accommodations for a water hook-up even though it may not be used at the time.

GE has introduced its Profile "Built-In Style" line, where only the door extends beyond the counter, and this series provides a flush appearance without the expense of the coil on top.

White-Westinghouse has 11- and 13-cubic-foot refrigerators that are small enough that all the contents can be reached from a wheelchair. They meet the accessibility requirements by keeping the midpoint of the freezer section less than 54 inches from the floor. This company also has a side-by-side model with adjustable shelves that can be positioned low to reach from a seated position or high to prevent the need for bending over.

All White-Westinghouse refrigerators feature an energy saver switch that conserves energy in less humid weather when cabinet moisture removal is not needed.

The Kohler Coordinates™ program offers an easy way to color coordinate kitchens and bathrooms with Kohler plumbing fixtures, major appliances from Amana Refrigeration Inc., Marvin Windows and Doors, Dal Tile, Bruce® Hardwood Floors, Soft Scrub® Cleanser, Martex® Towels, French Reflection, Inc., Mirrors, Wilsonart® Laminates, and Gibraltar® Solid Surfacing (Figure 9–3).

Nylon rollers are provided for moving or rolling the refrigerator out from the wall. If the refrigerator is to be moved sideways, a **dolly** should be used to avoid damaging the floor covering.

Ranges

Old-fashioned stoves have been replaced by **drop-in** or **slide-in** units or **free-standing** units. Slide-in models can be converted to free-standing by addition of optional side panels and a backguard. Some ranges contain the cooking units, **microwave,** and/or oven in one appliance, or the oven and cooktop may be in two separate units often in two separate locations in the kitchen (see Figures 9–2 and 9–3).

Some electric ranges have the controls and clock on a back panel. On separate cooktops, controls are in the front or at the side of the cooktop. Controls on the latest cooktops are electronic touch pads. Free-standing ranges vary from 20 or 30 to 40 inches wide, while slide-in ranges usually measure 30 inches.

Many 30-inch ranges now come with a second oven above the cooktop surface. This may be another **conventional oven** or a microwave. A ventilation fan is incorporated beneath some of the microwave ovens.

A free-standing range has finished sides and is usually slightly deeper than the 24-inch kitchen counter. This type of range may be considered if a change of residence will take place in the near future. The drop-in or slide-in units are designed for more permanent installation and are usually placed between two kitchen cabinets. The cooking medium may be gas or electricity. Some ranges have the cooking surface flush with the counter, while others are lowered an inch or so. The only difference is that if several large or wide pans are used at the same time, such as during canning or for large parties, the lowered surface is more restrictive. The flush surface permits the overhanging of the larger pans. The surface of ranges may be white or colored with porcelain-coated steel, stainless steel, tempered glass, or ceramic glass.

For those who wish state-of-the-art technology combined with authentic 19th-century styling, the old-fashioned ranges are now available with gas or electricity. These ranges have the decorative cast iron doors, which in some cases conceal a full-size self-cleaning oven. There are several companies manufacturing this type of product including Elmira Stove Works and Heartland Appliances Inc. The latter company also has a wood or coal burning stove similar to the old-fashioned cookstove. Also available on the market now are cooktops with two gas and two electric burners in combination with a downdraft exhaust system.

The Department of Energy estimates that the typical annual cost of operating an efficient gas range is

Figure 9–3

The provincial warmth and charm of the south of France provided the inspiration for this kitchen by Joe Ruggiero for the Kohler Coordinates program. The kitchen is divided into three areas: baking, preparation, and cleanup. Cabinetry: Wilsonart Laminate; tile floor: Dal Tile; wood parquet floor: Bruce Hardwood Floors; sinks and faucets: Kohler Fixtures and Faucets; windows and French door: Marvin Windows and Doors; solid surface material on center island: Gibraltar from Wilsonart; and appliances: Amana. (Photograph courtesy of Kohler)

about half the cost of operating an electric range. However, this only amounts to a dollar or two per month, so individual preference is more of a consideration.

Electric Ranges

There are several different types of element choices. The least expensive is the coil element, which is the most widely sold type. The most expensive is the European solid disk of cast iron sealed to the cooktop, which some manufacturers refer to as a **hob**. With the solid-electric element, a red dot indicates that the element is thermally protected and will shut down if a pan boils dry. Some elements have a silver dot, a pan sensor that maintains a fairly constant preselected temperature, sometimes with a variance of 20°.

Another type is the radiant **glass-ceramic cooktop,** or smoothtop. When first introduced in 1966 these were white, but today most are black. All these surfaces are heated primarily by conduction; however, some use halogen. Some smoothtops have quick heating elements and, for safety's sake, the indicator lights will stay on as long as the surface is hot. This type of cooktop has a limiter that cycles the burners on and off, restricting the temperature reached by the glass surface. Most smoothtops recommend cleaning with a special cream that both cleans and shines the ceramic.

Two new methods of heating are halogen and induction, both of which use glass-ceramic cooktops. The halogen units from Gaggenau have vacuum-sealed quartz glass tubes filled with halogen gas that filter out the white light and use infra-red as a heating source. The surface turns a bright red when turned on. This unit provides instant on and instant off with any type of cooking utensil, and as with the induction method, the surface itself does not get hot. The only heat the glass top may retain is absorbed from a hot pan.

In technical terms, induction uses electromagnetic force to heat cookware of ferromagnetic material (iron, nickel, cobalt, and various alloys). When controls are turned on, the coils produce a high-frequency alternating magnetic field which ultimately flows through the cookware. Molecules in the cookware move back and forth rapidly, causing the cookware to become hot and cook the food.

Plus, the cooktop's glass-ceramic surface is unaffected by the magnetic field since it contains no ferromagnetic material. The heat of the pot will warm the glass but will remain much cooler to the touch than other smoothtop surfaces.[3]

When induction-type smoothtops sense overheating, they beep and shut off the power to that burner. Because of the method of heating, induction units turn off the power when a pot is removed. Induction models use electronic controls while other types use knobs.

To obtain the most efficiency, all cooking utensils used on an electric range must be flat bottomed to allow full contact with the cooking unit, although induction units will work with slightly warped pans. Some smoothtops have quick heating elements and, for safety's sake, the indicator lights will stay on as long as the surface is hot. Usually there are four cooking units, but some of the larger glass cooktops have five or even six units.

Electric cooktops may be modular, with interchangeable coil elements, smooth top, **griddle, grille, and shish-kebab rotisserie** units.

The cooktops now have concealed or visible hinges that make it easy to clean under the cooktop, where the overflow from drip bowls ends up. Porcelain drip bowls are much easier to clean than the shiny metal bowls and can be cleaned in the oven during the self-cleaning cycle.

Gas Ranges

One advantage of using gas is that it is easier to moderate the temperature changes, and the required temperature is reached more rapidly (see Figure 9–4). Conventional gas burners have grates that hold the pan above the flame. These grates should be heavy enough to support the pans and also be easy to clean. Propane burns a little cooler than regular gas. Since sealed gas burners are fused to the cooktop with no drip pans, all spills remain on the glass surface.

Newer gas ranges have pilotless ignition systems that light the cooking unit automatically from either a spark ignition or a coil ignition. By eliminating the standard, always-burning pilot light, these ranges reduce the gas needed for cooking by 30 percent, keep the kitchen cooler, and prevent pilot outage caused by drafts or other conditions. Electricity must be run to the range in order to operate the pilotless ignition. In case of electricity failure, the burner may be lit by a match; however, as a safety precaution, the oven cannot be used by lighting a match. If electricity cannot be run to the pilotless range, models with pilot lights are still available.

Global Environmental Solutions (GES) is working on a new flameless gas burner made from silicon carbide ceramic fibers, which are chemically bonded together. Upon ignition at the surface, the ceramic burner material goes from cold to red hot in one second because of its low thermal mass. The hot burner surface radiates energy in the infrared wavelength and is ideal for transmitting energy by radiation and conduction through today's modern black glass ceramic CERAN™ cooktop panels like those used in electric smoothtops.[4]

One of the trends of the 1990s is the use of the multiburner restaurant gas range with six or even eight burners in home kitchens. These ranges are free standing and are very useful when catering for a large crowd, but the floor should be reinforced to support the extra weight. This problem can be overcome by using restaurant ranges designed for residential use, which are made to be installed touching the adjacent cabinet. Most are stainless steel, but Russell Range may be obtained in a solid brass edition.

Regency USA has a full trivet four-burner cooktop, which means that pots and pans can be slid and not lifted aside from the burner, as there is no level change. Russell Range also has all-over grids (see Color Plate Figure 6 for a commercial range and Figure 9–4 for an attractive kitchen).

Ovens

Electric ovens come in two types: self-cleaning (**pyrolytic**) or continuous-cleaning (**catalytic**). Self-cleaning ovens have a special cleaning setting that is activated by the timer for the required length of time. This cleaning cycle runs at an extremely high temperature and actually incinerates any oven spills, leaving an ash residue. One of the excellent by-products of a self-cleaning oven is that, because of the high temperatures required to operate the cleaning cycle, the oven is more heavily insulated than is customary and so retains the heat longer and uses less energy when baking. There are now some gas ovens that are self-cleaning.

The continuous-cleaning oven features a special porous ceramic finish that disperses and partially absorbs food spatters to keep the oven presentably clean. Running the oven at the highest temperature for a while will help clean up remaining spatters.

Figure 9–4
The Monogram Greenhouse Kitchen from GE Appliances features a center island with a five-burner gas cooktop. On the right is the 36-inch trimless, built-in cabinet-friendly refrigerator. A narrow storage cabinet separates the refrigerator from the built-in double oven. (Reproduced with permission of the copyright owner, General Electric Company)

Oven-cleaning products available at the grocery store may *not* be used on the continuous-cleaning surface.

Ovens cook by one of three methods: radiation, convection, or microwave.

Radiant baking is the one used in most ovens.

While a conventional oven uses radiant heat to warm the food, oven interior and air, **convection** uses a fan inside the oven cavity to circulate that warm air. The moving air strips away a layer of cooler air that surrounds the food, thus speeding up the baking or roasting process. Jenn-Air's convection ovens have radiant heating elements at the oven's top and bottom, with the fan built into the back for maximum space usage. Meats are juicier, since circulating air seals the outside surface and reduces the evaporation. For large items, cooking times are reduced up to 30 percent. Because of the way in which the air circulates, cooks can bake three racks of cookies, pizza or other items instead of just one or two.[5]

Therefore, it is possible to cook a greater quantity of food in a small convection oven cavity than in a larger conventional one. On low heat settings, foods can also be dehydrated for long-term storage. The defrosting setting works on the same principle. Convection ovens increase the cost of the oven.

Built-in ovens are required when using a separate cooktop. These may be single conventional oven units or double oven units with one a conventional type and the other a microwave. Sizes available are 24, 27, and 30 inches, with built-in gas ovens at 24 inches. The 24- and 27-inch ovens fit into a standard 27-inch cabinet, but not all 30-inch models fit into a 30-inch cabinet. Some require the 30-inch opening that only a 33-inch cabinet provides.

Electric ovens may have a solid door, a porcelain enamel door with a window, or a full black glass window door. The porcelain enamel is available in many colors. A glass door may be seen in Figures 9–3 and 9–4. Controls may be knobs or electronic touch pads. Electric ovens require the door to be left ajar when in broiling mode, or food will roast.

Most ovens have a drop-down door, but for people who are physically challenged, Frigidaire has a side-swing door that is reversible so it can be set to open from either side. Sometimes double ovens are used, but for the physically challenged they take away the advantage of waist-level shelves, as one is higher than waist level and the other requires bending over. Timers for the ovens vary in length from 99 minutes to 10 hours.

Warming drawers are becoming more prevalent in up-scale kitchens. These thermostatically controlled warming drawers keep foods moist or crisp prior to serving and may also be used for "proofing" bread.

Microwave Ovens

This method of cooking activates the molecules in the food about 2 1/2 billion times per second. It is the friction between molecules that produces the heat. Today, most microwave ovens are operated by means of touch controls that electronically monitor the amount of energy from full power to a warming setting or defrost cycle.

Microwave ovens may be programmed to cook whole meals on a delayed time basis. Some have recipes that are available at a touch while others use a meat probe to produce meat that is rare, medium, or well done.

Microwave ovens may be counter models, under-the-cabinet (UTC) without a vent, or the latest over-the-range (OTR) models with built-in recirculating exhaust fans. Spacemaker Plus™ from GE features higher wattage and a bottom-feed microwave distribution system. Some new features are Auto Cook, Auto Popcorn, and Auto Reheat. They rely on a humidity sensor to precisely determine when the food has been properly cooked.

Most microwave ovens have a door that swings open, but the GE Monogram® microwave oven has a door that pulls down to open. This particular microwave oven also may cook by convection either alone or in combination with the microwave. The combination method means that food can be browned while being cooked by microwave. Probably the most used feature on a microwave oven is the defrost cycle.

Unlike regular ovens, the cooking time varies with the amount of food to be cooked; thus, four potatoes require about 70 percent less energy when microwaved, but 12 potatoes bake more efficiently in a conventional oven.

Ventilation Fans

There are many methods of exhausting cooking fumes from the kitchen. Ducted fans may be either updraft or downdraft. With updraft, the hood over the cooking surface collects the heat, odors, and fumes and exhausts them to the outside. This method does take up some space in the cabinet over the cooking surface.

There are three types of downdraft on the market. The most well-known downdraft is Jenn-Air, the original manufacturer of cooktops and grill ranges, with a built-in downdraft ventilation. Jenn-Air has a vent that goes from back to front of the cooking surface. It will also vent fumes and heat that escape the oven during the self-cleaning cycle. Downdraft cooking is ideal for peninsulas.

Some have a raised vent at the back of the cooktop that may not always completely exhaust fumes from the front burners particularly if the pans are very high. Split downdraft consists of two vents on each side of the cooktop surface.

For outside walls an exhaust fan that vents directly outdoors may be used.

Ductless or recirculating systems have a **charcoal filter** that filters out odors, with a washable filter.

Dishwashers

Dishwashers are 24 inches wide and are usually installed adjacent to the sink so that the plumbing connections are easily made. Dishwashers discharge the dirty water through the sink containing the garbage disposal. For older-style kitchens with no undercounter space for a dishwasher, movable models are available that connect directly to the faucet in the sink and discharge directly into the sink. An undersink model is made by GE for small kitchens.

Available features in dishwashers include a heavy-duty cycle for cleaning heavily soiled pots and pans, a regular cycle for normal soil, rinse and hold for a small number of dishes requiring rinsing, and low-energy wash cycles.

If your utility offers lower off-peak rates, the delay-start feature may be desirable. Some models will display an alert message, such as "blocked wash arm" or "PF" should a power failure occur.

Dishes may be dried by the heated cycle or for energy efficiency, a no-heat drying cycle may be programmed. Most dishwashers require little or no rinsing of soiled dishes as a soft food disposer is built into newer dishwashers. Racks and even dividers are now adjustable, allowing for large size dishes or wider items that do not fit over the fixed dividers. Some dishwashers have a separate rack on top for silverware, making them easier to get at, easier to clean, and more scratch resistant. Water-saver dishwashers are now available.

Trash Compactors

Trash compactors reduce trash volume by 80 percent in less than one minute. Most have some form of odor control and use a compacting ram with the force of approximately 3,000 pounds. In today's society, where trash disposal has become a very expensive service, trash compactors do reduce the volume of trash considerably but may make trash less biodegradable because of its compacted volume. Trash compactors vary in width from 12 to 18 inches.

As a result of recycling laws, trash compactors are becoming obsolete as far as many designers are concerned. However, trash compactors can be used to crush recyclable aluminum cans and plastic bottles.

Kitchen Sinks

Kitchen sinks are constructed of stainless steel, enameled cast iron, enameled steel, or manufactured materials, usually compression-molded modified acrylic. Each material has its own pros and cons.

Stainless steel sinks give a very contemporary look to a kitchen and are less likely to break dishes that are accidentally dropped into them. However, any water spots will leave a spot on the shiny surface. Also, heat from the hot water dissipates more rapidly with a metal sink than with a porcelain enamel one. When selecting a stainless steel sink, the lower the number of the gauge is, the thicker the metal will be.

Porcelain enamel sinks do show stains more easily, and a scouring powder is usually required to remove such stains. The porcelain may become chipped when hit with a heavy object. However, enameled cast iron sinks do provide a colorful touch in the kitchen.

Enameled steel sinks are low cost and lightweight but also less durable than the other types. Sinks made of solid surfaces are easily cleaned, but colors are limited and require an experienced installer, which raises the cost.

Porcelain sinks are highly chip-resistant but can break when a heavy object is dropped into them. Porcelain sinks are made from high-fired clay with an enamel finish, a combination that is used more in Europe than in this country.

Composite or quartz acrylic is the latest material for kitchen sinks. This material produces a color-through sink impervious to stains and scratches. Composite sinks are a combination of natural materials and synthetics. Americast is a porcelain-enamel surface on metal backed by an injection-molded structural composite.

Some kitchen sinks, such as the stainless steel ones and those designed to be used with a metal rim, are flush with the counter. Any water spilled on the counter may be swept back into the sink. However, the self-rimming type are raised above the surface of the counter and any water spilled must be mopped up (see Figures 9–3, 9–5, and 9–6). Kohler has introduced the Madrigal triple basin kitchen sink with wide 18-gauge stainless basins bonded to decks that come in eight colors. The Black Black™ deck looks very sophisticated with the black marble or granite solid surface materials.

Some self-rimming sinks have predrilled holes that need to be ordered to suit the type of faucet to be used. The old standard had three holes, or four holes for a spray or soap dispenser. However, with the increasing use of single-lever faucets with self-contained pullout sprays, only one hole may be needed. Some models have knockout holes started in their undersides. An extra hole may be needed if a water purifier is desired. Undermounted, flush-mounted, and integral or molded sinks have the faucets on the counter.

Single-compartment models should be installed only where there is minimum space. One-bowl models do not provide a second disposal area if the bowl is in use. Two-bowl models may be the same size and depth, or one bowl may be smaller and shallower. For corner installations there are even L-shaped double models.

In triple sinks one of the bowls is usually shallower and smaller than the other two and may contain the garbage disposal unit. Some sinks with small bowls have a strainer to fit for draining pastas or cleaning off vegetables.

For those interested in composting waste, Kohler has the EcoCycle™ sink, which has two 10-inch deep basins and a chute system accessed by an opening in the wide saddle between the two basins. Accessories with the sink include the EcoCycle chute and bucket system, a cutting board, colander, and the Duo-strainer® Dry, a new remote control cable drain. The EcoCycle comes in self-rimming and tile-in versions (Figure 9–5).

Corian, when used as a material for kitchen sinks, may or may not be an integral part of the counter and is discussed on page 170 under Counters.

The width of a kitchen sink varies between 25 and 43 inches. Some with attached drainboards are almost 50 inches wide. New sinks have the drain at the rear, which means there is a flat area for food preparation and more accessible storage space under the sink.

Accessories for sinks may include a fitted cutting board, where waste material may be pushed off one corner into the sink. Also, wire or plastic colanders are

Figure 9–5
The EcoCycle™ kitchen sink from Kohler adds a convenient composting/recycling feature. The chute system is accessed by an opening in the wide "saddle" between the two basins. The EcoCycle is shown in a self-rim model. A tile-in version is also available. (Photograph courtesy of Kohler)

useful for holding food or vegetables that require rinsing (see Figure 9–5).

The Assure™ kitchen sink from Kohler extends accessibility into the kitchen. It is made from cast iron with high and low basins that make kitchen sink tasks easy to perform from a seated or standing position. An optional polyethylene cutting board, polypropylene colander, and drainboard with wire dish rack are all specifically designed for Assure. It is designed with a front apron that curves gently inward to bring the basins closer to a seated user and a wide front ledge that the user can grasp to pull himself/herself toward the sink and rest his/her arms while working. A polystyrene shroud designed to fit over the drain and water pipes prevents a seated user's knees or legs from coming in contact with hot pipes. The Assure kitchen sink was designed with the following points in mind: users' specific limitations of reach, upper body mobility, and gripping strength; the amount of room needed to turn or position a wheelchair, walker, or crutches; and accessibility to working surfaces and appliance controls from a seated position (Figure 9–6).

Maintenance. Kitchen sinks should be cleaned with only mild powders or paste cleaners. Do not use steel wool and avoid heavy-duty abrasive powders. A mirrored-finish stainless sink can be cleaned with a special automotive polishing compound to maintain its sheen.

Kitchen Faucets

Faucets do not come with the kitchen sink and can sometimes be as expensive as the sink itself. Faucets constructed of chrome-plated steel should be all chrome-plated steel with no parts chrome-plated plastic, since plating will gradually peel off with use. A mixing type of valve, where hot and cold may be blended with one handle, allows one-handed operation, which is useful when holding something in the other hand. One problem is that the handle may be accidentally turned on when in the hot position and a burn can occur. This problem should be eliminated by legislation enacted January 1, 1994, that requires all new and replacement faucet valves to have pressure

Figure 9–6
The new Assure™ wheelchair-accessible kitchen sink by Kohler becomes a complete work station with the addition of a polyethylene cutting board, colander, and drainboard. Coralais™ faucet with integral pull-out sprayhead brings the spout to the seated user. (Photograph courtesy of Kohler)

balance and antiscald controls by January 1996. The water heater should have the thermostat set at 120°F.

Several manufacturers have lifetime warranties on their valves. The Price Pfister Warranty covers the ceramic disc valve cartridge that is part of its washerless faucet construction. The valve is only 35 mm (smaller than most), is self-lubricating, and has back-to-back gaskets. The warranty covers finish and function for as long as the customer owns his/her home.

Moen warrants to the original purchaser that its faucets will be leak and drip free during normal domestic use for as long as they own them. If the faucet should ever develop a leak or drip during this time, Moen will provide free of charge the parts necessary to put the faucet back in good working condition.

A gooseneck faucet is higher than normal and may be used for the kitchen but is more frequently used in a bar sink (see Figure 9–3).

The Gourmet spray from Delta features a contemporary single-hole 10-inch spout that pulls out to 59 inches, enabling buckets and humidifiers to be filled from the floor. Vacuum-breaker ball design prevents contamination caused by backflow and back siphonage, should the spray be accidentally dropped into soapy or dirty water. The Gourmet series is available in polished brass as well as other standard finishes. Most kitchen faucets now have faucets that have a hose attached for spraying the sink and washing vegetables (see Figures 9–5 and 9–6).

Several hot water dispensers on the market provide very hot water (about 190°) for use in making hot drinks and instant soups. Franke and In-Sink-Erator have recently introduced models that dispense both hot and cold water through one faucet. The extra hole in the sink may be used for these dispensers as well as for purified water when desired.

Because of the tightening of water usage, plumbing manufacturers are now making 2.5 to 2.7 gallons-per-minute flow kitchen faucets.

KITCHEN CABINETS

Stock kitchen cabinets usually start at 15 inches wide and come in 3-inch increments up to 48 inches. The depth of lower cabinets is 24 inches and the depth of upper cabinets is 12 inches. Filler strips are used between individual cabinets to make up any difference in measurements.

Kitchen cabinets are usually made of all wood or wood with decorative laminate doors. Solid wood is required for raised panel designs. For dimensional stability, a Medium Density or Multi-Density Fiber-

board (MDF) is used for the case and shelves; the edges are banded with a wood veneer that matches the door and drawer fronts. The interior of the cabinets is often coated with a PVC plastic material that reflects light, making it easier to find items inside and easier to clean. Under-cabinet appliances are also popular and clear the counter of clutter.

One of the many products available from the St. Charles Companies is the steel cabinet. Because of the strength of steel, the cabinets are thinner and taller and feature an added shelf for more storage. They are resistant to temperature and humidity changes and won't twist, warp, swell, or absorb odors. The steel cabinets are also available in hypo-allergenic material, which is important for those clients who need a chemical-free environment.

The kitchen is a very personal room and the style of cabinets selected should reflect the client's life style. At one extreme are kitchens that have everything hidden from sight, in other words, behind solid doors, and empty counters. The other extreme is the kitchen with raised panel doors, often shaped at the top, often with glass inserts, and shelves where personal collections and/or kitchen utensils are displayed. Glass doors should have glass shelves when displaying decorative items, or the impact on the viewer is lost (see Color Plate Figure 7). Glass doors also require some thought as to what is going to be visible. Another style of kitchen uses open shelves for the storage of dishes and glasses, and a pantry is used for food storage. Most kitchens fall somewhere between these extremes but should be personalized for the client.

Wood cabinets may have flush overlay, reveal overlay, or, for more traditional styles, an exposed frame with a lipped door. The face surface of the door may be plane, have a flat or raised panel, or have mouldings applied for a traditional approach. Contemporary kitchens may have not only flush overlay doors, but flush overlay in combination with linear metal or wood decorative strips that also function as drawer and door pulls.

When decorative laminates are used, Perma-Edge® from Wilsonart has matching mouldings for doors and drawers (Figure 9–7). The traditional front frame construction and the European-style frameless construction (sometimes referred to as 32 mm cabinets) are both popular. Thirty-two millimeters is the spacing of predrilled holes in the cabinet sides for shelf spacing. Shelves in all cabinets should be fully adjustable to accommodate the needs of the user. A well-stocked kitchen requires a minimum of 50 square feet of shelf space and a minimum of 11 square feet of drawer space. Pots and pans are more readily accessi-

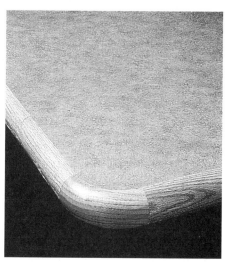

Figure 9–7
Perma-Edge® Mouldings from Wilsonart® make decorative edge treatments for work surfaces and cabinet doors easier and more attractive. (Photographs courtesy of Ralph Wilson Plastics)

ble if drawers are used for storage, rather than base cabinet shelves.

When the frameless type of construction is used, it will have an opening 1 1/2 inches wider than conventionally constructed cabinets. A quality frameless cabinet is as strong as a face frame cabinet with 1/2-inch-thick sides and 1/4-inch back. There is very little cost difference between framed and frameless.

Many special features may be ordered for the custom-designed kitchen. These will add to the cost of the installation but may be ordered to fit the personal and budgetary needs of the client. Base sliding shelves make all items visible, which eliminates getting down on hands and knees to see what is at the bottom of a base unit. A bread box may be contained within a drawer with a lid to help maintain freshness. A cutting board, usually made of maple, that slides out from the upper part of a base unit is convenient and will help protect the surface of the counter from damage. However, do not place a cutting board directly over a drawer that might be needed in conjunction with the cutting board.

Lazy susans in corner units or doors with attached swing-out shelves utilize the storage area of a corner unit. Another use for the corner unit is the installation of a 20-gallon water heater, thus providing instant hot water for the kitchen sink and the electric dishwasher and preventing waste of water. A second water heater can then be installed close to the bathrooms for energy conservation and for avoiding those long waits for the hot water to reach the bathroom lavatory.

Dividers in drawers aid in drawer organization, and vertical dividers in upper or base units utilize space by arranging larger and flat items in easily visible slots, thus avoiding nesting.

Bottle storage units have frames to contain bottles. Spice storage may be attached to the back of an upper door or built into a double-door unit, or a special spice drawer insert allowing seasonings to be easily visible may be utilized. Hot pads may be stored in a narrow drawer under a built-in cooktop. A tilt-down sink front may hold sponges, scouring pads, etc. Wire or plastic-coated baskets for fruit and vegetable storage provide easily visible storage. A wastebasket, either attached to a swing-out door, a tilt-down door, or sliding out from under the sink, also provides a neat and out-of-sight trash container.

Appliance garages are built into the back of the counter and enclose mixers, blenders, etc. The garage may have tambour doors or may match the cabinets.

Portable recycling units have been on the market for some time, but some states and cities have comprehensive recycling laws, and both custom and even stock cabinets now have multibasket units, with the four-unit being most popular.

The manufacturers recommend putting one single unit near the sink for compostables, and then two others away from the food preparation area, one for aluminum cans and the other for bottles. Check local building codes to see whether some type of venting is necessary for the cabinet under the sink.

Several of the kitchen cabinet companies have brochures that will help with kitchen planning. These include questionnaires that cover such issues as height of primary user, type of cooking to be performed, and what the client may or may not like about their current kitchen plan.

COUNTER MATERIALS

Counters may be of the following materials: decorative laminate, ceramic tile, wood, marble, travertine, solid surface materials, stainless steel, granite, or slate.

Decorative Laminate

In some areas decorative laminate is the most commonly used counter material. The construction is exactly the same as that used for laminates on walls. For counter top use, two thicknesses are available; a choice of one or the other depends on the type of counter construction. For square-edged counters, the general purpose grade is used. If it is necessary to roll the laminate on a simple radius over the edges of the substrate, a **postforming** type is specified. The postforming method eliminates the seam or brown line at the edge of the counter. Another method of eliminating the brown line is to use one of the "colorthrough" laminates.

Installation. Postformed counter tops must be constructed at the plant rather than at the job site, as heat and special forming fixtures are used to create the curved edge. The counter may be manufactured as a single unit, or each postformed side may be manufactured separately. By manufacturing each side separately, any discrepancy in the alignment of the walls can be adjusted at the corner joints.

For square-edged counters, the edge is applied first and then routed smooth with the substrate. The flat surface is then applied, and the overlapping edges are routed flush with the counter surface.

Another method is to apply the flat surface first and

rout the apron to accommodate such edge treatments as Perma-Edge® mouldings. These mouldings may be laminate with a beveled edge, all one color; laminate with a beveled edge, two different colors; half-round wood mouldings with 2-, 4-, or 6-inch radii to match; or wood with a laminate insert (see Figure 9–7).

For counters, the adhesive is applied to both the counter top substrate and the back of the laminate. When the adhesive is dry, scrap plastic, thin wood, or metal strips are placed on the substrate to prevent contact before the laminate is properly positioned. These strips are gradually removed, and the bond is complete. The excess at the front is then trimmed with the router.

A decorative laminate surface is durable, but it is not a cutting surface and will chip if heavy objects are dropped onto it. For areas where chemical spills or other destructive or staining substances may be used, a chemical and stain resistant laminate may be specified. Specific uses are chemistry laboratory tops, photographic lab tops, medical and pathology labs, and clinics.

For high-use and heavy-wear areas such as fast-food counter tops, supermarket check-out stands, or bank service areas, a .125-inch thickness of decorative laminate is available.

Maintenance. Decorative laminate may be cleaned with warm water and mild dish soaps. Use of abrasives or "special" cleansers should be avoided because they may contain abrasives, acids, or alkalines. Stubborn stains may be removed with organic solvents or two minutes of exposure to a hypochlorite bleach such as Clorox, followed by a clean water rinse. Consult manufacturers for specific instructions and recommendations.

Ceramic Tile

Ceramic tile has become a very popular material with which to cover kitchen counters. To facilitate cleaning, the backsplash may also be covered with tile. Ceramic tile is a very durable surface, but the most vulnerable part is the grout, which will absorb stains unless a stain-proof grout is specified. A grout sealer or lemon furniture oil will also seal the surface of the grout so that stains will not penetrate.

Around the sink area, ceramic tile counter may be carried down the front to the top of the doors below. This is reminiscent of old farmhouse kitchens and also protects wood cabinets from water.

Because of the hard surface of the tile, fragile items that are dropped on the counter will break, and if heavy objects are dropped, the tile may be cracked or broken. Always order sufficient tile for replacements.

Installation. When installing a ceramic tile counter, it is recommended that an exterior grade plywood be used as the substrate. The remaining installation procedure is the same as for floors and walls.

Maintenance. Maintenance is the same as that for ceramic tile floors.

Wood

Wood counters are usually made of a hard wood such as birch or maple and are constructed of glued strips of wood that are then usually sealed and coated with a varnish. Unsealed wood will permanently absorb stains. Wood counters should not be used as a cutting surface because the finish will become marred. Any water accumulating around the sink should be mopped up immediately; the surface can become damaged from prolonged contact with moisture.

Wood counters may be installed in a curved shape by successively adding a strip of wood, gluing, and clamping it. When dry, another piece is added.

Marble

In the past, marble was used as a material for portions of the counter top. Today in some expensive installations, marble may be used for the whole counter area. Some people like to use a marble surface for rolling out pastry or making hand-dipped chocolates. As mentioned in the marble floor section, marble may absorb stains and cause unsightly blemishes on the counter. Heavy items dropped on a marble surface will crack it.

Maintenance. Stain removal is the same as that for marble floors.

Travertine

When travertine is used as a counter material, it must be filled. Maintenance is the same as that for marble.

Solid Surface Materials

Corian®, a product invented by DuPont, is acrylic based and combines the smoothness of marble, the solid feel of granite, and the workability of wood. Corian is available in sheets of 1/4-, 1/2-, and 3/4-inch thicknesses and in a wide variety of double- and single-bowl kitchen sinks and lavatory styles. It is nonporous and highly resistant to abuse; even cigarette burns, stains, and scratches can be removed with household cleanser or a Scotch-Brite® pad. Because Corian is acrylic it can be formed to a very tight radius before the inside of the curve becomes too compressed and the outside too stretched. Most other brands are made of polyester, which resists tight radii. Dark colors may perform differently than light colors (Figure 9–8).

Thicker, built-up edges, made by using joint adhesive, can be routed into a variety of decorative treatments, including bull-nose edges and 'sandwich' inserts (Figure 9–9). Solid surface manufacturers may be able to supply custom colors for large projects.

GIBRALTAR® from Wilsonart is the latest addition to the solid surface market. This company has made its colored GIBRALTAR to match their laminates exactly, so that a coordinated look can be obtained although different materials are being used.

Fountainhead is the solid surface material from Nevamar and can be routed to provide curves. Contrasting color can be used to fill in the routed designs. FH Coordinates from Nevamar is a collection of hardware designed to coordinate with its solid surfacing material and laminates. Swanstone® is a fiberglass-based solid surface material.

The edges of solid surface materials may be shaped like wood, and seams may be made for longer lengths, provided there is support for the seam.

Maintenance. Most stains just wipe right off with a regular household detergent. Because of the solid composition of these materials, most stains stay on the surface and may be removed with any household abrasive cleanser or Scotch-Brite® pad gently rubbed in a circular motion. Cigarette burns and cuts may be removed with very fine sandpaper, 120–140 grit, then rubbed with the Scotch-Brite pad as above. If the surface was highly polished, it may need repolishing to blend the damaged area.

Stainless Steel

All commercial kitchens have stainless steel counters because they can withstand scouring, boiling water, and hot pans. Stainless steel counters can be installed in private residences if desired, providing a high-tech look.

Maintenance. One of the problems with stainless steel is that the surface may show scratches, and

Figure 9–8
A kitchen featured at the 1994 National Association of Home Builders Show in Las Vegas as the "New American Home," shows a Corian® counter. (Photograph courtesy of DuPont®)

Figure 9–9
Shown here are just a few of the more popular edge treatments available for Corian® counters. (Drawing courtesy of DuPont®)

with hard water the surface shows water spots. However, water spots may be removed by rubbing the damp surface with a towel, and scratches gradually blend into a patina. Apart from possible scratches and the spots, stainless steel is extremely easy to maintain.

Granite and Slate

Both these stones may be used as counter materials if desired, although construction of the cabinets must be strong enough to support the extra weight. As noted in the floor chapter, these stones vary in porosity, and care should be taken to prevent stains from penetrating the surface.

Maintenance. Maintenance is the same as that for granite walls and slate floors.

Other Materials

In composition, Nuvel™ does not fit any of the previous classifications. It is a surfacing material suitable for counter tops, kitchen and bath cabinets, shelving units, etc. It is a flexible, high-density mineral-filled thermoplastic polymer. Sheet sizes are 30 inches × 8 feet, 10 feet, and 12 feet; 4 feet × 8 feet; and 5 feet × 12 feet. It is available in five solid colors, all in the white and off-white range, with a matte finish. Nuvel may be used for postforming and thermoforming.

Nuvel is not manufactured with and does not contain or emit ozone-depleting compounds. Offall is a nonhazardous material under RCRA and has the potential to be reprocessed. Nuvel is completely recyclable.

Installation. Nuvel surfacing material is not recommended for application directly to composite substrates such as hardboard, cardboard, and solid lumber because of their dimensional instability. The recommended substrates for Nuvel are industrial grade particleboard, medium density fiberboard, hardwood-faced grade plywood or metal. While contact adhesives commonly used in high pressure laminate fabrication are suitable for use with Nuvel, it is recommended that Nuvel Seaming Cartridge be used.

Maintenance. While Nuvel will not be damaged with inadvertent and short-term exposure to extreme heat, it is advised that Nuvel not be exposed for prolonged periods to temperatures in excess of 175°. Nuvel may be cleaned with spray detergent and a damp cloth. More difficult stains may be removed with cleanser and damp cloth. A Scotch-Brite pad will aid in removing difficult stains.

FLOORS

Kitchen floors may be ceramic tile, quarry tile, wood, or any of the resilient floorings. The choice of flooring will depend on the client's needs and personal wishes. Some people find a hard-surfaced floor to be tiring to the feet, while others are not bothered at all. Wood floors need to be finished with a very durable finish that will withstand any moisture that may be accidentally spilled. Resilient flooring may be vinyl, cushioned or not, or the new rubber sheet flooring.

WALLS

Walls should be painted with an enamel that is easily cleansed of any grease residue. The backsplash may be covered with the same decorative laminate used on the counter, either with a cove or a square joint. Ceramic tile may be used in conjunction with a ceramic tile counter, or with a decorative laminate one. Mirror may also be selected for walls, which provides reflected light and visually enlarges the appearance of the counter space. A completely scrubbable wallcovering is another alternative material for the backsplash.

CERTIFIED KITCHEN DESIGNERS

A certified kitchen designer (**CKD**) is a professional who has proven knowledge and technical understanding through a very stringent examination process conducted by the Society of Certified Kitchen Designers, the licensing and certification agency of the American Institute of Kitchen Dealers. A CKD has technical knowledge of construction techniques and systems regarding new construction and light exterior and interior remodeling that includes plumbing, heating, and electrical.

A CKD will provide a functional and aesthetically pleasing arrangement of space with floor plans and interpretive renderings and drawings. In addition to designing and planning the kitchen, the CKD also supervises the installations of residential-style kitchens.

An interior designer would be well advised to work with a CKD.

BIBLIOGRAPHY

American Gas Association. *Buyer's Guide, Efficient Gas Ranges*, 1991.

Consumer Reports. "Cooktops, a Remodelers Dream?" (July 1994).

Consumer Reports. "Wall Ovens, a Cooktops Complement" (July 1994).

Jenn-Air Company. *Solid Element Cooktops*. Indianapolis, IN: Author, 1985.

Peter O. Whiteley. "Choosing a Kitchen Sink." *Sunset Magazine*, January 1993.

ENDNOTES

[1]Linda Trent, "Combining Kitchen and Bath Elements," *Interiors & Sources*, April 1994.

[2]*Buyer's Guide to Energy-Efficient Gas Furnaces & Appliances* (Arlington, VA: American Gas Association, 22209).

[3]Jenn-Air®, *Masterful Cooking—Induction*. (Indianapolis, IN 46226).

[4]Global Environmental Solutions, *Flameless Gas Burner*. (San Clemente, CA 92672).

[5]Jenn-Air®, *Masterful Cooking—Convection*. (Indianapolis, IN 46226).

GLOSSARY

Catalytic. A porous ceramic finish that accelerates the dispersion of food spatters.

Charcoal filter. A frame that contains charcoal particles that filter the grease from the moving air.

CKD. Certified Kitchen Designer.

Convection oven. Heated air flows around the food.

Conventional oven. Food is cooked by radiation.

Corridor kitchen. Two parallel walls with no contiguous area (see Figure 9–1).

Dolly. Two- or four-wheeled cart used for moving heavy appliances.

Drop-in range. Range designed to be built into the base units.

Free-standing range. Range having finished sides.

Glass-ceramic cooktop. A smooth ceramic top used as a cooking surface in electric ranges.

Griddle. A unit with a flat cooking surface used for cooking pancakes.

Grille. A unit specially for broiling food.

Hob. Sealed solid element providing a larger contact area with the bottom of the pan and better control at low-heat settings.

Kilowatt-hour (kwh). A unit of energy equal to 1,000 watt hours.

Microwave oven. Heat is generated by the activation of the molecules within the food by the microwaves.

Postforming. Heating a laminate to take the shape of a form.

Pullman kitchen. A one-wall kitchen plan (see Figure 9–1).

Pyrolytic. An oven that cleans by extremely high heat, incinerating any residue to an ash.

Rotisserie. An electrical accessory that rotates the food on a spit or skewer.

Shish-Kebab. A rotisserie accessory combining alternate small pieces of meat and/or vegetables on a skewer or spit.

Slide-in range. Similar in construction to a drop-in range except that the top edges may overhang the sides; therefore, this type must be slid in rather than dropped in.

Strip kitchen. One-wall kitchen plan (see Figure 9–1).

Studio kitchen. Also a one-wall kitchen plan (see Figure 9–1).

Work triangle. An imaginary triangle drawn between the sink, refrigerator, and cooking area.

Chapter 10

Bathrooms

The Greeks had many large public baths where one could take a hot and cold bath and then get a rubdown with olive oil. Public bathing was also practiced by the Romans. The Romans used aqueducts to bring the water to the people of Rome. After the fall of the Roman Empire, bathing became much less frequent during the Dark Ages. In the 1800s and early 1900s one often reads of the ritual of the Saturday night bath, where a metal tub was brought into the heated kitchen and hot water was poured in by hand. The last 25 years have produced almost 90 percent of all the progress in bathrooms.

It was American hotels that started the idea of bathing rooms, and the first one was built at the Tremont House in Boston in 1829. The idea proved very popular and spread to other hotels and private homes throughout the country. As a nation, Americans take more baths and showers than any other people in the world. The realities of the 1990s, however, include both energy and water conservation.

Other factors have led to additional changes:

The graying of America combined with new awareness of the needs of the physically challenged have increased demand for both safety features and barrier-free or accessible products that are attractive and functional, particularly in hospitality, commercial and multi-housing construction and renovation.[1]

As all bathrooms have the same three basic fixtures, it is the designer's challenge to create a bathroom that is not only unique but functional. A knowledge of the different materials used in these fixtures and the variety of shapes, sizes, and colors will help resolve this challenge.

PLANNING A BATHROOM

Eljer has the following suggestions for planning a better bathroom: The size of the family needs to be considered. The more people who will use a bathroom, the larger it should be. There should also be more storage, more electrical outlets, and perhaps more fixtures. If the bathroom is to be used by several people at the same time, compartmenting can often add to utility.

The family schedule should also be considered. Where several people depart for work or school at the same time, multiple or **compartmented** bathrooms should be considered. Two lavatories will allow a working couple to get ready for work at the same time.

The most economical arrangement of fixtures is against a single **wet wall**. Economy, however, is not the only factor to be considered. Plumbing codes, human comfort, and convenient use require certain minimum separation between and space around fixtures. The minimum size for a bathroom is approximately 5 feet × 7 feet, although if absolutely necessary, a few inches may be shaved off these measurements. Deluxe bathrooms may be very large and incorporate a seating area or an exercise room and/or a **spa**.

In a corridor-type bathroom, there should be 30 inches of aisle space between the bathtub and the edge of the counter or the fixture opposite. The bathtub should never be placed under the window because this will create too many problems—lack of privacy, drafts, condensation on the window, and possible damage to the wall when using a shower. There should be a minimum of 24 inches in front of a toilet to provide knee room. When there are walls on either side of the toilet, they should be 36 inches apart. If the **lavatory** or bathtub is adjacent to the toilet, then 30 inches is sufficient.

The lavatory requires elbow space. Five feet is the recommended minimum length of a counter top with two lavatories. The lavatories should be centered in the respective halves of the counter top. For a sitdown **vanity**, the counter should be 7 feet long with 24 inches between the edges of the lavatories for greatest comfort. Six inches minimum should be allowed between the edge of a lavatory and any side wall.

The location of the door is extremely important. The door should be located in such a manner that it will not hit a fixture because it will eventually cause damage both to the door and the fixture. A sliding pocket door may have to be used to prevent this from happening.

All bathroom fixtures, whether tubs, lavatories, toilets, or **bidets**, come in white and also in standard colors that are 20 percent more expensive. High-fashion colors—even black—are 40 percent more expensive than white. Care should be taken not to select fad colors that will become dated, because bathroom fixtures are both difficult and expensive to replace when remodeling. In order to obtain a perfect match, all fixtures should be ordered from the same manufacturer. Colors, even white, vary from one manufacturer to another.

FLOORS

Bathroom floors should be of a type that can be easily cleaned, particularly in the area of the bathtub, shower, and toilet (Figure 10–1). Ceramic tile may be used, but should not be highly glazed, because glazed tiles, when used on a floor, can be very slippery when wet. Other types of flooring material for the tub area

Figure 10–1
Using the Mix and Matchables glazed ceramic tile from American Olean creates a custom floor. A 6-inch matte glazed tile in a neutral is selected in an octagon or pentagon shape. Then a 1 3/8-inch accent dot available in a variety of glazes completes the design. A contrasting grout outlines the design. For the wall 6-inch Sizzle Strip® liners are used. (Photograph courtesy of American Olean)

can be wood with a good finish or any of the resilient flooring materials.

Carpeting may be used in the master bath but is not suggested for a family bath because of a likelihood of excessive moisture, causing possible mold and mildew.

WALLS

The bathroom is an area in the house where wallcoverings are often used. Vinyls or vinyl-coated wallcoverings are suggested because they are easy to wipe dry and maintain. Again, because of the moisture problem, the walls should be treated for possible mildew (see Chapter 2 page 13).

Most of the manufactured materials used for

counters can be used to cover vertical surfaces, either on the wall or as a shower enclosure. This would include Syndecrete® discussed in Chapter 1.

Only semigloss paints or enamels that can withstand moisture should be used on bathroom walls.

If an acrylic shower and tub **surround** is not used, ceramic tile is installed because of its vitreous quality.

BATHTUBS

The average bathtub is 5 feet long, 30 inches wide, and, in the less expensive styles, only 14 inches deep. However, 6-foot long tubs are available for those who like to soak, and the height, measured from the floor, may also be 15, 16, or even 22 inches. When bathing children the lower height is more convenient. However, the depth figures are the outside measurements and, making allowance for the **overflow** pipe, the 14 inches does not permit the drawing of a very deep bath. Most state laws require that all bathtubs installed today have a **slip-resistant** bottom. Many tubs also come with a handle on one or both sides that is extremely useful for the elderly or infirm.

The straight end of the bathtub contains the drain and the plumbing, such as faucets or **fittings** as they are sometimes called, and the overflow pipe; therefore, location of the bathtub must be decided before the order is placed. Bathtubs may be ordered with left or right drain, all four sides enclosed, enclosed on the front and two sides, front and one side, or for a completely built-in look, a drop-in model may be specified.

The drop-in model is sometimes installed as a sunken tub. While this may present a luxurious appearance, thought must be given to the problem of getting into and out of a tub that low. Attention must also be given to maintenance. Cleaning a sunken tub means lying flat on the floor to reach the interior. Another danger of a sunken or partially recessed tub is that small children may crawl into the bathtub and hurt themselves or, at the worst, drown.

Construction. Bathtubs are manufactured of several materials. The old standby is the porcelain enameled cast-iron tub. This was originally a high-sided bathtub raised from the floor on ball-and-claw feet with the underside exposed. This style is still available today in a slightly modernized version. The porcelain enamel gives better color than

other materials and is approximately 1/16 of an inch thick, but this finish can be chipped if a heavy object is dropped onto it. Therefore, bathtubs should be kept covered with a blanket, or a special plastic liner may be used, until construction has been completed.

A cast-iron bathtub is the most durable bathtub available but it is expensive and heavy; it weighs about 500 pounds. Therefore, the floor should be strong enough to bear the combined weight of the tub, a tub full of water, and the bather.

Formed steel tubs with a porcelain enamel finish were developed to provide a lightweight (about 100 pounds) tub that would be less expensive than cast iron. They are ideally suited for upper story installations or for remodeling because they are easier to move into place. A formed steel tub is noisier than the cast iron, but a sound-deadening coating may be applied to the underside at extra cost. Or, if the bathtub does not come with an insulated coating on the outside, a roll of fiberglass insulation can be wrapped around the tub. It not only helps the fixture retain the heat longer, but also helps reduce noise. Because of the properties of the steel, formed steel bathtubs may flex; therefore, they do not have such a thick layer of porcelain enamel as do cast-iron tubs.

When renovating old bathrooms with a badly stained or chipped cast-iron or steel bathtub (not fiberglass), there is now an alternative to tearing out the walls to get access to the old tub. This is done by using Re-Bath®, a bathtub liner made of nonporous ABS (Acrylonic Butadiene Styrene) acrylic, molded to fit into any bathtub without disturbing flooring, walls, or plumbing. Also available are Re-Bath wall systems designed to go over existing tile walls. A new overflow and drain are also provided.

One of the materials for bathtubs is heavy-duty polyester reinforced with fiberglass and surfaced with a **gel** coat. In specifying this type of tub, it is important to select a name brand. As there are currently many poor quality units on the market produced by a process that does not require a large investment, this field has many manufacturers, not all of whom are conscious of quality. Consequently, the tubs can crack easily and lose their surface fairly rapidly. Good maintenance practices and avoidance of abrasive cleansers are mandatory. Should the gel coat surface become dull in appearance, some manufacturers suggest using a coat of marine wax or a good automotive wax to restore the shine.

Another type of lightweight bathtub is acrylic reinforced with fiberglass with the color throughout. This type of bathtub does not have such a high gloss as the gel coated ones, but it is easier to maintain and the color does not fade.

There are several advantages to this new material. First, it is much lighter weight than steel or cast iron, though maybe not as durable. Second, the tub surround can be cast as an integral part of the bathtub and can include such features as a built-in seat, soap ledges, and grab bars. This latter type can be installed only in new construction, because the tub and surround are too large to be placed in a remodeled bathroom. For remodeling, there are molded tub units with wall surrounds in two, three, or four pieces that pass easily through doorways and join together in the recessed bathtub area to form a one-piece unit.

International Cushioned Products Inc. makes a Soft Tub, with foam cushioning inside bonded to a fiberglass outer shell. The tough, nonporous elastomeric surface is durable like porcelain, yet it will remain supple for the life of the bathtub. They are warranted for a limited 10-year residential and 5-year commercial use. The nonslip surface minimizes the risk of a fall, but should a fall occur the cushioned surface greatly reduces the chance of injury. The cushioned surface molds to the foot, providing stability when entering, exiting, or showering.

Soaking tubs are also made from reinforced fiberglass. Instead of sitting or laying in the tub, one sits on a molded, built-in seat and the tub is filled to the requisite depth. Some soaking tubs are recessed into the floor, and the bather steps over the edge and down into the tub; others are placed at floor level and require several steps to reach the top. Soaking tubs should not be installed in every bathroom in the house, as bathing small children is impossible and the elderly or infirm will find entering and leaving a soaking tub too dangerous. A regular bathtub should be installed in at least one bathroom in the house.

Whirlpool baths are generally bathroom fixtures; they must be drained after each use (Figure 10–2). Jacuzzi®, the inventor of the whirlpool bath, uses continuous cast acrylic, reinforced with fiberglass for added strength. Quiet jets are placed low in the bath for the best results in hydrotherapy (see Chapter 1).

Figure 10–2
The Fontana^{TM} whirlpool bath for two has water cascading down the spectacular stair step. The Fontana includes a European-style, hand-held shower; four PowerPro® fully adjustable whirlpool jets; dual Water Rainbow® spouts; and conveniently located fingertip jet control. Photographer © Oscar Thompson. (Photograph courtesy of Jacuzzi Whirlpool Bath)

These whirlpool jets create a circular pattern of bubbles as the air/water mixture flows into the tub providing deeply penetrating massage. For a problem corner, The Fiore™, from Jacuzzi, features a double Water Rainbow® spout system that creates the sight and sound of water gently cascading down the staircase waterfall sculpted into the bath design. Many luxury models have an accessory area with mirrored interior and hand-held shower head.

For those interested in a whirlpool bath and family spa combination, the Delfino™ provides a luxurious cleansing or a relaxing soak. Created for indoor use, this unit contains an in-line heater and filter system so it may be used as a spa or a traditional fill-and-drain whirlpool bath.

For the active elderly or for any person who might have difficulty stepping over the edge of a bathtub, Kohler's Precedence™ whirlpool bath with swing-open door is the answer (Figure 10–3).

Spas are similar to whirlpool baths but need not be drained after each use. They are equipped with heat and filtration systems. Since the same water is re-circulated, daily testing and maintenance of the proper water chemistry is required. Spas may be in-

Figure 10–3
The accessible ease of Kohler's Precedence™ whirlpool bath with swing-open door indicates the design for this stylish bath for the active elderly by Ethel Nemetz, ASID, IBD. The tile "rug" in front of the bath is both decorative and safer than using a loose area rug in the space. Heat lamps are recessed above the whirlpool for added comfort while bathing. The leaded glass clerestory reveals a faux outdoor scene, an effective technique for opening up an interior space. Plumbing fixtures by Kohler; floor and wall ceramic tile is by Ann Sacks Tile & Stone, a Kohler company. (Photograph courtesy of Kohler)

stalled outside in warmer climates or in an area other than the bathroom. They have many of the same features as the whirlpool baths but are larger, being 64 to 84 inches long, 66 to 84 inches wide, and 28 to 37 inches high. Spas come with factory-installed redwood skirts and rigid covers.

Tub surrounds and shower enclosures may also be reinforced fiberglass, as mentioned previously, or they may be decorative laminate, ceramic tile, solid ABS, or solid acrylic. Many of these have integrated tubs with built-in whirlpool systems. The all-in-one type eliminates the need to caulk around the area where the tub and surround meet. Failure to install and caulk the tub surround properly is the major cause of leaks in the tub area. When designing a bathroom, the bathtub should be placed where an access panel can be installed to facilitate future plumbing repairs. Access *must* be provided to any whirlpool equipment to facilitate future maintenance.

Ceramic tile is installed as described in Chapter 5. The substrate must be exterior grade plywood or a special water-resistant grade of gypsum board. The backer board mentioned in Chapter 4 also makes a suitable substrate. Particular attention must be paid to the application of the grout, since it is the grout that makes ceramic tile a waterproof material. Sometimes, particularly when a cast-iron tub is used, the extra weight may cause a slight sagging of the floor. Any space caused by this settling should be filled immediately.

SHOWERS

Showers may be installed for use in a bathtub or they may be in a separate shower stall. There should always be at least one bathtub in a house, but stall showers may be used in the remaining bathrooms. When used in conjunction with a bathtub, the tub spout contains a **diverter** that closes off the spout and diverts the water to the shower head. A bathroom with a shower instead of a tub is designated as a three-quarter bath.

The standard height of a shower head is 66 inches for men and 60 inches for women, which puts the spray below the hairline. These measurements also mean that the plumbing for the shower head must break through the tub or shower surround. Therefore, it is recommended that the shower **feed-in** be 74 inches above the floor. When placed at this height, the shower head should be adjustable so that it can be used for hair-washing or hit below the hairline.

A hand-held shower can easily be installed in any bathtub, provided the walls are covered with a waterproof material. These showers come with a special diversion spout and the water reaches the shower head by means of a flexible metal line. One type of shower head is hung on a hook at the required height. Another type is mounted on a 5-foot vertical rod and attached to the water outlet by means of a flexible hose. This full-range sliding spray holder or grab bar locks at any desired height. The spray holder is both adjustable and removable.

There are several positive attributes of the hand-held shower. One is that it can be hung at a lower level for use by children, and the hand-held unit can be used to rinse the hair of young children without the complaint of "the soap is getting in my eyes." A second factor is that the hand-held unit may be used to clean and rinse the interior of the bathtub.

Water conservation does not mean a skimpy shower. The Speakman Anystream showerheads will automatically adjust water flow to compensate for the available pressure. The output ranges from bracing needle spray to gentle rain.

Stall showers are 34 × 32 inches wide; a slightly larger 36-inch square is recommended if space is available. These are the minimum requirements, but of course the deluxe shower may be 48 inches or even 60 × 36 inches wide and usually includes a seat.

Stall showers may be constructed entirely of ceramic tile; in other words, the slightly sloping base and walls are all made of tile. When installing a shower area made from ceramic tile, particular attention should be paid to the waterproof base and installation procedures supplied by the manufacturer or the Tile Council of America. Other stall showers have a **preformed base** with the surround touching the top of the 5- to 6-inch deep base. This preformed base is less slippery than a base of tile but not quite as aesthetically pleasing. Shower walls may also be constructed of any of the solid surface materials.

The J-Shower Tower™ features a full-size whirlpool bath combined with an elegant, curved shower enclosure. The unit offers optimal hydrotherapy provided by four patented PowerPro® jets as well as convenient showering, all in one compact, yet stylish, area. Two sizes are available: 60 or 72 inches long × 32 inches wide × 96 inches high.

Water is kept within the shower area by several means. One is a shower curtain that is hung from rings at the front of the shower. A shower curtain is a decorative feature but, unless care is taken to ensure the placement of the shower curtain inside the base when using the shower, water may spill over onto the floor and cause a slippery area. Glass shower doors are also used, the type depending upon the local building codes (see Figure 10–4). All have tempered glass, but some codes require the addition of a wire mesh. These glass doors may pivot, hinge, slide, or fold. The major maintenance problem with glass doors is removing the soap and hard water residue from the glass surface and cleaning the water channel at the base of the door. A water softener does greatly reduce or even eliminate this residue. Some shower units are designed with close-fitting doors that completely enclose the front of the unit and become steam systems with a **sauna** effect. An example of multiple use is the J-Carré (see Figure 10–4).

Masterbath showers often are designed so no door or curtain is required. These shower stalls have walls so placed that the water is contained within the wet area.

The Freewill™ line of barrier-free bathing products from Kohler is designed to meet the strict ANSI standards, with slip-resistant bottom for safety and grab bars fabricated of rigid nylon to provide a firm grip even when wet. It features a removable transfer seat so that bathers can sit down and swing legs over the edge of the tub, instead of stepping into it. The fold-up seats make it ideal for installation in a residence where one family member may have limited mobility, but the others need no special assistance.

Wheelchair accessible stall showers are available varying in size from a 42-inch × 36-inch unit to the 65-inch × 36-inch unit with an interior threshold height of only 1/2 inch. Units with integral seats have the seat placed toward the front of the enclosure for easier access.

Kohler produces a Masterbath Series, personal and programmable retreats that combine the soothing elements of sun, sauna, steam, shower, and warm breezes with the added relaxation of a spacious whirlpool bath. The size of the unit itself measures 91 × 52 × 82 inches with the whirlpool bath measuring 66 × 19 1/2 × 33 inches. However, the recess area must be 96 × 106 × 94 inches in order to accommodate the necessary equipment. The luxury Environment™ features an upholstered deck, 24-carat gold trim, and genuine teakwood interior—the ultimate in sybaritic pleasure. The Habitat™ Masterbath has the same functional features as the Environment Masterbath, but the interior is acrylic instead of teak, has chrome interior trim, and comes in 16 Kohler colors. The padded deck is optional.

TUB AND SHOWER FAUCETS

The old-fashioned type of faucet is ledge mounted; the fitting is mounted on the edge of the tub or tub enclosure, usually with an 8-inch to 18-inch **spread**.

Tub/shower combinations may be of five different types. Two of them are wall mounted, including the single control, which is operated by pulling to turn on, pushing to turn off, and twisting to regulate the temperature. The single control may be operated with one hand. The other wall-mounted type has separate handles for hot and cold water. An 8-inch spread is standard.

Diverters include the diverter-on-spout where, when the water temperature is balanced, the diverter is pulled up to start the shower. To stop the flow of water to the shower head, the diverter is pushed down. The handle diverter design has three handles and, by twisting the middle handle, the water is diverted to the shower head. The two other handles control the hot and cold water. This handle diverter has 8-inch **centers**. The button diverter is often found on single control faucets where, by merely pushing the button, water is diverted.

Most shower heads are adjustable and change the flow of water to drenching, normal, or fine spray. Some shower heads have a pulsating flow that provides a massaging action. Conventional shower heads use from 6 to 8 gallons per minute. With conservation of water in mind, the plumbing codes are being amended to make 2.7 gallons of water per minute at 60 psi the maximum amount of water that can be used.

Epic has created a new fast-flowing Roman tub valve that features 27 gallons per minute at 40 pounds per square inch (psi) pressure, using 1/2-inch supply lines. This enables whirlpool baths to be filled rapidly provided a large capacity water tank is used.

For stall showers, the controls may be single control similar in action to the single control bath type. The second design has two separate hot and cold handles with a standard 8-inch spread.

Jacuzzi Whirlpool Bath offers a new addition to the J-Dream™ family of shower systems—the J-Carré. This state-of-the-art corner unit incorporates an 8-function shower nozzle and 16 programmable jets. Detailed design features include a sculpted seat, cascading waterfall, soothing steam bath, and transparent cap. A full-length mirror allows grooming convenience, while a built-in cabinet and shelves provide ample storage space. Two tempered-glass sliding panels facilitate entry and exit (Figure 10–4).

For a children's bathroom, Grohe America has shower heads featuring Disney characters.

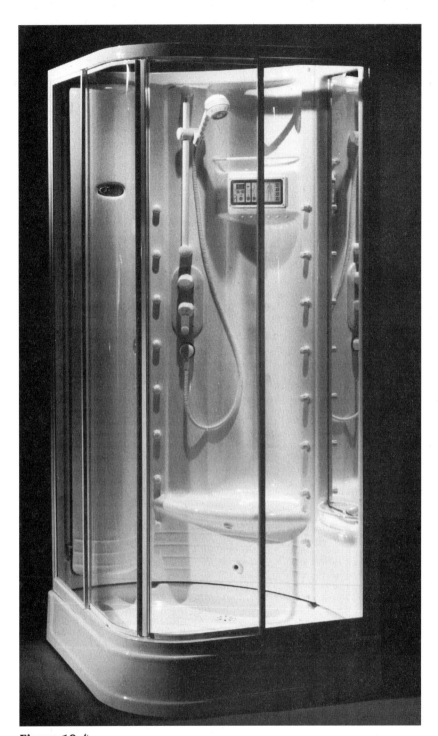

Figure 10–4
*The J-Carré is the new addition to the J-Dream™ Family of shower
systems. This state-of-the art corner unit incorporates an 8-function
shower nozzle and 16 programmable jets. Detailed design features
include a sculpted seat, cascading waterfall, soothing steam bath,
and transparent cap. A full-length mirror allows grooming
convenience, while a built-in cabinet and shelves provide ample
storage. Two tempered-glass sliding panels facilitate entry and exit.
The J-Carré measures 36 inches long, 35 inches wide, and 88
inches high. (Photograph courtesy of Jacuzzi Whirlpool Bath)*

LAVATORIES

Lavatories come in many sizes, shapes, and materials according to personal and space requirements. Some are **pedestal** lavatories and may be as streamlined or decorative as desired (see Color Plate Figure 8). Most are made of vitreous china, but some pedestals are even sculpted out of marble. Besides being made out of china, lavatories may be made from enameled cast iron, enameled formed steel, polished brass, or some of the solid surface materials.

Lavatories are usually round or oval, but they may also be rectangular, or even triangular for corner installations. Sizes range from 11 × 11 inches for powder rooms, to 38 × 28 inches for hair and other washing chores.

The pedestal lavatories are the latest style of lavatory to be used, but they are probably more suitable in a master bathroom because they do not provide the adjacent counter area usually needed in family bathrooms. To overcome this lack, some pedestal lavatories come as large as 44 × 22 inches, with a wide ledge surrounding the bowl area. The Console table from the Revival™ collection has an oval basin with a generously proportioned rim wide enough for toiletries (Figure 10–5).

Built-in lavatories may be one of five types. First, they may be self-rimming, where a hole is cut into the counter smaller than the size of the lavatory and the bowl is placed in such a manner that the edge is raised above the level of the counter. With a self-rimming sink, water cannot be swept back into the bowl, but must be mopped up (see Figure 10–2).

Figure 10–5
Console table from the Revival™ Collection of Kohler. (Photograph courtesy of Kohler)

Second, for a flush counter and bowl installation, the lavatory may be installed with a flush metal rim. This is a popular and inexpensive style but can cause a cleaning problem at the juncture of the rim with the counter top.

Third there is the integral bowl and counter such as the one made of solid surface materials. With this type, which may be placed virtually anywhere on the vanity top, the counter top and bowl are seamed for a one-piece look, with the faucets usually mounted on the counter.

A fourth type is the more old-fashioned wall-hung installation that is quite often used in powder rooms or for wheelchair users. The fifth type is installed under the counter and is generally used with a tile, marble, or synthetic counter top. With more types of solid surface materials available, the under-the-counter installation is becoming very popular. Under-

Figure 10–6
On the left a glass top sink from Robern, Inc., for mounting with its Series M mirrored-cabinet Stacking System. The sink wall-mounts directly into the mirrored cabinet, appearing almost effortlessly suspended in space. A chrome faucet from Kroin is mounted directly into the mirrored cabinet. All plumbing and support for the sink are hidden behind removable mirrored panels. Photographer: Tom Crane ©. (Photograph courtesy of Robern Inc.) Top right is Iris design from Sherle Wagner. The handpainted, china over-edge bowl is decorated with mauve and lavender blue irises, with coordinating basin set in 24-karat gold plate. (Photograph courtesy of Sherle Wagner) Bottom right is an undermounted VITRAFORM Glass sink in Starphire frosted finish, with engraved floral design. (Photograph courtesy of Cherry Creek Ent., Inc.)

the-counter installations require that the fittings be deck mounted (see Figure 10–6).

Robern Inc. has a 16-inch round, brightly polished stainless steel bowl set in a 3/4-inch clear glass top with an arc front (Figure 10–6). Cherry Creek Enterprises uses glass in a different manner. They laminate glass for their Vitraform sinks, which are available in clear, and several colors, all in a polished or frosted finish, with custom engraved options available (see Figure 10–6).

A specialty lavatory is the solid brass self-rimming bowl that adds a special elegant look to a bathroom. For a unique lavatory, a self-rimming painted ceramic washbasin may be used. These specialized sinks have wall- or counter-mounted faucets.

Some lavatories come punched with three holes. With single-control fittings and 4-inch centerset fittings, the third hole is for the **pop-up rod**. However, in wide-spread fittings, the third hole is used for the mixed water.

Other lavatories are punched with one or two extra holes. These are for use as a shampoo lavatory and have a retractable spray unit. The second extra hole is used for a soap or shampoo dispenser. These shampoo lavatories are extremely useful for a family with children, as the bowl is usually installed in a 32-inch high vanity as compared to the 36-inch height of a kitchen sink. Some styles even have spouts that swing away.

LAVATORY FAUCETS

There is also a wide choice of lavatory faucets. For the past few decades, **center-fit** faucet fittings have been used. On these units, the two handles and spout are in one piece, with a 4-inch spread. The single-control unit with a 4-inch spread has a central control that regulates both temperature and rate of flow. This single control unit may also work by means of a lever that, when pulled up, increases the flow of water and, when pushed down, decreases the flow. Temperature is controlled by moving the lever to the right for cold and to the left for warm or hot water. The lever is easier to operate for arthritis victims who cannot grasp and turn the knob type.

The placement of the faucets depends on the design of the sink. Some sinks have predrilled holes for the faucets and others require a deck-mounted style. Faucets must be ordered after the sink has been selected.

The popularity of center-fit faucets is declining; the use of spread-fit fittings now comprises 80 percent of the market and is growing. Spread-fit faucets have the hot and cold handles and the spout independent of each other. In order to make installation and choice of faucet sets easier, the fittings should be joined by means of flexible connectors. If these flexible connectors are not used, selection of faucets may be limited to the spread of the holes that come in the selected lavatory. When the center-fit fittings are used, the plate covers the center hole. When a spread-fit fitting is used, the center hole accommodates the spout (Figure 10–7).

Several companies are now manufacturing faucets designed as barrier-free products and also with water conservation in mind. When the electronic beam is broken by the hands, the water flows at the preset temperature. Savings of up to 85 percent of normal water usage are not unusual. Additional energy savings are realized by conserving hot water.

Moen produces a Riser® for lavatories. This spout lifts 7 inches above the sink for washing hair or watering plants. The spout tip swivels to convert to a water fountain.

Faucets may be polished chrome, black chrome, polished brass, or even gold plated. One of the current trends is to use two different finishes in the same faucet such as black chrome with polished chrome and/or polished brass, or wood and brass. Also, brushed nickel with brass is often used. Two finishes are often used on what is known as the ring handle. Delta Faucet Company has ring handles suitable for retrofit, so the bathroom can be given a new appearance without great cost. Translucent and metal handles have slight indentations in order to provide a nonslipping surface. Other handles may be of the lever type. The traditional shape for spouts is being replaced by the more delicately curved shape that is popular in Europe. The Roman-style faucets previously used for bathtubs are now being used for lavatories.

What has previously been a feature of kitchen faucets has now come to the bathroom. Delta has a 4-inch center-set faucet with a new pull-out spout that can extend to 21 inches and may be used for washing hair, bathing infants, filling containers, and even washing the family pet (in the utility room, of course).

For use by the handicapped are ADA-approved **wrist-control** handles that do not require turning or pulling but are activated by a push or pull with the wrist rather than the fingers.

(a)

(b)

(c)

(d)

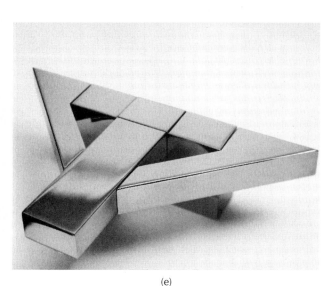

(e)

Figure 10–7

A wide variety of lavatory faucets are illustrated here. (a) The Moen® Model #5003/H-205P Concentrix™ widespread lavatory faucet, chrome finish with polished brass handles. (Photograph courtesy of Moen Inc.) (b) On the left Moen Model #441/H-105 P and on the right #4641/H-104P Concentrix™ 4-inch center-set lavatory faucets, chrome finish with polished brass handles. (Photograph courtesy of Moen Inc.) (c) A lavatory faucet with curved, tapered spout and faceted dome handles from the new Revival™ Collection of faucets and accessories. Available in either polished chrome or polished brass. (Photograph courtesy of Kohler Co.) (d) A lavatory faucet from Kohler's TABORET® line has a softly contoured, high arch spout and subtle brass accents. Shown with TABORET® faucets. (Photograph courtesy of Kohler Co.) (e) Contemporary faucet from Paul Decorative Products.

TOILETS

In Europe, a toilet is often called the "water closet" and the plumbing trade frequently uses that term or "closet" when referring to what the layperson calls a toilet. In some areas of the country, it may also be referred to as a commode. We will use the word "toilet" in the text as this is the more common word, but when talking to a plumber, "closet" is more correct.

Toilet bowls are constructed of vitreous china and in most instances so are the tanks. However, some tanks may be made of other materials. Only vitreous china can withstand the acids to which a toilet is subjected. Most toilets are designed with water-saving devices that are important considerations, both economically and environmentally.

There are two basic shapes to a toilet: the regular or round bowl and the elongated bowl. Toilets do not come with a toilet seat; therefore, it is important to know the shape of the toilet before ordering a seat. Some special shapes do come with a seat. Another design feature of the elongated bowl is that more space, usually 2 inches, is required for installation. Consult local building codes.

Toilets may be wall hung, which leaves the floor unobstructed for easy cleaning, or floor mounted. Wall-hung toilets have a wall outlet; in other words, they flush through a drain in the wall. In order to support the weight of a wall-hung toilet, 6-inch studs must be used and an L-shaped unit called a chair carrier must be installed.

Floor-mounted toilets flush through the floor or the wall. For concrete floor construction, wall outlets are suggested to eliminate the extra cost of slab piercing.

Another choice in the design of toilets is whether tank and bowl should be a **low profile**, one-piece integral unit, or whether the tank and bowl should be in two pieces for a one-piece toilet. For space saving in powder rooms or bathrooms, a corner toilet, an Eljer exclusive, is available. The nostalgia for the past can be created by using an overhead wall-hung tank with the traditional pull chain. In areas where condensation on the toilet tank is a problem, an insulated tank may be ordered.

All toilets are required to have a visible water turn-off down near the bowl on the back wall in case of a faulty valve in the tank.

Toilets for the elderly and infirm have an 18-inch high seat, while regular toilets have 15 1/2-inch high seats. This higher toilet may also have a set of metal rails or armrests for extra support. The height of the seat on the one-piece toilets may be even lower.

Toilets have different flushing actions. The washdown is the least expensive but is also the least efficient and the noisiest. The least inexpensive of the siphon-action toilets is the reverse trap, where the rush of water when flushed creates a siphon action in the trapway, assisted by a small water jet at the trapway outlet. More of the bowl is covered by water, so it stays cleaner. The siphon-jet that is used on almost all newer toilets is much quieter and more efficient but usually more expensive. However, most of the interior of the bowl is covered by water, thus aiding in cleaning.

Under the provision of the 1992 National Energy Policy Act, the law now limits new toilets to 1.6 gallons per flush, compared to the typical 3.5-gallon models. For a family of four, that means a savings of more than 11,000 gallons of water per year. A European import even has double-handed flushers to vary the amount of water used in each flush.

BIDETS

While common in Europe, bidets are only now becoming an accepted fixture in American bathrooms and then only in the more sophisticated types of installations. A bidet is generally installed as a companion and adjacent to the water closet or toilet and is used for cleansing the perineal area. Bidets do not have seats. The user sits astride the bowl, facing the controls that regulate water temperature and operate the pop-up drain and transfer valve. Water enters the bidet via the spray rinse in the bottom of the bowl; or the water can be diverted by the transfer valve to the flushing rim. A bidet may also be used as a foot bath when the pop-up drain is closed.

When, as in a bidet, the fresh water supply is below or directly involved with piping, a **vacuum breaker** must be installed.

COUNTER TOPS

The term "vanity cabinet" is not technically used in the architectural profession, but ready-made bathroom cabinets containing the lavatory are so often called and sold by this name that this term will be used for the prefinished cabinet with doors underneath the counter top. Vanity cabinets may be ordered with or without the finished counter top and, with this design, the lavatory is purchased separately. Other types of vanities may come with the counter top and bowl molded in one.

Figure 10–8

Dal Tile shows how Pattern 4" and Pattern 8" can be used to create a custom look, even on curved surfaces. Counter area is cut on 1" scores, using Pattern 8", and the bath wall on 2" scores using Pattern 4". Plumbing fixtures are from Kohler. Ellipse sink and faucets are Pillows™. Built-in bath area has deck mounted Pillows faucet with Flume spout. (Photograph courtesy of Dal Tile)

A ready-made vanity is between 29 and 30 inches in height. For a master bathroom in a custom-designed house, the counter can be raised to suit personal requirements; however, at least one of the vanities in the house must be at the lower height.

Dal Tile's 1900 Vitrestone Series, Pattern 4″, is an 8-inch × 8-inch tile that has been scored into 2-inch wide strips with an eased edge. The tile cutter cuts on the scored area and then each piece can be laid into place on flat or curved surfaces (Figure 10–8). Also available is Pattern 8″, where each tile is scored into eight 1-inch strips. Pattern 8″ on the curved surfaces and Pattern 4″ on the walls is an excellent choice for designers who wish to design a custom ceramic tile area without the expense of special custom orders (see Figure 10–8).

Most custom-designed bathrooms have specially designed cabinets containing the lavatory with a storage area beneath. A bathroom counter top may be made of the same materials as a kitchen counter, though marble is more frequently used in bathrooms than kitchens.

Solid surfacing materials for counter tops, vanities, lavatory bowls, showers, and bathtubs are becoming increasingly popular because they are versatile and attractive (Figure 10–9).

Figure 10–9
Syndecrete® was used to cast this monolithic bathtub, which has 1/2-inch tempered glass dividing it from the shower area. The panel on the right is a Syndecrete slab with acrylic rods cast in it for translucent light. The copper zig-zag pipe on the panel is a towel warming bar, which heats up when water is used. (Photograph courtesy of Syndesis Inc.)

ACCESSORIES

There should be 22 inches of towel storage for each person. Towels should be located within convenient reach of the bath, shower, and lavatory. Soap containers may be recessed into the wall, such as those used in the tub area. For the lavatory with a counter, a soap dish can be a colorful accessory. A toilet tissue dispenser should be conveniently located adjacent to the toilet.

Ground frequency interrupter (**GFI**) electrical outlets should also be provided for the myriad of electrical gadgets used in the bathroom. All switches should be located so that they cannot be reached from a tub or shower area. This is usually required by local codes.

Mirrors may be on the door of a built-in medicine cabinet or they may be installed to cover the whole wall over the counter area. When used in the latter manner, they visibly enlarge the bathroom. The top of the mirror should be at least 72 inches above the floor.

Robern Inc., the manufacturer of the sink shown in Figure 10–6, has a very wide selection of mirrored wall cabinets. All its swing-door cabinets include a swing-out magnifying mirror. When opened, the mirror projects out over the sink for comfortable use. Glass shelves are 1/4 to 3/8 inches thick. Most of these cabinets have mirrored interiors and are available in 4-, 5-, and 8-inch depths and come with optional defogging door and concealed 110-volt outlets for recharging and use of electric appliances.

Broan has a wall-mounted hair dryer with two-speed control. The flexible hose reaches 72 inches to allow ample freedom of movement while drying hair.

One recent item to appear in upscale bathrooms is the heated towel rail. This may be heated by hot water recirculating through the house or be activated by an electrical switch.

The materials selected for floors, walls, and ceilings should be compatible with the moist conditions that prevail in most bathrooms.

Certified Bathroom Designers (**CBD**) perform the same services for bathroom design as CKDs do for kitchens.

PUBLIC RESTROOMS

The bathrooms previously discussed were designed to accommodate one or two people at the most. However, in public restrooms, conditions and location may mean designing an area to be used by many people at the same time. This includes not only people who can walk, but also those who use wheelchairs.

Public restrooms receive much physical abuse, most of which is not premeditated, but occurs through normal wear and tear. Unfortunately, vandalism is a major problem; therefore, fixtures and materials must be selected for durability. Naturally, the two-stall restroom in a small restaurant and the multistall restrooms in a huge recreational facility will have to be designed differently with this factor in mind.

Another factor in the selection of materials and fixtures is maintenance. Floors are almost always made of ceramic tile or similar material and require a floor drain not only for an emergency flooding problem, but also to facilitate the cleaning and disinfecting of the floor.

Lavatories

To aid in cleaning the counter areas of public restrooms, vitreous china lavatories with flush metal rims are most frequently specified. They provide quick cleaning of any excess water on the counter. White sinks are usually selected in restrooms for two reasons: They are cheaper; and cleanliness is more easily visible.

Lavatories come with the normal three holes punched in the top, but soft or liquid soap dispensers may be installed in a four-hole sink. Or, the soap dispenser may be attached to the wall above each lavatory or between two adjacent ones.

For free-standing applications, wall-hung vitreous china lavatories may be specified.

For those who are confined to wheelchairs, a specially designed lavatory that meets ADA requirements must be installed to enable the seated person to reach the faucet handles. Again, a wrist-control handle or a push button that requires five pounds or less of pressure should be specified. Because some wheelchair occupants are paraplegic, it is necessary to take safety precautions that include either turning down the temperature of the water to 110° or wrapping the waste pipe with some form of insulation. These measures will prevent inadvertent burns.

Faucets

Some companies specialize in faucets designed to be used in public restrooms. These faucets are available with **metering devices**, usually of the push-button type, that can be adjusted to flow for 5 to 15 seconds. This, of course, conserves both energy and water and prevents accidental flooding (Figure 10–10).

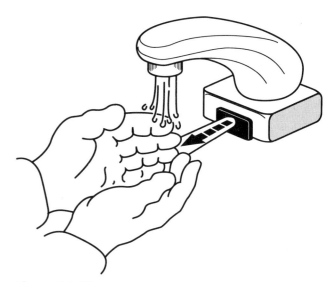

Figure 10–10
The Speakman SENSORFLO™ faucet requires no handles to turn on the flow of water. (Drawing courtesy of Speakman Co.)

Other faucets have an electronic eye, where, when the hands are put under the faucet, it turns on a temperature controlled stream, and when removed, the water stops flowing.

Toilets

Wall-hung toilets are quite often used in public restrooms to facilitate cleaning. Toilet seats do not have lids and must have an open front. To aid in quicker maintenance and to avoid vandalism, toilets in public restrooms do not usually use the conventional tank, but have a **flushometer** valve. This valve requires greater **water pressure** to operate but uses less water and is easier to maintain. This type of valve is not used in private residences because it is too noisy. It may be operated by hand or sometimes by a foot pedal.

Another method of flushing is electronic. After the toilet has been used and there is no longer pressure on the seat, it will automatically flush.

Several different types of **urinals** may be used in the men's room. All are constructed of vitreous china and all have integral flushing rims. One is the stall urinal mounted on the floor. Others may be wall hung, with a wall-hung unit with an elongated front for use by those who are physically disabled, as required by the ADA.

Stall Partitions

There are many different styles of stall dividers and many different materials from which to select. Marble is shown in Figure 10–11. The **pilasters** may be floor mounted with overhead bracing, floor supported, or ceiling hung. The latter type minimizes maintenance but also requires structural steel support in the ceiling. Doors for regular stalls are 24 inches wide and open into the stall. The actual width of the stall is determined by the width of the pilasters.

Stalls for the disabled must comply with the ADA and have wider, out-swinging doors that must meet applicable codes. The handicapped stall is usually placed at the end so that a passer-by is not hit when the door is opened from the inside.

The material used for partitions may be galvanized steel that has been primed and finished with two coats of baked enamel, stainless steel, seamless high-pressure decorative laminate, or even marble. All of these come in a variety of colors and may be coordinated with the colors used for washroom accessories, vanity centers, shelves, and counter tops.

When the design of restrooms dictates, entrance screens for privacy should be used. It is important to consider the direction the door opens and placement of mirrors to ensure privacy.

Another screen used in men's rooms is the urinal screen. These may also be wall hung, floor anchored, ceiling hung, or supported by a narrow stile going from floor to ceiling, in a similar manner to the stall partitions. They are placed between each urinal or be-

Figure 10–11
Marblstal® made of Georgia Marble® is perfect for toilet compartments and urinal screens as shown in this photograph. Marblstal is prefabricated, ready to install with rugged chrome-plated hardware included. (Photograph courtesy of the Georgia Marble Co.)

tween the urinal area and other parts of the restroom. (See Figure 10-11.)

Accessories

As was mentioned previously, soap dispensers may be installed on the lavatory rim itself. This type is probably preferable as any droppings from the dispenser are washed away in the bowl; the dry powder type usually leaves a mess on the counter area. Paper towel dispensers should be within easy reach of the lavatory, together with towel disposal containers. Sometimes both these accessories come in one wall-hung or wall-recessed unit. Another method of hand drying is the heated air blower. At the push of a button, heated air is blown out and the hands are rubbed briskly. This type of hand dryer eliminates the necessity of having the mess of paper towel disposal, but is a problem if the dryer breaks down. Newer hand dryers operate electronically, similar to the automatic faucets; in other words, they start when the hands are positioned under the blower and turn off when hands are removed.

Each toilet compartment requires a toilet tissue dispenser; an optional accessory is the toilet seat cover dispenser. Necessary in each toilet stall in a ladies' room is a feminine napkin disposal, and outside, near the toilet stalls, a napkin and tampon vending machine. Optional in a toilet stall is a hook for hanging pocketbooks and jackets. The preferred location is on the handle side of the door so that no personal items are left behind. Another optional accessory in the ladies' toilet stalls is a flip-down shelf that holds packages off the floor area.

In handicapped stalls, stainless steel grab bars are required by law to be mounted on the wall nearest the toilet. They are 1 1/2 inches in diameter and 1 1/2 inches from the wall and 33 inches from the floor. Local codes vary from city to city and state to state, so it is important to consult these codes for exact measurements.

There are two methods of transfer for wheelchair-bound people, depending upon their abilities. Those who are able to stand with support can pull themselves upright by means of the grab bars. Others have to use the side transfer method, where the arm of the wheelchair is removed and they lean across the toilet and pull themselves onto the seat. The side transfer method requires a larger stall, as the chair must be placed alongside the toilet; the front transfer requires only the depth of the chair, plus standing room in front of the toilet.

BIBLIOGRAPHY

Mazzurco, Philip. *Bath Design.* New York: Whitney Library of Design, an imprint of Watson-Guptil Publications, 1986.

ENDNOTES

[1]Linda Trent, "Combining Kitchen and Bath Elements," *Interiors & Sources*, April 1994.

GLOSSARY

Bidet. A sanitary fixture for cleansing the genito-urinary area of the body.

CBD. Certified Bathroom Designer.

Center-fit. Two handles and one spout mounted on a single plate.

Centers. Another way of saying "on centers"; in other words, the measurement is from the center of one hole to the center of the second hole.

Compartmented. Bathroom divided into separate areas according to function and fixtures.

Diverter. Changes flow of water from one area to another.

Feed-in. Where the rough plumbing is attached to the fittings.

Fittings. Another word for the faucet assembly; a term used by the plumbing industry.

Flushometer. A valve designed to supply a fixed quantity of water for flushing purposes.

Gel coat. A thin, outer layer of resin, sometimes containing pigment, applied to a reinforced plastic moulding to improve its appearance.

GFI. Ground Frequency Interrupter. A special electrical outlet for areas where water is present.

Lavatory. The plumbing industry's name for a bathroom sink.

Low profile. A one-piece toilet with almost silent flushing action having almost no dry surfaces on the bowl interior.

Metering device. A preset measured amount of water is released when activated.

Overflow. A pipe in bathtubs and lavatories used to prevent flooding. The pipe is located just below the rim or top edge of these fixtures.

Pedestal. A lavatory on a base attached to the floor rather than set into a counter surface. Base hides all the waste pipes that are usually visible.

Pilaster. Vertical support member, varying in width.

Pop-up rod. The rod that controls the raising and lowering of the drain in the bottom of the lavatory.

Preformed base. Shower pans or bases of terrazzo or acrylic.

Sauna. A steam bath of Finnish origin.

Slip-resistant. Special material on the bottom of the tub to prevent falls.

Spa. Whirlpool type bath for more than one person, with a heating and filtration system. Frequently installed outside in warmer climates.

Spread. Distance between holes of a bathtub or lavatory faucet.

Surround. The walls encircling a bathtub or shower area (see Figures 10–1, 10–2, 10–3, and 10–4).

Urinals. Wall hung vitreous plumbing fixtures used in men's rooms, with flushometer valves for cleaning purposes (see Figure 10–11).

Vacuum breaker. A device that prevents water from being siphoned into the potable water system.

Vanity. Layperson's term for a prefabricated lavatory and base cabinet.

Water pressure. Measured as so many pounds per square inch. Usually 30 to 50 psi.

Wet wall. The wall in which the water and waste pipes are located.

Wrist control. Long lever handles operated by pressure of the wrist rather than with the fingers.

Appendix A

Measurements, Manufacturers, and Associations

METRIC CONVERSION TABLE

This simple metric conversion chart contains equivalents only for the linear measurements taken from the textbook.

Some other quantities such as gallons, pounds, square yards, and temperatures may be converted from the following figures:

To convert square yards to square meters multiply square yards by .80

To convert gallons to liters, multiply gallons by 3.8

To convert pounds to kilograms, multiply pounds by 0.45

To convert Fahrenheit to Celsius, subtract 32 from the Fahrenheit amount and multiply by 5/9

IN.	CM	IN.	CM	IN.	CM	FT	M
1/000	0.003	4	10.16	36	91.44	1	3.05
1/16	0.16	4 1/4	10.80	37	93.98	2	6.10
3/32	0.24	5	12.70	39	99.06	3	9.14
1/8	0.32	6	15.24	40	101.60	4	12.19
5/32	0.40	7	17.78	42	106.68	5	15.24
3/16	0.48	8	20.32	44	111.76	6	18.29
1/4	0.64	9	22.86	46 1/2	118.11	7	21.34
5/16	0.79	10	25.40	48	121.92	8	24.38
3/8	0.95	11	27.94	52	132.08	9	27.43
7/16	1.11	12	30.48	54	137.16	10	30.48
1/2	1.27	14	35.56	55	139.70	12	2.7
5/8	1.59	15	38.10	59	149.86	15	4.5
3/4	1.91	18	45.72	60	152.40	22	6.6
7/8	2.22	19 1/2	49.53	64	162.56	25	7.5
1	2.54	20	50.80	66 1/2	168.91	28	8.4
1 1/16	2.70	22	55.88	72	182.88	37	11.1
1 1/4	3.18	23	58.42	78	198.12	64	19.2
1 1/2	3.81	24	60.96	82	208.28	66	19.8
2	5.08	27	68.58	84	213.36	100	30.0
2 1/4	5.72	29	73.66	90	228.60		
2 3/8	6.03	30	76.20	91	231.14		
2 3/4	6.99	30 1/2	77.47	96	243.84		
3	7.62	32	81.28				
3 1/8	7.94	33	83.82				
3 5/8	9.21	34	86.36				
3 7/8	9.84	35 3/4	90.81				

Some materials such as the stones do not have manufacturers and these materials may be found only through the Yellow Pages. For information on other manufacturers not listed in the Yellow Pages, write to the addresses in Appendix B.

Remember that the companies listed are just a few of those manufacturing that particular product. As far as possible, the listed products are nationally distributed items, but there are many local products that may be similar in quality.

Associations and Institutes represent their members in sales promotions and informational services only. They do not sell products, but many can provide a list of suppliers in your area.

CHAPTER 2

Paints*
Benjamin Moore & Co.
The Glidden Company
Porter Paints, Courtaulds Coatings Inc.
Sherwin Williams

Applied Finish
Duroplex® from Triarch Industries
Omniplex® from Seagrave Coatings Corp.

Multicolor Wall Coatings
Aquafleck® from California Products Corp.
Polomyx from Polomyx Industries
Zolatone™ from Surface Protection Industries International

Stains*

Danish Oil*
Watco Dennis Corp.

CHAPTER 3

The Carpet and Rug Institute (CRI) is the trade association representing the dynamic carpet and rug industry.
The Carpet Cushion Council represents the carpet cushion industry.

Painted Floorcloths
Grey Dun Studio

*Denotes that the local distributor may be found in the Yellow Pages under the particular product, brand name, or manufacturer's name.

Carpet Modules
Interface Inc.
Lees Modular Carpets

Carpet Manufacturers*
Bentley Mills
Image Carpets

Sisal, Coir and Natural Fibers
Alison T. Seymour
Merida Meridian
Ruskstuhl (USA) Ltd. Larsen Carpet

Painted Sisal
Linda Pettibone

Carpet Estimating Programs
M & Z Estimating Systems

Golf-related Areas
Playfield® Country Club Collection™

Natural Carpet Cushion
Dixie Manufacturing Corp.

Recycled Carpet Cushion
Dura Undercushions
Hartex® from Leggett & Platt

Dirt Control Foot Mats and Grating
J. L. Industries
Monsanto Chemical Co.
Nuway Matting Systems, Inc.

CHAPTER 4

Associations and Institutes
American National Standards Institute (ANSI) sets the codes and standards based on consensus of their membership.

American Society for Testing and Materials (ASTM) sets the standards for all types of products.

Hardwood Plywood & Veneer Association (HPVA) with ANSI sets the standards for hardwood and decorative plywood.

International Cast Polymer Association, formerly the Cultured Marble Institute, promotes the use of cast polymers that may be used on floors, walls, counters, sinks, and bathrooms.

Marble Institute of America represents the marble industry. It has a publication, *How to Keep Your Marble Lovely,* that is available from the address in Appendix B.

National Oak Flooring Manufacturers Association (NOFMA) sets the standards by which wood flooring should be installed.

National Terrazzo and Mosaic Association, Inc., represents the terrazzo industry.

National Wood Flooring Association represents the wood floor industry.

The Resilient Floor Covering Institute (RFCI) is a trade association representing seven resilient flooring manufacturers including Azrock Industries; Burke Industries; Congoleum Corporation; Domco Industries, Ltd.; Losetas Asfalticas, S. A.; Mannington Mills, Inc.; and National Floor Products Co., Inc. (NAFCO). To obtain a free copy of RFCI's brochure, "Recommended Work Practices for the Removal of Resilient Floor Coverings," write to the Resilient Floor Covering Institute at the address in Appendix B.

The Tile Council of America, Inc. publishes *CERAMIC TILE: The Installation Handbook* annually. These specifications cover all types of tile installations and are a guide for the tile industry.

Strip—Factory Finished
Bruce Hardwood Flooring
Chickasaw, Memphis Hardwood Flooring Co.
Kentucky Wood Floors Inc.
Memphis Hardwood Flooring Co.
Robbins Hardwood Flooring

Strip—Unfinished
Chickasaw, Memphis Hardwood Flooring Co.
Kentucky Wood Floors Inc.
Robbins Hardwood Flooring

Plank—Factory Finished
Bruce Hardwood Flooring
Chickasaw, Memphis Hardwood Flooring Co.
Kentucky Wood Floors Inc.
Robbins Hardwood Flooring

Plank—Unfinished
Chickasaw, Memphis Hardwood Flooring Co.
Kentucky Wood Floors Inc.
Robbins Hardwood Flooring

Parquet—Factory Finished
Bruce Hardwood Flooring
Chickasaw, Memphis Hardwood Flooring Co.
Kentucky Wood Floors Inc.
Robbins Hardwood Flooring

Parquet—Unfinished
Chickasaw, Memphis Hardwood Flooring Co.
Kentucky Wood Floors Inc.
Robbins Hardwood Flooring

Acrylic—Impregnated
Bruce® Wearmaster®
Gammapar, Applied Radiant Energy Co.
Hartco
PermaGrain

Foam-backed Parquet
Hartco

End Grain
Kentucky Wood Floors Inc.

Inlaid Borders
Kentucky Wood Floors Inc.

Laminated Wood Floors—Factory Finished
Kentucky Wood Floors Inc.
Robbins Hardwood Flooring

Custom Flooring
Bangkok International
Kentucky Wood Floors Inc.

Wood Adhesives
Bostik

Marble
The Georgia Marble Co.

Marble Veneers
Terrazzo & Marble Supply Co.
The Georgia Marble Co.

Backer Boards
Durock®
Hardibacker® from James Hardie Building Products
UTIL-A-CRETE® distributed by American Olean
Wonderboard® Glascrete Inc.

Grout Sealer
Portersept, Porter Paints

Agglomerate
Terrazzo & Marble Supply Co.

Granite*
The Granitech Corp.
Terrazzo & Marble Supply Co.

Flagstone*

Slate*
Buckingham-Virginia Slate Corp.
Structural Slate Co.

Ceramic Tile*
American Olean
Dal Tile
Florida Tile, Division of Sikes Corp.
Summitville Tile Co.

Ceramic Mosaic Tile*
Dal Tile

Pregrouted Ceramic Tile*

Quarry Tile*

Mexican Tile*
Vasquez Enterprises

Glass Block
Pittsburgh Corning Corp.

Monolithic Terrazzo*

Terrazzo
Fritz Chemical Corp.
General Polymers Corp.
Wausau Tile Inc.

Brick*

Floor Maintenance*
Hillyard

Vinyl Composition
Kentile Floors
VPI Inc.

Vinyl Tile
Kentile Floors
VPI Inc.

Conductive Vinyl Tile
Kentile Floors
VPI Inc.

Vinyl and Rubber Bases
Burke Flooring Products
Kentile
VPI Inc.

Rubber Tile and/or Sheet
Burke Flooring Products
Endura, Division of Biltrite Corp.
Johnsonite Inc.
Roppe Corporation
VPI Inc.

Sheet Vinyl
Altro Floors
Congoleum
Mannington Mills, Inc.

Custom-designed Vinyl
GMT Floor Tile Inc.

Cork
Ipocork

CHAPTER 5

Associations and Institutes

The Architectural Woodwork Institute (AWI) is a non-profit organization devoted to the elevation of industry standards, to continuing research into new and better materials and methods, and to the publication of technical data helpful to architects and specification writers in the design and use of architectural woodwork. Write for the price list covering all the books mentioned in this book as well as many others.

The National Association of Mirror Manufacturers promotes the many uses of mirrors and produces a compilation of outstanding mirror ideas by leading interior designers.

Granite*
Veneer, Stone Panels Inc.

Marble*
Georgia Marble Co.

Veneer*

Travertine*

Brick*

Concrete Forms
L. M. Scofield

Concrete Block*

Glass Block
Pittsburgh Corning Corp.

Plaster*

Gypsum Board
Gold Bond Building Products
FRESCO, from Pittcon Industries
SHEETROCK, USG Interiors Inc.

Vinyl-surfaced Gypsum Wall Panels
Gold Bond Building Products

Veneer Plaster
Domtar Gypsum
National Gypsum Co.
United States Gypsum (USG) Co.

Wallcoverings
Anaglypta®, Mile Hi Crown
Bradbury & Bradbury
Flexible Materials, Inc.
Katzenbach & Warren
Richard E. Thibaut, Inc.
Albert Van Luit & Co.

Paperbacking Fabrics
Custom Laminations, Inc.

Commercial Wallcoverings
Bay View Wallcoverings
Innovations in Wallcoverings Inc.
Koroseal Wallcoverings
Jack Lenor Larsen
J. M. Lynne Co., Inc.
MDC Wallcoverings
Numetal Surfaces
Tasso Wallcoverings
Tretford from Eurotex

Adhesives
Portersept, Porter Paints

Tambours
National Products
Flexible Materials

Redwood*
California Redwood Association

Solid Wood Strips*

Plywood Paneling*
Consult a member of the Architectural Woodwork Institute.

Prefinished Plywood*

Hardboard*
Masonite from Marlite

Decorative Laminate
Formica Corp.
Nevamar Corp.
Ralph Wilson Plastics

Glass
Edward Lowe Glass Design Inc. (ELGDI)
N. E. G. America
Restoration Glass™, Bendheim Co.
Transwall Corp.

Mirror*

Metal*

Acoustic Panels
Panel Solutions, Inc.

Other Materials
Pinecrest
Vitricor®, Nevamar Corp.

CHAPTER 6

Plaster Ceiling Tiles
Above View, Inc.

Wood*
Any of the wood flooring manufacturers

Manufactured Beams
Trus Joist MacMillan

Acoustic Ceilings—Residential
Armstrong

Acoustic Ceilings—Commercial
Armstrong
Forbo-Vicracoustics Inc.
Hunter Douglas Inc., Architectural Products
USG Interiors, Inc.

Mirrored Effect
The Gage Corporation, Int.
USG Interiors, Inc.
Ralph Wilson Plastics Inc.

Others
Barrisol North America, Inc.

Stamped Metal Ceilings
AA Abbingdon Affiliates, Inc.
Chelsea Decorative Metal Co.
W. F. Norman Corp.
Pinecrest Inc.
Shanker Industries

Strip Metal Ceilings
Shanker
Hunter Douglas Inc., Architectural Products

CHAPTER 7

The Door and Hardware Institute promotes those two
industries.

Mouldings
Driwood Moulding Co.
Formglas Interiors Inc.
NMC Focal Point
Old World Moulding

Doors
Customwood
Kentucky Millwork
Pinecrest Inc.

Hinges
Grass America
Hager Hinge Co.
Soss

Hardware*
Baldwin Hardware

The Broadway Collection
Gainsborough Hardware Industries Inc.
InteLock, Inc.
Sargent
Schlage Lock Co.
Stanley Hardware Division
Valli & Colombo (USA) Inc.
Yale Security

Glass Door Hardware
HEWI Inc.
Hiawatha Inc.

Closers*
Corbin Architectural Hardware, a Black & Decker Co.
LCN Closers
Rixson-Firemark

Keyless Locks*
InteLock®

CHAPTER 8

Shelving
Knape & Vogt Manufacturing Co.

CHAPTER 9

Kitchen Cabinets
Allmilmö
Amera Custom Cabinetry
Poggenpohl U. S., Inc.
Quaker Maid
The St. Charles Companies
Wood-Mode Cabinetry

Kitchen Appliances
Amana Refrigeration Inc.
DACOR
Gaggenau USA Corp.
Jenn-Air
KitchenAid
SubZero Freezer Co.
Thermador/Waste King
Traulsen & Co., Inc.

Restaurant Type Ranges
Russell Range, Inc.
Welbilt Appliance, Inc.

Wood/Coal Cookstoves
Heartland Appliances, Inc.

Under Counter Refrigerators and Coolers
Marvel Industries
U-Line Corp.

Ventilation Fans
Thermador
WCI

Kitchen Sinks
Elkay Manufacturing Co.
Moen Inc.
Kohler

Kitchen Faucets
Chicago Faucet
Delta
Elkay Manufacturing Co.
Kroin Inc.
Moen Inc.
Speakman Company

Kitchen Counter Materials
Formica Corp.
Wilsonart

Solid Surface Materials
Corian®, DuPont
Avonite®, Avonite, Inc.
Fountainhead®, Nevamar
GIBRALTAR®, Ralph Wilson Plastics
Surell®, Formica Corp.
Swanstone®, Swan Corp.

CHAPTER 10

Plumbing Fixture Manufacturers
American Standard
Eljer

Jacuzzi Whirlpool Bath
Kohler
Rebath
SoftTub, International Cushioned Products Inc.

Lavatories
Broadway Collection
Robern, Inc.
Sherle Wagner

Faucets
Chicago Faucet
Delta
Moen Inc.
Speakman Company
Kroin Inc.

Accessories
Broan Mfg. Co. Inc.

Commercial Bathroom Fixtures
Eljer

Stall Partitions
Accurate Partitions Corp.
The Georgia Marble Co.

Bathroom Accessories—Commercial
Bobrick Washroom Equipment Inc.
HEWI Inc.
Sanymetal Products

Appendix B

Resources

AA Abbingdon Affiliates Inc.
2149–51 Utica Avenue
Brooklyn, NY 11234

Above View Mfg., by Tiles Inc.
235 E. Pittsburgh Avenue
Milwaukee, WI 53204

Accurate Partitions Corp.
P.O. Box 287
Lyons, IL 60534

Allmillmö Corp.
P.O. Box 629
Fairfield, NJ 07006

Altro Floors
730 Los Altos Avenue
Los Altos, CA 94022

Amana Refrigeration Inc.
Amana, IA 52204

Amera Custom Cabinetry
Adrian, MI 49221

American National Standards Institute
1430 Broadway
New York, NY 10018

American Olean Tile
1000 Cannon Avenue
Lansdale, PA 19446–0271

American Society for Testing and Materials
1916 Rose Street
Philadelphia, PA 19103

American Society of Interior Designers (ASID)
608 Massachusetts Avenue NE
Washington, DC 20002–6006

American Standards Inc.
P.O. Box 6820
Piscataway, NJ 08855–6820

Anderson Hardwood Floors
P.O. Box 1155
Clinton, SC 29325

Applied Radiant Energy Co.
P.O. Box 289
Forest, VA 24521

Architectural Woodwork Institute
P.O. Box 427
Centreville, VA 22020

Armstrong World Industries Inc.
P.O. Box 3001
Lancaster, PA 17604

Avonite Inc.
1945 Highway 304
Belen, NM 87002

Azrock Industries Inc.
P.O. Box 34030
San Antonio, TX 78265

Baldwin Hardware Corp.
P.O. Box 15048
Reading, PA 19612

Bangkok International Inc.
Gillingham & Worth Street
Philadelphia, PA 19124

Barrisol Stretch Ceilings
1340 Depot Street, Suite 110
Cleveland, OH 44116

BASF Corporation/Fibers Div.
P.O. Drawer D
Williamsburgh, VA 23187

Bay View Wallcoverings
41 East Sunrise Hwy.
Lindenhurst, NY 11757

S. A. Bendheim Co., Inc.
61 Willett Street
Passaic, NJ 07055

Bentley Mills
14641 E. Don Julian Road
City of Industry, CA 91746

Blumenthal Inc.
42–20 12 Street
Long Island City, NY 11101

Bobrick Washroom Equipment Inc.
11611 Hart Street
North Hollywood, CA 91605

Bostik
Boston Street
Middleton, MA 01949

Bradbury & Bradbury
P.O. Box 155
Benica, CA 94510
Cost of brochure $10

The Broadway Collection
250 N. Troost Street
Olathe, KS 66061

Broan Mfg. Co. Inc.
Hartford, WI 53027

Bruce Hardwood Floors
16803 Dallas Parkway
Dallas, TX 75248

Buckingham Virginia Slate Corporation
P.O. Box 8
Arvonia, VA 23004–0008

Burke Flooring Products
A Division of Burke Industries
2250 South Tenth Street
San Jose, CA 95112

California Products Corp.
P.O. Box 569
Cambridge, MA 02139–0569

California Redwood Association
405 Enfrente Drive, Suite 200
Novato, CA 94949

Carpet & Rug Institute
P.O. Box 2048
Dalton, GA 30720

Carpet Cushion Council
P.O. Box 546
Riverside, CT 06878

Chelsea Decorative Metal Co.
9603 Moonlight
Houston, TX 77096

Chicago Faucet
2100 South Nuclear Drive
Des Plaines, IL 60018–5999

Congoleum Corporation
195 Belgrove Drive
Kearny, NJ 07032

Corbin Architectural Hardware, a Black & Decker Co.
225 Episcopal Road
Berlin, CT 06037

Custom Laminations Inc.
P.O. Box 2066
Paterson, NJ 07509

Customwood
Box 26208
Albuquerque, NM 87125

DACOR
950 South Raymond Avenue
Pasadena, CA 91109–7202

Dal Tile Corp.
P.O. Box 17130
Dallas, TX 75217

Delta Faucet Co.
P.O. Box 40980
Indianapolis, IN 46280

Dixie Manufacturing Corporation
P.O. Box 59
Norfolk, VA 23501

Domtar Gypsum
P.O. Box 543
Ann Arbor, MI 48106

Door and Hardware Institute
14170 Newbrook Drive
Chantilly, VA 22021–2223

Driwood Moulding Company
P.O. Box 1729
Florence, SC 29503

Dura Undercushions Ltd.
8525 Delmeade Road
Montreal, Quebec H4T 1M1

Edward Lowe Glass Design Inc. (ELGDI)
P.O. Box 2000
Arcadia, FL 33821

E. I. DuPont de Nemours & Co. Corian Products
Market Street Room X39196
Wilmington, DE 19898

Eljer Plumbingware
901 10th Street
Plano, TX 75086

Elkay Manufacturing Co.
2222 Camden Court
Oak Brook, IL 60521

Endura, Division of Biltrite Corp.
Two University Office Park
Waltham, MA 02254–9045

Environmental Flooring Products
P.O. Box 125
Lithonia, GA 30058

Envirosense Consortium, Inc.
100 Chastain Blvd., Suite 165
Kennesaw, GA 30144

Eurotex
165 West Ontario Street
Philadelphia, PA 19140

Flexible Materials Inc.
11209 Electron Drive
Louisville, KY 40299

Florida Tile, Division of Sikes Corp.
P.O. Box 447
Lakeland, FL 33802

Forbo Industries Inc.
P.O. Box 667
Hazelton, PA 18201

Formglas Interiors, Inc.
250 Rayette Road
Concord, Ontario L4K 2G6

Formica Corp.
10155 Reading Road
Cincinnati, OH 45241

Fritz Chemical Company
P.O. Drawer 17040
Dallas, TX 75217

The Gage Corporation, Int.
803 S. Black River Street
Sparta, WI 54656

Gaggenau USA Corp.
425 University Avenue
Norwood, MA 02062

Gainsborough Hardware Industries Inc.
1255 Oakbrook Drive, Suite C
Norcross, GA 30093

The Georgia Marble Co.
P.O. Box 9
Nelson, GA 30151

GE Monogram
GE Appliances
Louisville, KY 40225

General Polymers Corp.
145 Caldwell Drive
Cincinnati, OH 45216

The Georgia Marble Company
Structural Division
Nelson, GA 30151

Glascrete Inc.
13001 Seal Beach Blvd.
Seal Beach, CA 90740

The Glidden Company
925 Euclid Avenue
Cleveland, OH 44115

GMT Floor Tile Inc.
1255 Oak Point Avenue
Bronx, NY 10474

Gold Bond Building Products
2001 Rexford Road
Charlotte, NC 28211–3498

Granitech Corp.
P.O. Box 1780
Fairfield, IA 52556–1780

Grass America Inc.
P.O. Box 1019
Kennersville, NC 27284

Grey Dunn Studio
311 Pooles Hill Road
Ancram, NY 12502

Hager Hinge Co.
139 Victor Street
St. Louis, MO 63104

James Hardie Building Products, Inc.
10901 Elm Avenue
Fontana, CA 92337

Hardwood Plywood & Veneer Association
P.O. Box 2789
Reston, VA 22090

Harris-Tarkett
P.O. Box 300
Johnson City, TN 37601

Hartco Inc.
P.O. Drawer A
Oneida, TN 37841

Heartland Appliances, Inc.
5 Hoffman Street
Kitchener, Ontario N2M 3M5

HEWI Inc.
2851 Old Tree Drive
Lancaster, PA 17603

Hiawatha Inc.
4450 W. 78th Street Circle
Bloomington, MN 55435

Hillyard, Inc.
P.O. Box 909
St. Joseph, MO 64502–0909

Hunter Douglas Inc. Architectural Products
11455 Lakefield Drive
Duluth, GA 30136

Interface Flooring Systems, Inc.
P.O. Box 1503
Lagrange, GA 30241

InteLock, Inc.
6723 Sierra Court
Dublin, CA 94568

International Cast Polymer Association
1735 N. Lynn Street, Suite 950
Arlington, VA 22209

International Cushioned Products Inc.
202–8360 Bridgeport Road
Richmond, BC V63C7

International Interior Design Association (IIDA)
341 Merchandise Mart
Chicago, IL 60654–1104

J. L. Industries
4450 W. 78th Street Circle
Bloomington, MN 55435

Innovations in Wallcoverings, Inc.
22 West 21st Street
New York, NY 10010

Ipocork
1590 N. Roberts Road
Building 100, Suite 104
Kennesay, GA 30144

Jacuzzi Whirlpool Bath
P.O. Drawer J
Walnut Creek, CA 94596

Jenn-Air Company
3035 Shadeland
Indianapolis, IN 46226–0901

Johnsonite Inc.
16910 Munn Road
Chagrin Falls, OH 44023

Katzenbach & Warren
200 Garden City Plaza
Garden City, NY 11530

Kentile Floors
4532 South Kolin Avenue
Chicago, IL 60632

Kentucky Millwork Inc.
4200 Reservoir Avenue
Louisville, KY 40213

Kentucky Wood Floors Inc.
P.O. Box 33276
Louisville, KY 40232

KitchenAid
701 Main Street
St. Joseph, MI 49085

Knape & Vogt Manufacturing Co.
2700 Oak Industrial Drive N. E.
Grand Rapids, MI 49505

Kohler Company
Kohler, WI 53044

Koroseal Wallcoverings
3875 Embassy Parkway
Fairlawn, OH 44333

Kroin Architectural Complements
14 Story Street
Cambridge, MA 02138

Lees Modular Carpets
3330 W. Friendly Avenue
Greensboro, NC 27410

Leggett & Platt, Inc.
Fiber Cushion Products
P.O. Box 758
Villa Rica, GA 30180–9858

Jack Lenor Larsen Inc.
41 East 11th Street
New York, NY 10003

LCN Closers
P.O. Box 100
Princeton, IL 61656

J. M. Lynne Co., Inc.
59 Gilpin Avenue
Hauppauge, NY 11788

M & Z Estimating Systems
4700 Ashwood Drive
Cincinnati, OH 45241–2423

Mannington Mills Inc.
P.O. Box 30
Salem, NJ 08079

Mannington Wood Floors
1327 Lincoln Drive
High Point, NC 27260–9945

Marble Institute of America Inc.
33505 State Street
Farmington, MI 48025

Marlite
P.O. Box 250
Dover, OH 44622

Marvel Industries
P.O. Box 997
Richmond, IN 47375–0997

MDC Wallcoverings
1200 Arthur Avenue
Elk Grove, IL 60007

Memphis Hardwood Flooring Co.
1551 Thomas Street
Memphis, TN 38107

Merida Meridian, Inc.
P.O. Box 1071
Syracuse, NY 13201

Mile Hi Crown, Inc.
D/B/A/ Crown Corporation
1801 Wynkoop Suite 235
Denver, CO 80202

Moen Inc.
377 Woodland Avenue
Elyria, OH 44036

Monsanto Chemical Co.
320 Interstate North Parkway
Atlanta, GA 30339

Benjamin Moore & Co.
51 Chestnut Ridge Road
Montvale, NJ 07645–1862

National Association of Mirror Manufacturers
9005 Congressional Court
Potomac, MD 20854

National Gypsum Co.
Gold Bond Building Products
2001 Rexford Road
Charlotte, NC 28211

National Oak Flooring Manufacturers Association
P.O. Box 3009
Memphis, TN 38173–0009

National Particleboard Association
18928 Premiere Court
Gaithersburg, MD 20879

National Products
900 Baxter Avenue
Louisville, KY 40204

National Terrazzo and Mosaic Association
3166 Des Plaines Avenue
Des Plaines, IL 60018

National Wood Flooring Association
11046 Manchester Road
St. Louis, MO 63122

N. E. G. America
650 East Devon, Suite 110
Itasca, IL 60143

Nevamar Corp.
8339 Telegraph Road
Odenton, MD 21113

NMC Focal Point Inc.
P.O. Box 93327
Atlanta, GA 30377–0327

W. F. Norman Corporation
P.O. Box 323
Nevada, MO 64772

Numetal Surfaces Inc.
235 Pavilion Avenue
Riverside, NJ 08075

Nuway Matting Systems Inc.
8 Sagamore Street
Glen Falls, NY 12801

Old World Moulding & Finishing Inc.
115 Allen Boulevard
Farmingdale, NY 11735

Oscoda Plastics Inc.
731 Morley Drive
Saginaw, MI 48601

Panel Solutions, Inc.
P.O. Box 11
Hazelton, PA 18201

PermaGrain Products Inc.
13 West Third Street
Media, PA 19063

Linda Pettibone
144 Parnassus 19
San Francisco, CA 94117

Pinecrest Inc.
2118 Blaisdell Avenue
Minneapolis, MN 55404–2490

Pittcon Industries Inc.
6409 Rhode Island Avenue
Riverdale, MD 20737–1098

Pittsburgh Corning Corp.
800 Presque Isle Drive
Pittsburgh, PA 15239

Playfield International Inc.
P.O. Box 8
Chatsforth, GA 30705–0008

Poggenpohl U. S. Inc.
5905 Johns Road
Tampa, FL 33634

Polomyx Industries
400 Charter Way
North Billerica, MA 01862

Porter Paints
Courtaulds Coatings Inc.
P.O. Box 1439
Louisville, KY 40201–1439

Quaker Maid
Route 61
Leesport, PA 19533

Rebath
1055 South County Club Drive
Mesa, AZ 85210–4613

Resilient Floor Covering Institute
966 Hungerford Drive, Suite 12B
Rockville, MD 20850

Rixson-Firemark
9100 W. Belmont Avenue
Franklin Park, IL 60131

Robbins Hardwood Flooring
4785 Eastern Avenue
Cincinnati, OH 45226

Robern, Inc.
1648 Winchester Avenue
Mensalem, PA 19020

Roppe Corp.
1602 N. Union Street
Fostoria, OH 44830

Ruckstuhl (USA) Ltd.
dba Larsen Carpet
1480 Ridgeway Street
Union, NJ 07083

Russell Range Inc.
325 South Maple Avenue
South San Francisco, CA 94080

The St. Charles Companies
1401 Greenbrier Parkway, Suite 200
Chesapeake, VA 23320

The Sanymetal Products Co. Inc.
1705 Urbana Road
Cleveland, OH 44112

Sargent, Unit of L. B. Foster Co.
P.O. Box 9725
New Haven, CT 06536

Schlage Lock Co.
P.O. Box 193324
San Francisco, CA 94119

L. M. Scofield
6533 Bandini Blvd.
Los Angeles, CA 90040

Alison T. Seymour Inc.
5423 W. Marginal Way SW
Seattle, WA 98106

Shanker Industries Inc.
P.O. Box 3116
Seacaucus, NJ 07096

Sherle Wagner International Inc.
60 East 57th Street
New York, NY 10022

Sherwin Williams Co.
101 Prospect Avenue N. W.
Cleveland, OH 44115

SieMatic Corporation
One Neshaminy Interplex
Suite 207
Trevose, PA 19047

H. Soss & Co.
P.O. Box 45707
Los Angeles, CA 90045

Speakman Company
P.O. Box 191
Wilmington, DE 19899–0191

Stanley Hardware Division
Box 1840
New Britain, CT 06050

Stone Panels Inc.
1725 Sandy Lake Road
Carrollton, TX 75006

The Structural Slate Co.
P.O. Box 187
Pen Argyl, PA 18072

SubZero Freezer Co.
P.O. Box 4130
Madison, WI 53711–0130

Summitville Tiles Inc.
Summitville, OH 43962

Surface Protection Industries International
400 Charter Way
North Billerica, MA 01862

The Swan Corporation
One City Centre
St. Louis, MO 63101

Tasso Wallcoverings
1239 E. Newport Center, Suite 118
Deerfield Beach, FL 33442

Terrazzo and Marble Supply Co.
5700 South Hamilton Avenue
Chicago, IL 60636

Thermador/Waste King
5119 District Boulevard
Los Angeles, CA 90040

Richard E. Thibaut, Inc.
480 Frelinghuysen Avenue
Newark, NJ 07114

Tile Council of America Inc.
P.O. Box 326
Princeton, NJ 08542–0326

Transwall Corp.
P.O. Box 1930
West Chester, PA 19380

Traulsen & Co., Inc.
P.O. Box 169
College Point, NY 11356

Triarch Industries
10605 Stebbena Circle
Houston, TX 77043

Trus Joist MacMillan
P.O. Box 60
Boise, ID 83707

U-Line Corp.
P.O. Box 23220
Milwaukee, WI 53223

United States Gypsum (USG) Co.
P.O. Box 806278
Chicago, IL 60680–4124

U. S. A. Solarq
14560 Woodruff Avenue
Bellflower, CA 90706

USG Interiors Inc.
101 South Wacker Drive
Chicago, IL 60606–4385

Valli & Colombo (USA) Inc.
P.O. Box 245
Duarte, CA 91010–0245

Albert Van Luit & Co.
23645 Mercantile Road
Cleveland, OH 44122

VPI Inc.
P.O. Box 451
Sheboygan, WI 53082

Vasquez Enterprises
811 W. Warner Road
Tempe, AZ 85284

Watco-Dennis Corp.
19610 Rancho Way
Rancho Dominguez, CA 90220

Wausau Tile Inc.
P.O. Box 1520
Wausau, WI 54402–1520

Welbilt Appliance, Inc.
P.O. Box 3618
New Hyde Park, NY 11042–1287

WCI White Consolidated Industries
P.O. Box 182056
Columbus, OH 43218

Ralph Wilson Plastics Co.
600 General Bruce Drive
Temple, TX 76501

Wood-Mode Cabinetry
Kreamer, PA 17833

Wood Mode Inc.
One Second Street
Kreamer, PA 17833

Yale Security Inc.
P.O. Box 25288
Charlotte, NC 28229–8010

Index